Facing Out
to Sea

D1306074

SCEPTRE

Facing Out
to Sea

PETER ADAMSON

SCEPTRE

First published in 1997 by Hodder and Stoughton
A division of Hodder Headline PLC
A Sceptre Book

A CIP catalogue record for this title is available
from the British Library.

ISBN 0 340 69564 1

Typeset by Palimpsest Book Production Limited,
Polmont, Stirlingshire
Printed and bound in Great Britain by
Mackays of Chatham PLC, Chatham, Kent

Hodder and Stoughton
A division of Hodder Headline PLC
338 Euston Road
London NW1 3BH

For Lesley

Part One

The slums had been built, long before anyone could remember, in the gardens of what had once been well-to-do homes in the north and east of the Pettah. But with the influx of the poor into every interstice of the city, the wealthy had fled to the suburbs, leaving their grand homes to the landlords and the speculators who had brutally divided them into tenements and built tight rows of slums down the sides of what had once been spacious gardens. Today, throughout the wards of New Bazaar and Maligawatta, the old garden walls compress the lives of the poor as once they preserved the space of the rich, and it is for this reason rather than any horticultural attraction that the city's slums are officially known and numbered as 'the gardens'.

Without any proper entrances of their own, the gardens find their way out via narrow alleyways so that, from the outside, the only evidences of their existence are the stygian clefts in the sun-white façades of the city's streets. Through these restricted throats, the lungs of the slums breathe into the Pettah. But as the alleyways lead only into the gardens, and as there is usually only an evil-looking drain to be seen flowing from within, there is no reason for anyone to enter save those who live there; and despite housing a hundred thousand souls, the slums are never seen by those who go about their business in the capital.

The entrance to Slum Garden 178 in Maligawatta West, for example, could easily be missed; only an inconspicuous gap, barely wide enough for a hawker's barrow, serves as entrance and exit for its forty or fifty homes and two or three hundred inhabitants. Inside the crack, stone steps, shallow and slimy on either side of the foul drain, lead up into a damp-walled passage which squirms its way through into the slum.

Here in this private world the two rows of houses confront each other, their overhanging roofs leaving only a narrow strip-light of sky down the whole length of the garden. Permanently shaded under these deep eaves, each of the houses has its own small sitting-out verandah where neighbours, adjacent or opposite, can sit and pass the time of day. From the front edge of the verandahs, painted wooden posts rise to prop the continuous roof, and nailed between the tops of the posts is a matching wooden trellis, carved and fretted in a poor man's version of the Dutch colonial style. All down the garden these proud, peeling posts mark off the individual homes, their dark mouths opening into each other over the drain until, at the far end, the alleyway opens out into a bare patch of beaten earth where are to be found the latrine blocks and the washhouses. Here the slum comes to a full stop at the old end wall of the garden.

On the verandah of No. 29, Vijay Jayasinghe is slowly smoking a cigarette. It is a little after seven in the evening. Light swarms of midges are gathering over the drain and the strip of sky between the roofs has turned to indigo, smudged with the smoke of fires. On the latrine wall a neon light fizzes. A few of the older children of the garden are sitting beneath it, doing their homework under an inspectorate of insects. Somewhere a voice is raised and a dog begins to bark. As is usual for the hour, the women are embedded in the recesses of their homes, scouring pans with ashes from the dying fires, stacking the blackened pots, pouring the cooking oil back into its bottles, lowering the bed-boards, smoothing the worn covers, spacing out the garments that have bunched together in the middle of coir ropes slung diagonally across dark rooms. Outside, the men are relaxing on the verandahs, talking in tones which fall imperceptibly with the light, their glowing cigarette ends tracing their eloquence in the evening air.

Vijay Jayasinghe narrows his eyes against the smoke, frowning slightly at the harsh, incessant barking. Through his shirt pocket, a packet of Gold Leaf shows plainly. Somewhere he has read that one cigarette, ritually enjoyed at the same time each day, can give more pleasure than ten or twenty smoked carelessly, without postponement or anticipation. The notion had taken lodging within him, meeting his need for economy while permitting the dignity of choice, a sense that all was not necessity. He slowly releases the smoke, letting it burn in his nostrils. The smell of evening meals lingers comfortably under the deep eaves. This, the first cool of evening, and the first calm hour of the day, is his chosen time.

A sweeter scent briefly brushes aside the pungent tobacco smoke as Chandra appears from the doorway and steps down into the alley. In a mood to savour, Vijay watches his wife make her way between the verandahs, wafting aside the midges as she goes, the deep red of her sari dispersing the darkness that is gathering its strength in the open space around the latrines. Most of the other men in the garden are also following Chandra with their eyes, there being just enough light left. Almost without exception they draw on their cigarettes after she has passed, all eyes still upon her as she nears the gap in the garden wall and slips gracefully into the gloom.

Vijay's eyes return to his half-smoked cigarette. He hesitates over an old dilemma: whether to make it last by letting it burn away slowly in his fingers, or to draw on it, burning the paper and tobacco more fiercely, taking the smoke deep into his lungs, torn between the anticipation and the act. There is no movement in the garden, and his eye is drawn only to a flimsy cockroach scraping across the concrete of the verandah. He flicks the remaining centimetre of cigarette over the low wall and hears it hiss in the drain. Without the tobacco smoke, the faint smell of the latrines begins to re-establish itself. Tilting back in his chair, he sets his feet up on the low concrete surround, one naked foot over the other, staring at the break in the wall through which his wife has just disappeared. Like the gentle curve of the *dagoba*, or the saffron glow of a priest's robe, the dark shape of the broken brickwork is an icon for Vijay Jayasinghe, an image that summons unbidden a whole universe of meaning. Idly, he closes one eye and lines up a bare toe so that it exactly fills the gap in the garden wall, just discernible against the darkness beyond.

❀

The dispute over the breaching of the old end wall in Slum Garden 178 was long past. But while it had lasted it had been an ice age in community relations, scooping deep valleys of division, amassing mountains of solidarity, and sculpting the social landscape for years to come. The cause of this colossal upheaval was, of course, the world beyond the wall. What had once been just a grassy slope down to the dubious waters of the canal had become a flourishing shanty town of cadjan and cardboard, of thatched palms and bamboo poles, of scavenged planking and rusting corrugated iron. It was a sink of stench and heat, of puddled alleyways and mournful music, of dark, smoking hovels eking out their unvaried food, of wild-eyed dogs with starved rib-cages picking over festering refuse, of energyless children on whose unresisting faces flies played undisturbed. Such settlements are to be found almost everywhere in the city, growing like weeds on land which nobody else wants, at the edges of canals and railway lines, against the walls of slaughter houses and public latrines, around the rotting rubbish dumps and out over the waterlogged marshes on the north-east fringe; they are the running sores from which the respectable citizenry averts its eyes and holds its breath, and from which it imagines all kinds of fearful vices to be breeding as freely as the families who live there.

Such was the community that was to be found beyond the wall of Garden No. 178 in the ward of Maligawatta West.

It would be too simple to say that the battle lines between the wall-breachers and the wall-builders had been drawn between the sexes, although that was how it had begun. By climbing over the wall of the garden and walking for perhaps two hundred metres along a path behind the shanty, it was possible to reach the bridge at the other side of which were the vegetable market, the clinic, and both schools; it was a good five minutes quicker than leaving the garden through the alleyway and walking to the bridge via the main road. At first it had been only the children who had scrambled over the wall, pleading that they were late for school; but as they were always late for school the route had come to be depended on, and it had been only a matter of time before some of the younger women had also taken to climbing over with the help of two or three large stones that had one day appeared on the garden side of the wall. There had been some muted grumbling from one or two of the older women, but this would have amounted to little had it not been for the kindly action of Mr P. D. Norman Stanley, the retired cinema projectionist who lived alone at No. 42, the last house in the garden.

P. D. Norman Stanley, being adequately supported by his daughter who had gone to the Middle East as a housemaid, spent most of the day on his verandah, occasionally indulging in a *beedi* which he took longer to make than to smoke, but mostly just listening to the radio or chatting to his neighbours. To reach the back wall of the garden it was necessary to pass P. D. Norman Stanley's verandah, and it warmed the old man's declining years to see first the children and, later on in the morning, their pretty young mothers walking by on their way to the shops. Some of the children had even fallen into the habit of stopping by for a few minutes on their way home from school, encouraged no doubt by the supply of Fair Ladies and Delta Dots which he kept ready in a screw-top glass jar. Gradually, the balance of traffic had shifted so that most people were passing by P. D. Norman Stanley's verandah at some time during the day. It was a small thing, perhaps, but P. D. Norman Stanley woke up every morning the more cheerful because of it.

There was only one detail that disturbed him: he did not like to see graceful young women being forced to adopt what he considered to be ungainly positions in struggling over the garden wall. He was sure, also, that they were scraping their delicate skins, and what he liked to imagine was the silk of their saris, on its rough concrete facing. It offended his sense of chivalry; and one morning, having time on his hands, he had solved the problem by knocking out a dozen bricks with the help of a borrowed cold chisel.

It was the dislodging of the bricks that precipitated the crisis. Half of the garden, including most of the older inhabitants, had risen up against the breaching of the wall; it left them exposed; it disturbed social comfort; it punctured the status of the community. The gap was an open invitation, it was said, to all that was undesirable, all that they wished to be separated from. Now every kind of shiftless, work-shy, shanty-dweller would be able to wander freely into the slum. Hundreds of surly, foul-mouthed, drug-addicted men with bloodshot eyes and alcoholic breath would use the garden every morning to get through to Kochchikade on their way to look for casual labour at the docks and the fisheries. They would burgle the houses and molest the women while the menfolk were away; they would foul the latrines and break the brass taps on the stand-pipes; they would bring smells and disease and vermin and head lice; most alarming of all, their limitless offspring would mingle freely with the children of the slum.

The horror at the breaching of the wall was by no means unanimous. Most of the younger women and several of the men rallied to the hapless P. D. Norman Stanley's defence: the gap in the wall saved a lot of time and effort; no one in the shanty would ever dare come through into the quiet, private, slum garden; and any who did could be firmly discouraged by the family of Tamil hod-carriers at No. 4.

The next morning, after an uproarious night of verandah oratory and raised voices in which many a long-suppressed grievance was given an unexpected outing, the garden had woken to find the wall rebuilt, bare but neatly cemented bricks standing out like a red sentinel in the old white-limed wall to show where the offending gap had been. All that day, smirks and scowls had identified the two parties; but by the following morning the bricks had been cleanly knocked out again and those who were yesterday smirking were today seen to be scowling. The bricks themselves had vanished completely, only to be replaced the next night by gritty, grey breeze-blocks, crudely cemented in and scratched with a *hooniam*, a curse, on anyone attempting to reopen the wall.

It was on that morning that the battle lines had really been drawn, with the wall-breachers forbidding their wives and children to use the alleyway and the wall-builders forbidding those in their thrall to use any other exit. Under penalty of the strap, the children of the wall-builders were forbidden to play with the children of the wall-breachers, and elderly dependants, suddenly finding themselves in one camp or the other, felt obliged not to speak to those with whom they had gossiped amicably for half a century. Even the tacit agreement about the tuning of radios to the same station had been suspended, so that evening time in the garden had become a cacophony of classical and popular refrains as transistors were brought out onto the verandahs and tuned to the different stations chosen by the two camps.

Sometimes guards were mounted at night when the wall had been breached or rebuilt, but such vigilance could not be sustained and, within days, built walls were breached and breached walls were built again until, after several exhausting weeks, a wordless process of compromise had begun. First, the wall-building party had left a few bricks out when, in the small hours of one Sunday morning, it had rebuilt a breach in the wall that had remained open for several days. The following Thursday, the wall-breachers went to work again, but this time they did not remove all of the replaced bricks, leaving a smaller passageway than usual. And so the negotiations continued, a brick offered here and surrendered there, so that the difference between what was considered a wall and what was considered a breach grew narrower and narrower until one day, in the hottest part of the year, the gap stabilized to an irregular opening, wider at the top, which bit into the wall to within four bricks of the ground and was just wide enough for all but the stoutest to squeeze through. Within a month, a few more bricks had been dislodged by the increasing traffic but by that time no one had cared, and within six months all but the most die-hard wall-builders were using the gap to reach the bridge and most were exchanging pleasantries with P. D. Norman Stanley as they passed by the last house in the garden.

On the verandah of No. 29, Vijay Jayasinghe had lowered his toe from the gap and was straining to catch the exact moment at which the silhouette of the broken brickwork could no longer be distinguished against the darkness beyond. Most of the children were asleep and the garden was settling for the night. The few remaining radios had been turned low and the women, their chores done, had come to sit out for a few moments before bed. It was almost six years since the wall had first been breached, and little had changed in the garden. Except, that is, for the arrival of Vijay Jayasinghe and his family, who at the time of the dispute had been living in a shack on the other side of the wall, in the heart of the shanty, on the banks of the St Sebastian Canal.

2

The early morning is the only time of day when Galle Face Green, the half-mile stretch of worn grass and beaten earth that runs between the sea wall and the Galle Road, could be considered empty. Only a grizzled few who had been sleeping rough interrupted its long sweep towards the distant silhouettes of dockside cranes and the few high-rise buildings of the city centre. On the seaward side, the waves journeyed steadily in from India, thudding without urgency into the sea wall and occasionally sending up a lazy crescendo of spray that left damp patches here and there on the deserted promenade.

On the landward side the morning traffic was beginning to build up, tensions rising as trucks and cars became frustrated by barrow-boys and bullock carts. The lights changed and a bus blared its horn as an ancient bullock, all shoulder bone and worn leather, lumbered into a slow, disdainful motion. The conductor had given up trying to fight his way through the press of passengers and was lighting a cigarette; most of those inside, as well as those hanging from the window bars, would travel free at least as far as Havelock Town.

As the bus slowed for the Kollupitiya roundabout, Vijay Jayasinghe dropped from the platform. Edging through a stream of pedestrians, he reached a small door crudely hatched into a wooden gate facing out onto the Galle Road. The security guard nodded him through into a cobbled courtyard, deserted apart from a dozen or so heavy bicycles wedged between rusting cylinders of propane gas. The clock showed fifteen minutes to seven as he punched his card, the brass button worn bright by the heels of many hands. A flight of stone stairs led down into the locker-room, heavy with the damp, familiar smell of centuries of food and heat, of dirt and disinfectant, and of the salt sea. He bent to remove his shoes, noticing that the holes in the soles were spreading outwards, as if the leather were burning from within. Passing through into the kitchens, he helped himself to a saucer of bread and curry and poured sweet, milky tea into a tin mug. A few moments later, after splashing some water on his face and running a comb through his hair, glossy with coconut oil, he checked himself in the full-length mirror at the foot of the stairs. He lingered a moment, tugging at his tunic, accosted by the notion that the uniform did not perhaps hang quite so well on him as it did on the others. He was just progressing to the thought that it must be something about himself, something in his bearing perhaps, when the daylight was cut off from above and he knew that the captain would be looking down the stairwell. He snapped a loose thread and turned to climb the worn stone steps towards the light.

By seven o'clock, Vijay had emerged into his upper world. Slim and statuesque in the white floor-length sarong and tight tunic top, he stood at one end of the verandah restaurant and let his soul be captured, as it was always captured, by the most perfect hundred yards of this earth he had ever seen. The verandah, arched and pillared in whitewashed stone, was the first of a double cloister along the seaward side of the hotel. On the upper level, the thirty or so dining tables were so perfectly matched to their surroundings that he was reminded of the serenity of the temple. Gentle white table-cloths, washed a thousand times, were draped diagonally on faded purple undercloths that fell gracefully to the worn tiles. The gleaming glasses and place settings were as yet undisturbed, and the slim mahogany chairs with their mellow basketwork seats were all in their rightful places. Along the length of the verandah, tall green plants stood in stone pots between tables that looked out across the lawns to the sea. At regular intervals, shallow steps descended to the lower cloister, where cane recliners and glass-topped tables awaited the hour of afternoon tea. More steps led to gravel walks, edged with mature shrubs whose serrated leaves were also, alternately, purple and green. One of the walks led out across the lawns to the black and white stone squares of a chessboard patio. Beyond, the path narrowed between two large urns, shaped by the morning sun, and came to an end at the strip of sand behind the sea wall, edged by palm trees whose extravagant silhouettes swayed against a dazzling sea.

Each morning, Vijay beheld this scene with a brimming sense of its fineness, a feeling of becoming lighter, less substantial, floating towards its beauty for an instant of fleeting union that died almost as it was born, leaving him feeling crude and separate, as if he had foundered on some dross in himself which prevented any finer fusion. In the long day ahead, he would occasionally experience again this sensation invading him, exquisitely, though he was unable to prolong the moment and must endure its fading, watching with the impotence of one who watches a wave withdrawing down the shore, retreating as if it had tried and failed to find a place within him.

For a few moments more, the verandah remained at peace, the only sound the tireless thudding of the waves on the sea wall. On a spur of rock, a cormorant stretched out its wings to dry, while out to sea the pale silhouette of an oil tanker stood anchored to the horizon. Vijay and the two other waiters were at their posts, watching as the day captain performed his little rituals, inspecting the guard of white tables, occasionally straightening a napkin, holding a glass critically to the light, or motioning for a suspect spoon to be replaced. Upstairs, in the wing of the hotel that was still occupied, the guests would still be taking bed-tea. Below, all appeared to be to the captain's satisfaction, and he took up his place at the antique desk in the centre of the verandah restaurant.

Vijay turned towards the ocean. The fronds of palm trees were already being torn to shreds by the brightness of the sun. He closed his eyes to the morning and asked himself whether it would not be normal to stroll over and join the others for a minute or two before the first guests arrived. But an invisible wall held him in his place, and he turned to look again down the verandah, feeling the yearning to reach toward something whose essence he seemed on the verge of comprehending but could not quite grasp, like the sensation of being inexplicably unable to swallow.

A discreet burst of laughter erupted from the group of figures by the desk. He closed his eyes against the brightness, but still the sun forced its way through. Sometimes he felt sure that the wall that kept him apart had no real substance, save his own lack of ease; but there were other times when he so bruised himself that he had no doubts about the wall's reality, times when he knew that it was solidly built on the foundations of a common background, its bricks the comfortably shared assumptions, its cement the common reference points, the little idiosyncrasies of tone and manner. Behind such a wall there could be this easy intimacy, the certainty of belonging, the unquestioning assurance of the right to be as and where they were, the level looks from unclouded eyes, lacking the scared inner light. Another burst of restrained laughter broke up the group in the centre of the verandah as the captain walked a little circle to compose himself before rejoining the others. Vijay opened his eyes. Out over the ocean, hidden in the dazzling light, he conjured up the lascivious, naked figure of assurance dancing before him, unashamed, taunting, ready to leap back into the sunlight should he reach towards her. He blinked and turned to face the verandah. The captain glanced towards him and he lowered his gaze to the tiles. After a moment or two he raised his head again. They were still there, on their firm, unconscious ground. And from his heart, he envied them their place to stand.

Soon after seven the first guests began to arrive in ones and twos, pushing through the double doors from the lobby, invading the verandah in safari jackets or chrome-yellow shorts, breaking into its hues and patterns, ruffling its plumage, leaving its cutlery displaced, its glasses lipsticked, its napkins soiled, its chairs scraped and left askew, sullying the glory of his morning.

Half a dozen guests still lingered over their coffee. By the deserted stretch of tables, a few jackdaws had taken up their positions on the low, whitewashed wall between the two levels of the cloister, threatening to invade, to get in amongst the remains of the papayas and bread rolls, the pineapple cores and open marmalade pots. But Ananda was patrolling the wall of his sector, clapping his hands to prevent any of the birds from taking the final, unforgivable step of doing more than look, heads thrust forward greedily, at the debris of the morning's breakfasts.

Vijay stood at the top of the steps which led down to the second cloister. From across the lawns he heard a faint scraping and saw the slim silhouette of a girl, swaying rhythmically from the waist, sweeping the gravel paths. He imagined for a moment that it was Chandra, and wished that she could see him here on his verandah. But he knew that she would have been too awed to take in the quiet elegance of his surroundings, the steady grace of the cool white arches and the well-watered lawns; Chandra, who had never seen a table properly set, never heard a wine glass ring, never seen blue eyes close up. The girl with the *ekel* brush had gone, but Vijay stared still across the lawns and his name had to be called to bring him back to his post. He moved down to the end sector, thighs and shins stretching the sarong that sheathed his legs. He deliberately slowed his pace, struggling for dignity, aware that others had somehow mastered the art of gliding across the tiles in the discipline of the sarong.

After he had covered for Ananda for a few minutes, he returned to his own position and took stock of the remaining guests: the Indian businessmen had paid their bill and hurried off to catch the morning flight to Trivandrum; the two Swedish engineers, regular guests, had left by car for the Mahaveli; only a few tourists remained on the verandah, most of them Scandinavians, either very pale or very pink depending on whether they were on their way to or from the beach hotels along the southern and eastern coasts of the island. The only new arrival was a blonde, fair-skinned woman of about thirty who would have to be careful for at least the first few days; even now, though it was barely half past nine, the sun was blazing its morning path across the ocean and renewing its attack upon the lawns.

The captain strolled down the verandah to the antique desk where the bills were prepared. In a moment, he would put on his spectacles with due ceremony and begin checking through the spike to see that no mistakes had been made on the breakfast shift. From his station by the first of the whitewashed pillars,

Vijay's eyes returned to the new arrival. Foreign magazines left behind by guests regularly filtered down from the room boys to the waiters, but of all the women who had made their entrances and their exits on his verandah over the years he had never seen one who really measured up to the women in the advertisements for clothes and cosmetics, perfumes and wrist-watches, airlines and holidays. He held his gaze on the new arrival, ready to avert his eyes if she should look his way, and conceded to himself that this was a woman who might have stepped straight from the pages of a magazine. The only difference was that she did not appear to be wearing any make-up; in fact she wore no ornament at all save for the plain gold earrings, in the shape of a half open fan, which flashed in the sunlight as she tossed aside the deep fall of her hair.

By the little desk, the captain had begun balancing his spectacles on the end of his nose so that he could look down with a sufficiently sceptical air at the little pile of chitties. In the double doorway which led into the lobby, the Food and Beverage Manager made a brief appearance, looking down the length of the restaurant, chin lifted, checking that all was well. When the captain had finished and bustled off importantly for his nine thirty cigarette, Vijay strolled casually down to the desk and began leafing through the arrivals list. After eliminating one or two possibilities, he came to the name of Clara Lane. Nationality: British. Date of birth: 29.9.53. Home address: Holland Park, London. Occupation: company director. Purpose of visit: holiday. Duration of stay: twelve days. A white business card was stapled opposite her name. He tilted the card against the light to read the embossed lettering. The name of the company was 'Boston International'; and underneath her own name were the words 'Director of Planning' in small block capitals, followed by a long list of telephone and fax numbers in London, Boston and Strasbourg.

Vijay made his way back to his post. The sun had risen higher and the horizon had lost its focus. Soon he would go down to the boot room for his break. For the moment there was nothing to do but occupy his station and face the emptiness of his morning. He moved closer to the stone pillar, leaning unobtrusively against its cool surface, and suddenly his dissatisfactions were besieging him with bared teeth, attacking in waves, mouths agape, tearing at his composure until the water all around him was stained by the blood of his disquietude. For several minutes he stared miserably out to sea, focusing on everything and nothing, until a forced cough from the captain brought him back to his post and he moved away from the pillar.

The verandah was deserted, save for the new arrival. Pushing back her hair, she turned to look out through the arches and across the bright lawns to the sea. Vijay could now observe her without the risk of meeting her eye, and he moved closer to the end of his sector. It was usually possible to pick out a first-morning guest by certain small signals: a self consciousness in new surroundings, a curiosity over things which tomorrow would be familiar, a tentativeness about the way things were done, a hesitancy over this or that detail. But the woman at table ten offered no such concessions, giving instead the impression that she would have been equally at home wherever in the world she had happened to wake up that morning. He continued to watch her, absorbed by the manner in which she held her head just a little higher than was natural, suggesting a self-possessed authority, almost a defiance, an unapproachability flashing from her eyes, a lighthouse lamp constantly sending out a warning. But as he watched he was sure that she too was drinking in the beauty of her surroundings, appreciating the verandah in the same way as himself. He surveyed the disordered tables, feeling a foolish yearning for all to be restored to its former perfection.

Although it was only just after ten, half a dozen German tourists were sitting drinking imported beers at the low tables scattered around the entrance to the verandah. A snap of fingers brought him to their side. He presented the bill and watched as one of them scribbled a name and room number underneath a figure which exceeded two months' wages. Without looking at him, the young man tossed the bill onto the polished table top, covered now in fragments of peanut and scatterings of cigarette ash.

Back at his station, Vijay thought idly about changing the carbon in his pad. Instead, he turned to face the ocean. A few gulls hung motionless on fixed wings, like kites over Galle Face Green. From the pool by the pagoda came the first splashes, followed by shouts of joy at the freshness of the water. He stiffened the muscles of his legs and stared fiercely out to sea, the better to focus on things closest to him. A breeze stirred the palms and the ocean swept up onto the shore as he steadied himself and tried to sip at the substance of his disquiet through the froth of his agitation. His throat contracted with an almost physical pain as a mass of unarticulated feeling pushed towards the light; he was Vijay Jayasinghe, a man with a salaried position, the legal tenant of a proper home, the holder of a diploma from the City Catering College, a speaker of the English language, with a beautiful, modest wife, a fine, healthy son, a man looked up to in his community, respected by all for lifting his family out of the shanty. He screwed up his eyes and tried to return to normality, but the sea and sky seemed to be as one, and shame flooded into him as he acknowledged his blessings that were as easy to count as the little numbered blocks of polished teak that stood on the tables of his verandah. The empty skies stared back at him; he could give no name to the tremors which threatened the tower of teak and, unnamed, his disturbance subsided again into dumbness, its efforts spent, leaving him only with aching muscles in the jaw and a smarting in the eyes from staring too long at the sea and sky. He turned back to his deserted verandah and looked down the perfect perspective of arches and pillars, at the steady sunlight on the smooth white surface of the stone.

3

Clara Lane sipped the thick, dark coffee, turned her face to the sun, and attempted to give herself up to a purely sensuous appreciation of the finest of first mornings. There was a wonderful freshness in the pure air blowing in from the ocean, and already a huge sunlight had overwhelmed the fringe of palm trees and set up camp on the lawns. Through jet-lagged senses she took in the glow of the terracotta on the verandah, the slow, redundant turning of the ceiling fans, the unnaturally clear edges of the plants against the warm white wall of the hotel. This was what she had wanted, she said to herself, removing a grain of coffee from the rim of her cup, to be in a world where everything was different, a world where the air had a different taste, where the look of all ordinary things, of grass and stone, of earth and sky, of sunlight on the bark of trees, was subtly different from anything she had ever known.

For a few moments more she was able to give herself up to the thoughtless touch of the sun. But even as its warmth gently seized her bare arms, she felt her mind sinking away from the lightness of the surface, falling into the murky struggle that was to do with her presence in this place. A waiter approached, barefoot over the tiles, to replenish her cup. She smiled as he withdrew. The verandah was almost empty now, and she saw only the retreating rhythm of its arches; but still it was as if she were looking at an uninvolving film, as if some transparent barrier of anxiety stopped her from entering into its tranquillity. She drank her coffee and looked down again at the old-fashioned newspaper: reprisals had been taken for the blowing up of an army lorry near Trincomalee; one day she would like to go to a place called Trincomalee. At first she had thought only of a few days in Cornwall or the Cotswolds, but something had told her that this would not be enough, that such places would lack the power to jolt her, to give her respite. Scanning the travel pages of a weekend supplement, she had chanced on an item about 'the last great unspoilt hotel of the East' and had felt the small stirrings of an enthusiasm: it held a certain appeal, a different continent, a place with none of the associations of Europe or North America, a place where she could be released from the weight of her own predictable reactions to her surroundings. On the Thursday she had asked her secretary to rearrange her appointments and informed her colleagues that she was taking two weeks' leave. Within an hour there had been two calls from Boston to ask if everything was all right. She had chatted lightly about seeing a window for her first holiday in three years. Only later, when making the bookings, had she discovered that the last great unspoilt hotel of the East was in fact owned by Stateline Hotels, a subsidiary of Boston International. Now it was Sunday and she was here, blinking out across the bright lawns to the Indian Ocean, and feeling something close to panic.

The waiter was threatening to advance once more with the coffee pot but she forestalled him by shaking her head and covering her cup with her hand. After a few moments, she withdrew from the vast and vapid light over the lawns and collected herself behind familiar walls: there was nothing in the least bit unusual about taking a break; most people did it every year; and after a few days she would have everything sorted out, ready to return with all her old resolution.

She pursed her lips in optimism. The hotel was exactly as she had hoped it would be, old and quiet and slightly run-down, mustiness fighting with the fresh sea air, the smell of polish in long corridors where elderly room-boys in white sarongs waited all day in the gloom. Most of the rooms had been closed for years, and the few that remained in use were vast and airy with dark wooden floorboards, plain white walls, parchment lamp shades, old cane-backed chairs, sepia photographs of colonial days, comfortable old-fashioned beds, and a silence broken only by the sound of the ocean. And best of all, there was the faded beauty of the verandah on which she had just breakfasted.

She raised the china cup to her lips and drank the last of her coffee.

Signing the bill, she stepped down through the lower cloister onto the path which led across the lawns towards the ragged palm trees whose swaying fronds struggled to retain even their silhouettes against the brightness of the morning sky. A small breeze blew in from the ocean and she caught the smell of spices in the warm air. Between the palm trees and the sea wall was a narrow strip of freshly raked sand, a secluded balcony overlooking the ocean. Here and there, ancient thatched umbrellas shaded wooden loungers, facing out to sea. To her left was a kind of pagoda with a curious oriental roof in red tile under which uniformed attendants stood ready to serve cool drinks at the poolside. The pool itself was not, she was pleased to note, kidney shaped: it was a large, oblong, sea-water pool, its sides painted a dull duck-egg green; at each corner, white-painted steps descended into the water between old-fashioned brass hand rails, rusting green at their joints.

Slowly she made her way back along the path towards the black and white squares of the patio. Never before had she experienced such effects from a long flight: all sensation seemed to be at one remove, the pageant of her mind in slow motion, and there was a strange, muffled, feel about the world. But through it all, the enormous freshness and tangibility of her surroundings seemed to stare at her like an outlandish stranger, intimidating the vagueness of her reasons for coming to this place. The suddenness of her decision, the long expectant flight, the unfailing novelty of arrival – all had worn away, and she was left only with alarm at how out of character it all was, how inexplicable by any of her normal lights. She slowed her walk across the lawns, and for a few seconds the clouds in her mind seemed to pull apart, showing her that it was some stranger in her inner counsels who had prevailed on her to make this journey, invited her here to confront something which could not be confronted in her normal world but which could no longer be ignored. Slowly the clouds closed over again and the sun touched the tops of her shoulders, reducing all to absurdity. She would have to go inside; even at this hour, she was in danger of burning. She turned her back to the hotel, the vast brightness of the sea and sky bullying the feeble flame of her motivation, leaving her feeling frightened, alone, absurdly without purpose, on this most glorious of first mornings, standing in the centre of a stone chessboard in the sunlight of South Asia.

The path brought her to a side door of the hotel. Inside, the gloom was a relief, but when her eyes had adjusted she found herself in a part of the hotel that was disused, the floorboards bare and unpolished. Ahead of her, a staircase seemed as if it might lead back in the direction of her room. On the first landing, she saw that she was at one end of a long gallery lined with disused hotel furniture, grey with the dust of years. She began to pick her way between broken tables, ancient washstands, and fraying cane chairs until, passing the half-unhinged door of a wardrobe, she was startled by the sight of an old man, a hotel servant, asleep among the dusty skeletons of chests and drawers. She edged past. Further along, the gallery became a musty balcony which looked down through peeling white arches into what seemed to be a vast disused ballroom. Far below her was a wooden floor, scuffed and worn in a great oval by the feet of forgotten dancers. Around the walls, blind arches and fluted pilasters were separated by gilded ornamental wall lights reflected in tall, pitted mirrors. Such a room, she thought, must once have shimmered with excitement and romance; now it stood in the warm, dusty silence of another century.

As she had thought, the gallery brought her back to the main landing from which a corridor led to her room. In her absence, the bed had been neatly made and the yellow curtains drawn against the sun. Clara lay on the cool sheets and breathed in the smell of sunlight and wood polish; the place itself was perfect, she thought, stretching her arms out wide on the bed. It was only just after eleven o'clock. On the desk downstairs she had noticed a block of polished wood hand-painted with the words 'Tailor-made Tours', but she already knew that to plunge into sightseeing would be to retreat to the safe side of the divide that she had crossed in coming to this place. She thought instead of the days stretching emptily ahead, and decided that she would spend her time under one of the thatched sunshades, on the little balcony of sand looking out over the ocean, calmly working out what had brought her here and what she needed to do about it. She pulled her knees up to her chest and bit her lip in an unaccustomed attitude. The tenseness she felt was, at least, not of the normal kind; it was the tenseness only of leaving the beaten path.

For a fitful hour she dozed, drifting between over-vivid dreams which seemed to overburden so frail a sleep until, tired of resting, she stripped and smoothed herself all over with a high-protection sun cream, planning to progress to lower numbers as the days went by. Slipping a fine cotton dress over her black bikini she paused, wondering whether she could risk leaving her passport in the bedside drawer. She stood as if transfixed in the middle of the room, trying to decide if she had everything that she would need for a morning of lying in the sun: sun cream, sunglasses, sunhat, towel, cassette player, earphones, tapes, novels, tissues, moisturiser, mints, handbag, purse, room key, and a notebook and pen in case she thought of anything. Using the ballroom gallery and the disused staircase, she descended once more to the verandah and found the plant-fringed path towards the strip of sand on the edge of the ocean.

After an hour on one of the sunloungers under the shade of the thatched umbrella, trying the back-rest up and then down, picking up first one book and then the other, reapplying her sun cream, trying her sunglasses on and off, raising her chin to avoid a pale half-moon at the throat, changing the cassette, Clara admitted to herself that she was not relaxing. She watched, semi-hypnotised, as the waves came in one after another, but she could not still the teeming images in her mind nor soothe the surge of her concerns. Even after another hour, the best that she could achieve was a surrender to the randomness of her preoccupations rather than the struggle to impose order. Several times she made a determined effort to think about nothingness, to listen only to the voice of the ocean; but plans, eagernesses, doubts, anxieties, welled up from the flat surface of her nothingness, advancing towards her, swelling slowly as they approached, finally breaking in the shallows of her consciousness and seething with uncontrolled agitation through her mind before receding in an undertow of dissatisfaction while, out in the nothingness, another wave was welling.

She decided that a swim might relax her. She would time herself over twenty lengths, trying to improve on her time each day. Then she would lie out in the open sun for just fifteen minutes, increasing the time by, say, five minutes a day. She could use the alarm on her cassette player. Better still, she could quickly write a ten-line programme on the palm-top computer in her bag, an alarm routine that would increment by five minutes each day; it should be easy – subtract today's date minus one from the first two digits of the built-in date function, multiply the remainder by five, increment the result into a simple ten-minute loop, set the sound . . .

The cawing of jackdaws along the sea wall woke her and she came round as if from a drug, fighting free of the elastic chains of her dreams and screwing up her eyes against the ineffable brightness. Slowly she realised that she was not in her bed in Holland Park but lying on a ledge of sand on the edge of Asia, and she came suddenly awake, jolted by the full force of what she had done, of the inexplicability of her coming here, motivated by nothing that she could clothe in any rags of reason. A shadow fell across her and she turned her head to look into the eager face of one of the pool attendants.

'Miss, wanting?' he said. Clara smiled, lying back again, shaking her head. Although almost silhouetted by the dazzling light, there was an undeniable life about the young man, an unignorable person-ness. Then he was gone. And for an instant, lying under the hot sun, she caught again a glimpse of what her being here might be about, a rare sighting of that momentous world before words which has life and sway and which moves in a subtler sea than consciousness but which, just for a moment, looked as though it might be trawled to the dockside by some particularly fine mesh of thought and weighed out by the pound as if it were the ordinary stuff of the world. But the glimpse passed as quickly as it had opened up before her, and she sank back on her lounger.

Clara swam her twenty lengths, applied her lotion, and lay in the sun until the brightness and the heat became oppressive and she decided it would be more pleasant to lie down indoors.

The curtains diffused the strong sunlight into a yellow glow as she lay on the cool bed. Breathing deeply, she told herself that she was ignoring the obvious, that she had been working at full stretch for months, years, and that what she needed was to just relax and do nothing, swim herself fit, read novels, eat mostly fruit and vegetables, lose four pounds. Feeling better, she reached out for the hardback copy of *Teachings of the Buddha* which lay on the bedside table. On the first page, an ornate red stamp thanked her for not removing the book from the room. She turned over the preliminary pages. *'The human mind in its never ending changes,'* she read, *'is like the flowing water of a river or the burning flame of a candle; like an ape, it is for ever jumping about, not ceasing even for a moment.'* Clara yawned on the cool bed, her body clock all awry. She needed to sleep. The ancient air conditioner battled away valiantly in the corner of the room.

4

Chandra Jayasinghe, too, was preoccupied as she sat in the Bandaranaike clinic surrounded by thirty or so other women from the slum gardens of Maligawatta. The clinic had a smell all of its own, a smell of dried out wood and warm baby milk, of frequent antiseptic laid over years of heat and flies, with an occasional faint whiff from the slaughterhouse when the wind blew in over the docks. Some of the women were breastfeeding infants, rocking gently to and fro on the wooden benches; others were fanning themselves with health cards or wafting the free ends of their saris to fend off the heat. Three or four were uncomfortably pregnant.

Chandra covered her mouth to yawn and was reminded that she had been awake for much of the night with Susil, nursing him out on the verandah in the darkness, trying to stop his cries from waking the others. She straightened her back and looked around at the clinic walls where faded posters illustrated 'Seven ways to prevent worm infestation', 'Taking care of elderly parents', and 'Bringing up children in the slums'. Outside, the sound of car horns and children's shouts slid in through the slatted wooden blinds.

In the middle of the room, the health education officer was struggling with the ancient projector, trying to persuade it to throw its light squarely onto the wall. By the time the frame had steadied, the film was already running; a sharp-suited businessman was handing his coat to a blonde woman whose admiring eyes followed him as he strode briskly over to the camera. The businessman leaned forward and addressed the women from the slums of Maligawatta in a familiar manner. 'Hi there, glad to see ya all out there,' he said in an over-personal way that brought a small giggling from the benches in the clinic. The health officer asked for silence, wondering whether 'Management the American Way', made in black and white by the General Electric Company in the nineteen-sixties, was really the best that the Town Hall could provide for his classes on 'Coping with your problems'.

'We have a problem,' the businessman confided to the group of women. 'Here, in this company, we've just lost a major order.' He glanced over his shoulder and then leaned even closer. Chandra had never seen a human face so big. 'You know why?' He raised one eyebrow. 'Delays in manufacturing and despatch.' He leaned back suddenly, the face rapidly shrinking to normal size. 'This morning,' he continued, the face growing slightly bigger again, 'we have a conference of heads of department to look into the problem.' The blonde woman was sitting with a note pad, chewing gum, smoothing her skirt over her thighs, almost to her knees. The women of the Maligawatta slums gazed at her. There was silence now inside the room, save for the chattering of the old projector.

Chandra could follow most of what was being said, but most of the other women stared uncomprehendingly at the jumping screen, fascinated by the overwhelming confidence of the businessman that seemed to push out into the little room. A large bee sawed in through the window slats and murmured obtrusively around the benches before deciding that there was nothing of any interest and drifting out again into the corridor. On the wall, the film jumped to a dozen middle-aged men sitting around a table. They were arguing and waving papers. The camera closed on the back of one of the group. He turned in his chair. It was the hero of the previous scene, smiling familiarly again at the women from Maligawatta. He lit a cigarette and the other voices faded. 'The trick,' he whispered confidentially, blowing a stream of smoke down his nose, 'is to arrange these discordant characters so that they're all playing the same tune, just like you would arrange the flutes and the oboes in an orchestra.' He winked ostentatiously to indicate that he was about to show his audience how it was done, and there was another burst of muffled giggling in the clinic. Tapping the glass of water in front of him with his pen, the businessman addressed the meeting with patient authority: 'Gentlemen, gentlemen, if we're ever going to solve this problem . . .' Inside the little room the heat seemed to be building up. Chandra's eyes began to droop.

She awoke as the film fell silent and the health officer picked up the commentary in Sinhala, while on the screen the businessman conducted his mute orchestra.

'The men in this film,' the health officer was saying, 'are doing what we all have to learn to do – getting together to scrape away the earth from around their problems, getting to the roots of them.' The women in the room were listening intently now, staring at the screen, distracted only by the shortness of the woman's skirt as she places a cup of coffee before each of the men. 'That's what we have to do here in Maligawatta. We have to clean our problems off, we have to see them clearly before we can even begin.' Soon there was only the most tenuous of connections between the health warden's words and the images on the screen, but the film was in any case becoming more and more difficult to see, its lights and darks obliterated by the tropical sun invading the room, slanting from every crack, even though the shutters were closed and the heat was becoming unbearable. Chandra sat up straight again, wondering how long it would be before Susil would begin to sleep through the night.

'The main thing is – we shouldn't just accept our problems,' the health officer was saying. 'We musn't just accept that things are bad. We must have a different attitude of mind. We must believe that things can be changed. We must believe that we ourselves can make things better. That's the lesson of this film from America.'

The film itself had faded to irrelevance, but most eyes were still on the flickering wall as the health officer made the long connection. 'It is no use just hoping and dreaming things will be better,' he urged. 'Like in America, you have to make a plan. And like in the film, it is better if you can get together with others to make your plan. If you have a problem, any problem at all, if you cannot keep yourself clean, if your children are always getting sick, if your mother-in-law is being cruel to you, if your husband is drinking, drinking, drinking, if your son is being led astray, – then the first thing to do is clear away the soil, see what the root of the problem is. Then you have to decide what can be done. Then you have to think who might help you do it. That is what your Garden Councils are for, so that you can discuss your problems with others instead of worrying about them all the time in your own houses.'

The health officer's darting look always seemed to come to rest on Chandra. She lowered her eyes. 'Remember,' he was saying, putting a clenched fist to his head in emphasis, 'you have to begin somewhere, even if the beginning is only small. Even making a list of your problems on a piece of paper is a good beginning. Like these fellows in the film, you have to get the problem outside of yourself before you can do anything about it.'

Chandra's concentration was intense, but just at that moment the projector shuddered into silence and the old film died on the wall. The health officer, thankful that the power-cut had waited until the session was almost over, began opening the wooden shutters so that the women of the Maligawatta slums had to blink and look down at the tiled floor where dirt gathered between the cracks and ants struggled endlessly to fetch and carry their insignificant loads.

Chandra Jayasinghe walked back up the Sri Sumanatissa Mawatha with the other young women from the gardens. It was four o'clock and the heat had not yet relaxed its grip on the city. Stopping for a moment on the crown of the bridge, she looked upstream at the line of shanties on either bank, stretching back into the distance as far as the eye could see, their tinder-dry colour broken only by the lush green of the Mahendra park. She did not need to scrape away any earth. She knew what the problem was. Vijay had not spoken to her about it, but she had pieced the picture together. At the time of their marriage, he had borrowed the money for the year's rent in advance that had been demanded by the landlord of the house in Slum Garden 178. Without security, the only person willing to lend such a sum had been K. W. Matthew, moneylender of Kochchikade, and at a rate of five per cent per month. It was extortion, but Vijay had been sure that they would only need the loan for a year at most. Just his tips from the restaurant would pay it off in less than a year, Vijay had said at the time. From his wages he had planned to save the next year's rent, so that he would not have to borrow again. But when the bombings had begun, first of all in the North and then in the capital, the tourists had stopped coming and the tips had dried up. Ever since, Vijay had been struggling just to pay the interest, and when the time came to pay the next year's rent he was having to borrow virtually the whole sum all over again.

As Chandra looked down on the shanty, it struck her that it would be impossible now to scavenge for fuel as she had once done; every scrap of wood or palm frond or peeling bark, even the scrubby bushes that used to grow from under the walls, was now woven into the spreading tapestry of the shanty itself. She knew, also, that they should have waited to be married, that if they had saved up the rent before moving to the slum garden, then they would not be in this trap. But homes in the slums almost never became available, and Vijay had been so sure. Her eyes travelled up the embankment. Last month's meeting of the Garden Council had considered a petition objecting to a slum-clearance scheme that would replace Mahendra's few acres of grass and trees with high-rise blocks of municipal flats. Everyone had known that none of the flats would ever be occupied by anyone who lived in the slums, and the vote to sign the petition had been unanimous. They also knew that the scheme would go through. The park would soon be gone.

Chandra turned down the stone steps to the embankment. It was at the same meeting that she had first learned of the loans for women who wanted to start small businesses in the slums. There had been laughter when the notice had been read out by the Garden President, along with the other official communications from the Town Hall, and he had passed on to the next item with a 'whatever will they think of next' expression on his face.

She picked her way along the back of the shanty. In places the path had become almost a tunnel where the low eaves of the huts reached towards the wall. Over long hours queuing at the water tap, at the latrine, at the washroom, at the clinic, at the ration shop, she had worked out an idea which, in her wildest moments, she thought might be a way of helping Vijay. A hundred times she had gone over the plan in her own mind, but she had done nothing, spoken to no one, and now, as she approached the gap in the garden wall, she thought about it with renewed anxiety. She knew that she was allowing her plan to become nothing more than a comfort to her, and the health officer's words of that afternoon kept returning: somehow she had to get the plan outside of herself. She slipped through the wall. Down the full length of the garden, washing lines looped their way from verandah post to verandah post, crisscrossing between the houses, clothes and sheets hanging motionless in the heat. Reaching No. 29, she ducked under the line and pressed one of Vijay's shirts to her lips. It was as dry as the humid air would allow. Against the strip of light between the roofs, she noticed the streaks left by the brackish water; it was the time of the year.

Once inside the darkness of the house, she found herself alone. Her mother-in-law had taken Susil to pay a call on Mrs Weerakone, and Godfrey was nowhere to be seen. On the display cabinet the radio stood silent, awaiting the return of the men. She carried the pile of cottons through into the dim bedroom and began arranging them over the line, wondering if they might be getting the broken chest of drawers from the hotel. Through the ill-fitting planks, she could hear the music of next door's radio. Swaying just slightly to its rhythm, she draped the last of the garments over the line and began running through the figures in her head. Mixed dozens sold for fifty rupees in the cake shops all along Grandpass. Even if the wholesale price was only half that, that was still twenty-five rupees a dozen. The ingredients could not cost more than fifteen; probably less if her father-in-law could do the buying at trade. But long before she had reached her familiar conclusion, she was chastising herself for indulging in easy figures. Make a start, even a small start, the health warden had said. Get things outside yourself. Make a list. She tightened the coir line on the hook and took a pencil from the pot on the shelf. Soon the problems were pouring out onto the inside of an empty sugar packet. How to find out about the interest-free loans? How much would the repayments be? How much for a second-hand oven? How much for a cylinder of calor gas? How many firings would it do? What would the ingredients cost? Would the shops buy the cakes? What would happen if she could not repay the loan?

Her heart beat quickly as she wrote in the dimness of the kitchen. Somehow the very act of writing out the list had made her idea more real. She stared at what she had written, and the enormity of it overwhelmed her, followed by a feeling of wrongdoing, a wave of shame that she should be writing lists of such things in her own home. She stood with the paper in her hand, her mind racing ahead to what would happen if it were to be found. She bent to burn it in the smouldering fire, but as she tried to stir the ashes into a little life she saw with a sudden certainty that if she did not have the courage to keep the list then she must forget about her plan. Straightening, she tucked the scrap of paper into the top of her bodice and looked around for a more familiar focus of her attentions. It was then that she realised she had brought the washing in before sweeping the house. Sighing to herself, she picked everything up again and carried it back out onto the verandah.

Tiredness beckoned her to the plastic chair, but its call was not as strong as the fear that her mother-in-law might return and find her sitting down. Back in the gloom of the kitchen, she turned the pots and pans upside down, flicked water over the floor with her fingers, and began to sweep. The only light came from the dim oblong of the doorway and the narrow shafts of dusty sun which drove through the ceiling. Over the door, a plank held cooking powders and spices, a plastic mesh for making string hoppers, and an arrack bottle three-quarters full of coconut oil. Chandra looked at the bottle, glinting in the gloom, remembering the first time that she had taken a stand against Vijay's mother. That, too, had begun with a talk at the clinic on 'Ten tips for a safer home'. Even if you can get three rupees for a good bottle, the nurse had said, don't keep your oil in broken bottles. There had been photographs of jagged, black-stitched cuts on the hands and faces of children, and Chandra had returned home determined to throw out the broken-necked arrack bottle in which Premawathie had always kept the coconut oil. But on that occasion, also, her courage had failed her as she had imagined what her mother-in-law's reaction would be. There would be only one interpretation: Premawathie's ways were no longer good enough; Premawathie did not know how to bring up children; Premawathie was an ignorant old woman; Chandra had no respect; Chandra was getting above herself; if Chandra had had to raise a child in the shanties with no wage at the end of the week then she would appreciate the value of a good arrack bottle. And the worst of it was that none of this would have been spoken: it would have been implied by a mixture of spiteful silence and sly, double-edged remarks extending over several days. Imagining all that would follow, Chandra had decided to forget about the broken bottle, but no sooner had she made this resolve than the image of Premawathie's fierce features had been replaced by Susil's tender face, black stitches pulling together the purple, swollen edges of a cut.

Chandra was lost now, staring at the pale golden liquid in the bottle, remembering what she had gone through over something as trivial as keeping oil in a new bottle. She had known that Vijay would be no help. He was not aware of the effort she had made to keep the peace in the face of the thousand small, daily provocations from his mother. He would simply tell her to change the bottle if she wanted, as if the solution were that simple, not appreciating that this would make things ten times worse; on top of her other crimes, she would then be guilty of underhand behaviour, of going behind her mother-in-law's back. The silence would have been deafening.

Chandra felt tears pricking and began to sweep the floor vigorously. She had made a stand then and she would make a stand now, she told herself, bullying a little pile of dust towards the bedroom door.

There had been no premeditated moment. One afternoon, she had simply lost patience with herself. Moved by anger at her own cowardice, she had taken Godfrey's empty arrack bottle from the display cabinet and walked with it into the kitchen. Without further thought, she had poured the oil into the new bottle and taken the old one to the bin on the main road. It was done. Choice was gone. And beyond a distant dread, she had refused to think about the matter for the rest of the afternoon. Now, in the kitchen doorway, her hands gripped the broom as she remembered the hours rushing by towards the moment when she had heard Premawathie's footsteps mounting the verandah. Not waiting for the discovery to be made, she had followed her mother-in-law through to the back of the house. It had been dark in the small kitchen, and she had sensed rather than seen Premawathie against the end wall. 'Amma,' she had said into the darkness, speaking in Sinhala, trying to keep her voice light, 'I've put the oil into another bottle. The nurse told us about the accidents with broken bottles. She said if we could afford it we should use good bottles, when there is a child in the house.' In the gloom, she had seen Premawathie's glance dart to the shelf. The older woman's eyes had spoken before her lips, but as she had mustered her forces Chandra had spoken again. 'I decided to do it, Amma,' she said, keeping her voice low but walking towards her mother-in-law and stopping just an inch or two closer than was normal, 'because we can afford it. And because I'd never forgive myself if anything happened to Susil when I'd been told.' Chandra had smiled at her mother-in-law, politely, a daughter-in-law that Premawathie had never seen before: gone was the modest casting down of the eyes, the self-effacing, deferential tone, and in their place there was an unflinching look, an uncompromising tone. Something deep inside Premawathie had been shocked, the sediments of the years stirred at a level deeper than she had thought her daughter-in-law could reach. For a moment the two women had looked at each other in the darkness of the little kitchen, and it had been unutterably clear that a line had been drawn in the dust.

It had been Premawathie who had looked away first, confused, intensely aware that in some unspoken way the rules of the game had been changed. Chandra had waited until the moment had fully passed. Then she had spoken again in her old, modest way.

'I will bring some tea now, Amma.'

Chandra had bent to build up the fire between the three stones. Premawathie, lips pursed, had left the dark kitchen and walked through to the verandah, moving slowly in a way which deliberately exaggerated her age and frailty.

Now, as she swept, Chandra felt her resolve growing. She would speak with Premawathie that afternoon. She tried to wield the broom less violently, her feet in a cloud of grey dust, silently cursing the kitchen floor. Whoever had first laid the concrete had been seized with the idea of relieving its primitiveness by scoring diagonal grooves with a pointed stick so that the whole floor was divided into rough diamond shapes; but the dirt, instead of being pushed smoothly over the surface, took lodging in the grooves and had to be vigorously swept out along the diagonals, stirring up a dust which settled over everything in the house. It had obviously been a man, she thought to herself as she stepped in and out of the dusty bars of light and backed towards the kitchen door.

For a moment she let herself imagine that the old lady would approve of her idea. Baking light and delicately turned out cakes for special occasions was a refined activity, an accomplishment of middle-class ladies, possessed by few in Maligawatta. And it was, after all, Premawathie who had taught her. During the long years in the shanty, she had kept Vijay fed and decently clothed by baking and selling cakes which looked and tasted every bit as good as shop-bought but which sold for half the price. Her oven had been a blackened oil drum set into the clay of the riverbank, and her only fuel had been whatever she and Vijay could scavenge from the muddy margins of the canal. They had brought the old oven to the slum garden, but nowadays Premawathie baked only rarely. There was no need when her son had a proper job, and it was no longer suitable to her position to wander up and down the embankment picking up anything that would burn. If there was reason to bake a few cakes, she used bundles of wood bought from the Tamil cart that came once a week down the Masjid Road.

Chandra's imaginings ran on. There would be no scavenging. A real oven would run on calor gas. And it would probably do four or five dozen cakes at a time. There would be nothing to be ashamed of, nothing inappropriate to their status in the slum garden. There would be just the ingredients to fetch and carry, and the cakes to bake and deliver. Surely they would be able to sell to one of the shops that had sprung up all over Maligawatta, New Bazaar, Grandpass. Even Premawathie had admitted that she had learned quickly, and had a light touch. If she asked her mother-in-law just to supervise the baking, to make sure the cakes were as good as shop-bought, if she made it seem as if it all depended on Premawathie's high standards, then maybe the idea would not be vetoed out of hand. She flushed with guilt at such scheming in the darkness of the bedroom.

Hearing footsteps on the verandah, her heart raced at the thought that this might be the moment. Caution fought with impulse. All would be lost if she failed to read aright the treacherous tides of her mother-in-law's moods. But the footsteps stopped, and she heard only the creak of the plastic chair. After a few seconds, a feeble short-wave warbling filtered through from the verandah. Chandra carried on sweeping, stirring up the little gusts of dust in the gloom. The radio was turned off, and she guessed that Godfrey would be settling down for his afternoon nap.

A little more light from the front door reached into the bedroom as one by one she stacked the boards, wooden sides outwards, against the concrete wall. She began to sweep gently around them. The grooves in the floor were shallower now, and she guessed that the unknown artist's enthusiasm had waned as the initial thrill of creativity had turned into the monotony of repetition. Reaching up to the shelf, she replaced a fallen candle stub next to a plastic nit-comb and a small stock of partly used soap tablets from the hotel. Last week Vijay had told her about a shirt, worn by an American lady of middle years, with the words 'Just do it' written in big black letters all over the front. But the fear she had felt at the thought of speaking to Premawathie had brought her back to earth, her excitement replaced by a realisation that her resolve was not solid. And as she swept through from the bedroom, she caught a glimpse of the something else that was restraining her, something deeper, some relative of conscience which, unconfronted, would not allow her to bring to bear the full weight of herself, some unknown charge from which she had yet to be acquitted.

The front room, giving out onto the verandah, was airier and had gradually been made more homely. Apart from the open door, there was a barred window at which a torn nylon fly-screen flapped uselessly. Opposite, on the inside wall, stood the display cabinet with its glass-fronted shelves and, at one end, a cupboard into which an ugly lock had been roughly cut by a previous owner. Next to it in the corner, sitting on a shelf supported by battens nailed into the concrete wall, was a plump blue Buddha in shiny plastic; Chandra thought it hideous, but Premawathie had insisted on having a religious statue in the home, and she had not enquired too closely of its provenance when Godfrey had bought it back after an evening playing cards. She wiped over Vijay's framed diploma and their own wedding photograph, knowing that even if her mother-in-law chose not to disapprove she would still have to talk to Vijay. And if her husband allowed her to take out a loan, then there would still be the test of whether the shops would buy the cakes, and whether they could make a profit when all the costs were taken into account. And in a cold moment, she knew that she had daydreamed too far, that she had faced none of the real obstacles, and that her precious plan had no more substance than the shafts of spangled sunlight through which the broom handle moved rhythmically to and fro.

Godfrey smiled in a nonplussed way as she emerged onto the verandah, not fully awake but making an effort to lift both feet off the floor so that she could sweep underneath him. Chandra swept the dust off the verandah into the drain and collected the pile of washing from the bench.

In the darkness of the bedroom, rearranging the clothes on the line, she tried to focus on that other difficulty that she sensed inside herself, and just for a second she saw it as more real than all the barriers in the world outside. But then the moment was over, leaving only the shadow of its disturbance. She walked through to the front room and stared vacantly at the clock on the display cabinet; it had no numbers to denote the hours, and the gilded hands silently traversed a picture of Lake Interlaken with snow-covered alps in the background. On the other walls hung calendars for various years: one advertised an imported whisky under a faded picture of the cool glens of Scotland; another displayed a gleaming sports car photographed on the wet sand of a deserted beach; the third was a calendar of the current year and had no picture but was simply divided into squares with large black numbers and, across the foot of each page, the words 'K. W. Matthew – Your Friend in Finance'.

Chandra turned and walked out of the house, leaving Godfrey on the verandah, heading for the gap in the garden wall.

As she made her way along the back of the shanty, heading away from the bridge, the mean shacks dwindled away to a narrow path along the water's edge. Soon she had reached the patch of tough grass in the shade of a tree whose gnarled, muddy, knuckles gripped fiercely into the bank of the canal. Here she sat for a few moments, staring out across the water, guilt and shame cawing at her like jackdaws from the overhanging roofs, chiding her for taking time for herself, threatening to drive her back along the canal bank to the thousand tasks that awaited her in the garden. She tensed and remained where she was, shooing away her guilts.

Here were no obtruding uglinesses, no sharp-edged shanty roofs, no rotting refuse, no raised voices, only the wide, still waters of the canal and the gracious green trees of the Mahendra park. The noise from the road had grown faint, and at her feet she could hear the small slaps of the water on the stones. The peace of the place began to seep into her. Screened by the struggling tree, she removed her *chapals* and let her feet and ankles slip into the cool green waters of the canal.

But soon the jackdaws began to reappear all around her, arising from the shanties and the slums, telling her in shrill, censorious tones that she should not be thinking of involving herself in business and money, the taking of loans and the signing of papers, the discussion of prices and the calculation of profits; telling her that what she was contemplating was not for women such as herself, that her modesty was becoming tainted, that she was committing the sin of not knowing her place. For a few seconds more she gave herself to their harsh, insistent chiding, hearing them cry that it was not seemly to assert herself, especially as her husband held such a position, especially as she had been so fortunate in her marriage, especially as she was from the Maligawatta shanty, especially as she was virtually black. She stared into the broken reflection of the tree on the slowly flowing waters of the canal, watching the curled leaves and the palm fronds being carried unresistingly past. Slowly she lowered her head and observed the monotonous lapping of the water at her feet, the shadows of her unregarded routines, the unquestioned obligations, the constant round of coping, the endless fulfilling of expectation. For a moment, she held in her mind the things that were too close to see, but at her feet the gently lilting water lulled her senses and she recognised, too, the security in the dark reflections of her self-effacement. Impatiently she plashed her feet in the water, breaking up shadows that failed to disperse.

5

A narrow road that ended at the sea wall and was used only by the waiting taxis and rickshaws was all that separated the whitewashed steps of the hotel from the expanse of Galle Face Green. In former days the Green had been a polo field where ponies grazed or sought shade under awnings of plaited palm, but now it served as a recreation area in the heart of the city and a few hundred people were always to be found strolling on its tired grass. Here were the gently retired and the tensely unemployed, the blind and the lame begging with their children, the con men collecting for their non-existent hospitals, the three-card-trick artists working the gullible, the barrow-men selling orange barley and Elephant House ginger beer, the trolleys of roasting peanuts in twists of newspaper, the segregated groups of teenagers promenading up and down the seafront, the bold young boys flying their kites, and the furtive drug-addicts whose kites had long ago fluttered back to earth.

To the north stood the small growth of tall buildings which constituted the downtown area of the city, starting with the five-star Meridian Hotel beyond which rose the Intercontinental, the Hilton, and the concrete cylinder of the National Bank. Inland, across the Galle Road and partly screened from it by a long line of palm trees, lay the Hotel Capricorn. To the south, facing out onto the end of the Green, stood the oldest and most dignified of the capital's hotels, its low white façade arched and pillared on either side of a dark doorway from which Clara Lane now stepped down into the sunlight.

She ignored the calls of the cab and rickshaw drivers and crossed over to the Green. Blinking constantly, she headed for the sea wall, intending to walk along the ocean front. The grass, almost colourless after weeks without rain, reflected the sun like glass, and it was quite impossible to look out to sea. She had walked about thirty metres and was just beginning to be able to keep her eyes open for more than a few seconds when she became aware of a figure approaching her, a dark girl, furiously gesturing, tight, tense fingers rising and falling to her mouth as she called out 'akka, akka, akka' in a voice harsh beyond her years. Clara had no time to compliment herself on having expected something of the kind as she fumbled in her bag, searching for one of the small denomination notes which she had obtained only a minute ago from the hotel reception desk. She gave ten rupees to the fierce little girl, not wanting to look at her, seeing only the dust in her hair and assuming she must belong to one of the families of professional beggars she had been warned of. She lifted her head again and walked on, summoning her most unapproachable look, flashing the lighthouse lamp all around her. But out in the glare of Galle Face Green the lamp that was so intimidating in her own world could not be seen at all, and she could already hear more cries and the sound of bare feet thudding purposefully on the grass behind her. Two boys were alongside her now, mimicking the act of eating as they uttered the strange guttural cry, 'akka, akka, akka', that was beginning to unstring her nerves. Almost tripping over something, she realised with a shock that one of the boys was trying to clean her shoes with a rag as she walked along. Without stopping, she opened her bag and held out two ten-rupee notes. Immediately the girl was back again, the same girl, she was sure of it, dark and fierce and insistent, 'akka, akka, akka'. Clara decided to ignore her. But the girl would not be ignored, running alongside her, 'akka, akka, akka, buth, buth, buth', tugging at her skirt to make her see the empty pinched fingers miming to and fro from her mouth. Clara pulled her skirt away from the clutching fingers and looked for a second into the girl's dark, intense face and burning, determined eyes. She gave her another note, and hurried on. Other children were coming towards her now, shouting for their fellows, and Clara felt the first emptying of panic. She had to get off the Green, but she would not be driven back to the hotel. She made instead for the main road. But now several children were dancing in front of her as well as alongside, holding out their hands, pulling insistently at her clothes, shrieking and trying to rub her shoes with sleeves and hems as she strode along. She dispensed some more notes and bought herself ten more metres towards the road.

A fierce shout assaulted the heat and in an instant the dozen or so children evaporated into the afternoon. Just ahead of her she saw the black-bereted soldier and managed to recover enough composure to give what she hoped was a reasonably calm smile of thanks in acknowledgement of his salute. He was still watching her as she stepped into the road, perspiring more than she could ever remember, exhaust fumes swirling all around her as she took stock in the comparative safety of a traffic island in the middle of the Galle Road.

She decided that it would not do to go straight back to the hotel. She would walk back up the main road and, no matter what happened, she would stay calm and keep walking. For fifty metres all went well. She negotiated the Kollupitiya roundabout and was starting to look around her for the first time, noticing the crumbling edges of the pavements, the heat-weary façades of the buildings, the dust of dead insects in the bottoms of shop windows and the faded, fly-blown window dressings.

'Miss, what is country?'

A man, smaller than herself, was striding just alongside her. She stuck to plan and kept walking as if she had not heard, forcing herself not to hurry. The sun bounced off the white buildings and the traffic fumes made it difficult to breathe.

'Miss, what is country?'

'I'm from England,' she said, feeling absurd.

'Miss, it is nineteen fifty-six. I am opening batting at Lords.' He spoke with an eager pride. 'It is versus MCC, Miss. All are there Miss, Tony Lock, Jim Laker, fiery Freddy Trueman. Now I am suffering great misfortune, Miss.'

Clara gave the man a note, not knowing what it was, and hurried on leaving his profuse thanks behind. The heat followed her. At the very next doorway another man whom she did not look at, began to walk with her.

'Gem stones, Miss? I give you special price.' A pause. 'Change money Miss? What is country?'

A few hundred metres ahead she could see what looked as if it might be the entrance to a hotel, but on the corner she also saw an ambush of people, a family, lying in the street under the little shade of a whitewashed wall. As she neared, trying to see without looking, she saw that the tableau against the wall was dominated by an old, tired-looking lady, her steel hair hanging in loose wires, her face lined and defeated. The woman beside her was bent forward, breastfeeding her baby, and Clara saw weeks of road dust in the young mother's hair. Next to her, in a cardboard box lined with a filthy red blanket, a girl of about two years slept, slack-limbed, thumb pushed into a perfectly shaped mouth. Clara walked on by. Her eyes hurt with the glare from the white walls and the joints of her jaws were aching. She closed her eyes for a second against the sun and immediately saw the peaceful face of the sleeping child who would have to wake up in a cardboard box at the side of the Galle road. Perspiring and irresolute, she turned and hurried the thirty metres back, giving the family all the notes in her handbag and not waiting for the response. She hurried on towards what she hoped was a hotel, but her way was barred again by a teenage boy offering her sheets of cardboard amateurishly wrapped in crinkled cellophane, and asking, cheerfully, 'What country, Miss? You buy stamps? *Sie kaufen briefmarken?*' She had no money left and almost fell over him in her haste to reach the gateposts of the hotel where a uniformed guard shouted the boy away and saluted her through.

There was no footpath, only the drive. She slowed down, breathing deeply and searching for a tissue in her bag as she approached the low white portico. The faint spray from a fountain fell across her face as she passed by a lily pool, and she became aware that the drive was shaded by well-watered shrubs and blossoming trees and that the ground in between was covered with pieces of tree-bark to keep down the weeds. As she neared the entrance, a liveried doorman swung open the great glass doors and she passed serenely through into the vast air-conditioned coolness of the Oberoi Hotel.

Soft armchairs and deep sofas were arranged in a low maze

of seating on the half-acre of raised and carpeted dais where Clara Lane now sat sipping tea from a patterned china cup. All around her rose the galleried quadrangle of the hotel while, far above, suspended from the roof, hundred-foot-long batik pennants of red and gold, gloriously lit by discreet spotlights, fell majestically into the central well. To her right, on one corner of the hushed dais, a handsome Indian pianist in evening dress was sentimentally caressing the keys of a grand piano, sending the saccharin notes of 'Some Enchanted Evening' up into the perfect acoustics. Clara had not heard the tune since her childhood; it had been one of several songs of which her father had known the first two lines and which he had occasionally bellowed out unexpectedly on Saturday mornings when times were good.

After washing her face in the white-tiled washroom, she had called at the desk to change more travellers' cheques and then, quite herself again, had decided to take tea. She refused to think about her walk on Galle Face Green, having long ago learned not to admit anything distressing into her mind until, at a time of her own choosing, when the experience was no longer raw, she could render it tolerable, keeping it in the outside porch of her thoughts until it could be trusted to behave itself in the inner sanctum. Clara therefore drank her tea, sitting in the great cool well of the Oberoi, determined to think about anything except her afternoon walk. But on this occasion she could not entirely keep at bay the notion that, despite having wanted to leave behind familiar associations, her first slight contact with Asia had sent her scurrying for this oasis of air-conditioned westernisation. Is this the only environment I can survive in, she wondered, looking around her, part scornful, part grateful, into the vast cool. For an instant all was absurdity, sitting alone on a pink armchair on a raised dais five thousand miles from anywhere she had reason to be and listening to a grand piano which had now elided smoothly into a rendition of 'Edelweiss, Edelweiss'. How could this possibly help her with whatever it was that she had to resolve? From nowhere, the absurd thought came to her that the little girl sleeping in the box on the Galle Road was probably just as happy as any other child so long as she remained asleep.

She shook herself free of the memory and looked around

her. Graceful trees of just the right height bordered the dais, four on each side, their delicate green deciduousness breaking the formal lines of the rosewood balconies. The waiter glided towards her.

'What kind of trees are these?' She half raised a hand towards the leafy branches behind the pink settee.

'Sorry, Miss. Not knowing. I am thinking they may be English trees.' He poured another cup of the dark, orange tea through the strainer.

'They're lovely now,' said Clara, 'but what happens when the leaves fall?'

'Miss, I am asking.' He had gone before she could tell him it didn't matter.

The dais was occupied by a few youthful Westerners, most of them dressed in cut-off jeans and drinking thick papaya juice through fat plastic straws with a corrugated hinge. Here and there, a few locals in shirts and ties or smart western sports clothes drank imported beers, shirt pockets square with cigarette packets, chromium watch straps hanging loosely on too-slender wrists. Clara's eyes travelled round the balconies above. Already the walk on Galle Face Green seemed like an incident from a previous life. Idly, she picked up the bar menu. A different waiter appeared. 'No, nothing, thank you.' She replaced the menu on the table and noticed a smudge on her skirt. She stared at the dark fingermark; it was as if a detail from a nightmare had turned up on the breakfast table. In the cool of the Oberoi, the image of the fierce little girl broke through to her, disturbing her more than she had thought possible, and for some reason she thought of the only time in her life, back in her early teens, when she had ever really been hit; as her cheek bone had stung and swelled, an unbearable sensation had welled up inside her and her whole world had seemed to change not because of the pain but because it could happen, because someone could at any time do this to her, because of the depths of the other world into which she was suddenly forced to look, vertigo rising.

She folded the fullness of her skirt over the fingermark. Despite the tea, she was beginning to feel light-headed, shimmering over the raised lounge, floating with the notes of the piano, rising between the red and gold banners towards the glass roof high above. She focused on the mundane, on the softly glowing reception desks, the seductive gem arcades, the exotic flower arrangements by the elevators, until finally her gaze travelled to the distant restaurants set behind glass walls through which she could see the silent rise and fall of glasses, cups, forks, spoons. She contrasted the scene with thoughts of her own hotel, old, discreet, quiet, but her complacency was soon ruffled by the thought of the walk back down the Galle Road. Then she remembered the line of taxis in the drive. She would have a look at some gems and then leave. The waiter was there almost as soon as she looked round, handing her the bill in a folder of red leather deeply imprinted with the hotel crest.

'Miss, trees are being made in Singapore. Costing one lakh each, Miss.'

Clara reached to hold one of the plastic leaves between her thumb and finger, and smiled at the young man. The pianist was drifting into a sentimental rendering of 'When I Grow Too Old to Dream' as Clara left the lobby and passed through the great glass doors into a waiting taxi.

6

The brickwork pulled Godfrey Jayasinghe's sarong loose as he squeezed through the wall and he paused to retie it, pulling it wide to one side and wrapping it just tightly enough to hold around his middle. There being no one sitting out at this time of day, he made his way down the garden and stepped up onto his own verandah. Two minutes of fiddling with the short-wave radio produced nothing more than a warbling of morse and he eventually settled back in the plastic chair, crossed his arms on his belly, and closed his eyes. From deep inside the house he could hear the sound of sweeping and he wondered if Chandra would soon be bringing him a brew.

Normally, a light doze came easily to Godfrey Jayasinghe, but on this particular afternoon he remained awake for all of two or three minutes, turning over in his mind the notion that had preoccupied him for most of the day. Last evening, the Cheltenham Corner had refused to take his larger-than-usual bet after a delayed start in the two o'clock at Worcester. It often happened with the unlicensed bookmakers who stood to lose too much on a particular horse, but what had caused Godfrey to ponder the incident was that he had himself listened to the two o'clock at Worcester a quarter of an hour earlier, sitting on his own verandah, courtesy of the World Service of the BBC.

Without a word, Chandra came out of the house and set off up the garden towards the wall. He wondered where she could be going. Vijay would soon be home. Godfrey resigned himself to waiting for his tea. Soon he had fallen into a gentle slumber.

The war in Europe had ruined Godfrey Jayasinghe. Summoned from his village by the call to arms which had sounded through the colonies, he had passed quickly from training ground to troop ship and thence to Algiers, where he had been inducted into the Eighth Army as it prepared to launch itself at the heel of Italy. Joining a British survey regiment as a replacement for a gunner who had been killed at Monte Cassino, he had suddenly found himself a player on the stage of empire rather than just one of the countless spectators in the worst seats in the house. What had been privations to soldiers from comfortable British homes had to him seemed luxuries, and the moments of real fear and hardship had been but brief and weighed but little against the dignity and significance with which the war in Europe had invested his existence. For there, in Italy, he had experienced the intoxicating mix of purpose and brotherhood which, though ill-defined, he was to long for all his life but never quite know again. He had drunk long and deep of the satisfactions of comradeship, of shared dangers, shared boredoms, shared amusements, shared beefs, shared slang; but above all it had been the acceptance of the men he had looked up to, men who in other circumstances, he knew, could never have been his friends, that had made him feel acceptable to himself and sown so extravagantly the seeds that in the years ahead would become the luxuriant, choking weeds of nostalgia. In those months on the beach-head at Anzio he had watched the contours of race and background being beaten into shallower relief by the shell-fire falling night after night on sandy trenches smelling of a common fear under common stars, and he had known that this state of being, this satisfying inebriation with the wine of acceptance, was what he wanted from his life. But after they had crossed the Po he had known it was coming to an end, and soon he had found himself once more on board a troop ship, steaming home with a sinking heart.

He had quickly found his village intolerable. The company he had kept, the places he had seen, the events he had been part of, made it unthinkable to live in the backwater he had grown up in, and even the capital city was robbed of all glamour by the excitements of his past and the promise of his future. For he had mentally committed himself to England, to the job in Luton promised by the Eighth Army captain at whose side he had sworn and sweated from Taranto to Ferrara. And in the months after his return, the enormousness of the hope had so occupied his mind that it had prevented him from entertaining any ambition more within his own powers of realisation. It was this that had allowed him to maintain his pride while he took temporary work and brought his bride to a temporary shack on the banks of the St Sebastian Canal. But the months had passed, and to his few jobs he had brought neither ambition nor application, seeing them only as a stop-gap before life really began, never looking to the top of the rise on which he stood but always to the distant hills beyond. Sometimes his jobs had come to an end because of some imagined insult, because he felt he had been treated like a common peon rather than a man who was waiting to take up a position in England; but the fact was that the glamour of war behind and of Luton in front had sapped his will for the tedium of working life in his native land, and it was the constant friction between the gritty details of his daily realities and the tender imaginings of his dreams which had eventually made his every job unbearable.

As a year passed, and then two, he had ceased going down to the Fort post office as he had ceased looking for work and ceased folding his trousers under the bed-board at night. Long before middle age he had found that, in the heat, his sarong fitted him much more comfortably than trousers and, soon afterwards, his shirts with the pockets and buttoned epaulettes had given way to a sleeveless cotton vest which spread gently out over his growing paunch. The years had become decades, and he had sat in the shade of the thatched hut, unwashed and stubbled, waiting to be fed, becoming increasingly nostalgic for the British Army and increasingly impatient with the BBC. He could not understand, as he often told his son, why the British paid so much attention to tin-pot dictators and jumped-up Arabs whose entire armies would not, in his professional opinion, have lasted more than five minutes against a handful of Gurkhas on their day off.

After the first year or two in the shanty, he had hit upon the idea of earning a little money by means of the one trade he had learned in the British Army. Early humiliations in long evenings playing poker for tens of thousands of *lire* in shored-up sand trenches on the Anzio beach-head had eventually taught him to control his natural effervescence when sitting on anything higher than a single pair. And this, added to a prodigious memory for anything he wanted to remember, and a genuine talent for assessing odds, had eventually hardened him into a formidable player. Back home, he had quickly dismissed *booruwa gahanawa*, the local card game, as being fit only for women and children, and had set about teaching schools of men in the shanties to play first stud-poker and then the high-gambling Eighth Army variant known as 'seven-card roll 'em blind'. Once the game had become established, his own well-honed skills, assisted not a little by his virtual monopoly of the rules, had begun to yield him an unpredictable income from the tea shops and the dimly lit arrack bars in the sidestreets of Maligawatta.

Through the years in the shanty, these skills had earned him a fitful income, though it was true that a higher proportion of his earnings than he would have liked came in the form of pawn-brokers' markers, clothing club coupons, lottery tickets, co-op chitties, broken wrist-watches, teeth which purported to have gold fillings, and paper IOUs which he himself had introduced and later regretted. But it was also true that his poker evenings provided him with something more important: they were his source of solace, his feeling of acceptance, his sense of an order in which he felt he had a place and to which he had something of his own to bring, some milieu in which he felt forgiven. By and large, he had avoided the drunkenness and brawling that were endemic to the places he frequented, although there had been the night when he had returned home with a small stab wound in his hand after attempting to claim a sizeable pot through the injudicious evocation of a retrospective rule. The fact that the other players in the unwindowed, smoke-filled room would not have been ignorant of this rule if they had ever played poker with Lance-Bombardier George Stokes had commanded less respect than he had thought was due, and his attempt to claim the untidy flutter of worn rupee notes had been forestalled by the point of an upturned knife suddenly appearing where the pile of notes had been.

Eventually the epidemic of poker in the shanties, and his own undisputed pedigree in the game, had opened up another conduit through which a doubtful income had trickled into his temporary life. Late one evening, long after the oil lamps had been snuffed and darkness had descended on the shanty, two men had appeared outside his hut, hissing his name in low, agitated tones. After a swift and unreassuring survey of his recent conscience, Godfrey had been relieved to find that the two men, whom he barely knew, had come to ask him to adjudicate in a dispute over a poker game at Varindra's arrack house near the New Bazaar Bridge. There, in the darkness of the canal bank in the heart of the Maligawatta shanty, Godfrey had delivered himself of a judgement of Solomon: he had congratulated the two men on the high bluff they had both been playing at the time of the dispute, but pointed out that, technically, both had been in infringement of the admittedly complicated 'when to roll'em' rule, and that therefore, on this occasion, they should split the pot. After news of this adjudication had spread, other gambling disputes began to be brought to Godfrey's shack or, as his wife preferred, to the Bodhiraja Bar where he could usually be found on the two main poker nights of the week. It did not, of course, take Godfrey long to institute a small fee of ten per cent of the disputed stake, a charge easily acceded to as it was paid from money which belonged to neither party at the time the service was performed. And as it tended to be the higher games which caused the more bitter disputes, his honorarium, as he began to call it, often came to ten, twenty, fifty rupees at a time. Once established as the guru of gaming, he had eventually found himself adjudicating also on sweepstake disputes, chitty draws, election bets, pigeon races, and even, in time, neighbourhood disputes and matrimonial quarrels.

Apart from the war, the only other great event in Godfrey's life had been the birth of his son, and the immense new love that had been born in a man approaching middle age. But his wife had claimed Vijay, rebuffing all his attempts to be a father, and he knew in his heart that she was right, that he had no grounds for opposing her monopoly, that he offered no model for the boy to live up to.

The one thing that could not be denied him was that he had taught his son to speak the English language. At a time when the local schools were attempting cultural decolonisation by bending their pupils' minds to the reign of King Dutugemunu and the poetry of P. B. Alwis Perera, Godfrey had been introducing Vijay to the well-thumbed collection of Biggles comics and P. G.

Wodehouse paperbacks that he had brought back in his kit-bag. He had also tutored the boy extensively with his own oral history of the North African and Italian campaigns, palate-knifing local colour onto his accounts and employing numerous visual aids such as the piles of used radio batteries which marked the relative positions and strengths of Rommel's Africa Corps and Montgomery's Eighth Army. All of this was something the boy felt the lack of in the reign of King Dutugemunu, and he had effortlessly absorbed the English language, including several words which his father had not explained to him in detail but which he had been told conspiratorially, one man to another, were never to be uttered in the presence of ladies of the opposite sex. And most evenings as Vijay was growing up, father and son had sat together on the canal bank, heads cocked to one side, trying to catch the fragments of the World Service on the short-wave radio which Godfrey had purchased with the last of his wife's dowry.

Soon his wife would no longer listen to his reminiscences, her face permanently wrinkled in disgust at the life he had brought her to. But the telling of his adventures to Vijay had kept his memories alive over the years and sometimes, if the heat and the mosquitoes from the canal kept him awake at night, he would seek sleep by trying to remember the names of each of the men in his platoon. And when, as the years went by, he occasionally fell short by one or two names, he could barely wait for the morning to take down the bamboo-framed photograph, yellowing now and showing patches of mould, to search through the fading signatures on the brown-paper backing until he had discovered the men who had gone AWOL during the night. Sometimes, he had felt a small moment of bitterness on coming across the flamboyant signature of the captain whose casually broken promise had been such a watershed in Godfrey Jayasinghe's life; but when he saw his own signature among that band of men, he stirred with a pride that no one could ever take from him and he forgave heartily this small betrayal, wishing that he could once more shake the captain by the hand and tell him everything was A-Okay.

He awoke still thinking about the strange business of the Cheltenham Corner. There was movement now inside the house and he guessed that Chandra had returned. After a few moments, he pulled the radio towards him again and began to twiddle the dial, hoping to find *Letter from America*. A bookie couldn't always refuse bets on the winner, he reasoned. And if a man were careful, if he did not show his hand, there might be a little money to be made of a weekend. He warned himself not to overdo it. He knew the Mahmoud brothers, and did not want them to know him. But he might just milk them very gently, not so as anyone would notice. And for a moment he entertained the thought of being able to present his son with a cash sum large enough to pay the year's rent in advance, thereby allowing him to dispense with the services of K. W. Matthew, his Friend in Finance.

Through the afternoon quiet of the garden, he could just about pick up the measured, reassuring cadences of Alistair Cooke. But the batteries were definitely fading. Expertly he sprang them loose from the radio and set them in a line on the stone wall for the sun to warm them into a little more life, looking idly up and down the garden to see if anyone might be lingering on a verandah in anticipation of a game of cards. After a few minutes, Chandra appeared, bringing his tea and carrying two metal bowls.

'Funny thing happening maybe eight o'clock last evening,' he began.

'In dream?'

'No, not in dream!' He lowered his voice as Chandra smiled and began chopping greens from one bowl to the other. 'It is getting dark and I am turning on, and what is happening to be on BBC but bloody horse racing.' He looked round to see if anyone might be listening and pulled his chair a little closer to Chandra.

'And then I am just popping out for five minutes only . . .'

'Little flutter, I am thinking.'

'Shush! That is it, only small little flutter. But this fine day very odd thing is happening.'

Convention had it that a girl as dark as Chandra was beyond the pale of beauty. But the first time Vijay had brought her home,

Godfrey had stood up and offered her his chair, something he had not done for a woman in forty years, such were the looks and the presence of the eighteen-year-old girl from the other side of the St Sebastian Canal. Although educated to tenth grade, she had not at first had the confidence to speak English with her new family. But soon after the wedding she had approached her father-in-law, through Vijay at first, to see if he would give her lessons. Before long Godfrey's stories of the war years, which had long ago gone dull from the want of a new audience, had been brought out and burnished on the sleeve of memory, inspiration stepping into the breach when recollection fell wounded, until they had shone with all their former glory while Premawathie cleaned or sewed with pursed lips and occasionally looked up from her work and remembered the dashing young man who had first told her these stories so long ago.

At first, it had been Chandra's freshness which had cheered the old man. Nothing gave the old soldier more joy than to see her eyes lowered in modesty as he recalled some off-colour episode of his wartime experience, or the sceptical look which very slowly came over her face when the twists and turns of one of his stories had mounted such preposterous paths that it became obvious even to her that he was merely seeing how far credulity could be stretched. But as time went by the effect became more profound; her youthful beauty and the unjaundiced way she smiled at him were like oxygen to something in him that had long been suffocating. The truth of the matter was that his daughter-in-law had stirred anew the aspiration towards self-respect in Godfrey Jayasinghe. For many years he had had no status in his home. It was his own fault, he knew. But since his one great failure there had been no expectations to live up to, no pride to maintain, no approval to be earned, not even the incentive of a warm look to spur any effort. Chandra, by contrast, seemed to look for the good, reaching out until it came to meet her, giving it strength with her touch. From the beginning, she had shown an interest in his little arbitrations and, as her English improved, he had fallen into the habit of occasionally discussing one of his 'cases' with her, especially on the increasing number of occasions when his opinion was sought on a domestic issue rather than on a gambling technicality. On one particular day, when he had finished telling her about a dispute he had failed to solve and which had led to one of the parties setting fire to the other's shack in Henamulla, she had offered consolation by reminding him that over the years he must have prevented hundreds of fights and injuries, family ruptures, neighbourhood feuds, broken friendships, and heaven knows what other troubles in the slums and shanties. Tears had pricked behind the old man's eyes, and he had looked away across the verandah to the top of the garden; he had never thought of his little adjudications in this way, and through brimming tears he had a brief vision of himself as a rough diamond of the slums, a small defiance growing in his breast, a brave little stand against his life's guilts. The thought came to him that he had probably done more good than all the upper-class social workers who came and went through the lives of Maligawatta's poor, and before long the old gambler had begun to see himself as a kind of unsung Mother Theresa and to contemplate whether or not he might be justified in implementing a modest increase in his fees.

Godfrey was finishing his account of the previous evening's events at the Cheltenham Corner. Normally he could count on Chandra's attention, but this evening she seemed preoccupied.

'So,' concluded the old man, leaning back in his chair, 'intelligent chap like me is working it out. Other fellows doing it wrong way round. First placing bet, then listening to race. I am thinking it is better strategy to be first listening to race.' He sat back, his eyes gleaming at Chandra, but he had the feeling that she had not really been following his story.

She smiled vaguely, aware that her response should have been more specific, but before he could embark on another episode she had put her bowl down and moved to sit opposite him on the low wall.

'Now I am wanting to ask something,' she said, taking a deep breath.

Godfrey sensed that something important was coming and wondered if he might be about to become a grandfather again. He composed himself suitably, his hands resting in the broad lap of his sarong. Quickly Chandra told him about her notion of applying for one of the interest-free loans from the Women's Bureau.

'I am thinking we can be having calor gas oven,' she told him hurriedly, 'so we can be doing baking for cake shops and tea-houses and all. Such places springing up all over place, Maligawatta, New Bazaar, even Grandpass. I am thinking we can be offering cakes cheaper.'

'What is Amma saying?' he asked knowingly.

'I am not mentioning. I am waiting for just right moment.'

Godfrey smiled a long smile of understanding and began to ponder, wanting to help.

'Amma is doing only supervising,' said Chandra. 'All other things I myself am doing. Amma is not having to be fetching and carrying and going all about here, there. We are not having scavenging at all, calor gas only.'

Godfrey nodded at the wisdom of all this.

'Only, I am needing to know what oven is costing, second-hand,' she said, holding out her arms to indicate the size. 'Also about gas. How much costing, and how much we are needing for one baking only.'

The old man rubbed his chin and warmed to the task of ransacking his wide acquaintance for possible contacts in the world of second-hand ovens.

'Also,' said Chandra, hurrying on in case Premawathie came back, 'we must be knowing how much cake shops themselves are paying, wholesale price I am thinking.'

Godfrey nodded, working the business through. They would need to know what price to charge to undercut the bakeries and still make a profit.

'And most important thing also, Thatha, is knowing if you can be buying at trade. We are needing flour, sugar, fat, also caster sugar, dried fruits, nuts, all such things as well as gas. Eggs we are also needing.'

Godfrey's eyes gleamed as he began to see all the ways in which an old soldier could help.

'Needing maybe one day only to be telling all these things,' he said, spreading his hands expansively as if he would have preferred to have been asked to do something more difficult. Chandra smiled. Godfrey could find out almost anything in

Maligawatta by calling in a small favour, passing on a tip for a horse, tearing up a worthless IOU, or buying a glass or two of toddy.

'Not mentioning to Amma?' asked Chandra, just to be sure.

'I am not mentioning, but even if I am mentioning she is not listening'.

'Only thing is,' said Chandra, her smile changing to a frown, 'what to do if we cannot be paying loan.'

Godfrey smiled and passed her his empty cup.

'If worst is coming to worst, then I am thinking we may be getting little bit of help from Cheltenham Corner.'

7

Feeling refreshed and determined, Clara seated herself at table ten. Her morning newspaper had been accompanied by a typed note from the general manager of the hotel, a Mr Miles Perera, graciously requesting the pleasure of her company for a light luncheon in the private dining-room. Guessing that he had looked more closely at her business card, she had smiled to herself and telephoned her acceptance to the desk. She ordered coffee and mango, looking forward bravely to the day ahead. Beyond the lawns, the sun was already dazzling the sea and the palm trees were stirring lazily in the warm, spicy air.

'Black or white, Miss?' She glanced up at Vijay.

'Black, please.' He poured carefully from the heavy coffee pot into a porcelain cup bearing the red hotel crest.

Clara felt more settled. The violent vibrations of her sudden removal were dying away and, after a night's sleep, she was feeling less jittery, more justified in taking a little time for herself. She started slightly as a jackdaw landed on the next table, its needle-claws puckering the purple undercloth, cawing angrily at nothing in particular until the captain bustled towards it clapping his hands. Screwing up her eyes, Clara could make out the pale silhouettes of two oil tankers, motionless on the horizon. Today, she decided, she would be more determined in thinking things through, staying on the tightrope of sequential thought. The slices of ripe mango were placed before her by the agreeable young waiter who was now picking up her napkin from the tiles and unobtrusively placing it before her.

She sipped the delicious, bitter coffee and wondered whether she might not take another tour of the city during the course of the week. The driver of the taxi outside the Oberoi had not been pleased when she had stated her destination: 'That hotel only just down road, Miss,' he had said in a mournful voice, and she had realised that he had lost his place in the queue for the sake of a four-hundred metre fare. She had asked him to take her to see the old part of the city; there was always, she had found, an old part of any city.

As they crawled past street-lights whose concrete posts had been covered in layers of posters urging 'Don't Drive Drunk', 'Avoid Accidents', 'Jaycees Welcome You', and what looked as if they might be home-made announcements offering rewards for missing children, Clara had found herself entering more and more into the world outside her window. Here, every business spilled its identity onto the street – 'Tinkering and Spray Painting Done Here', 'Tyres remoulded', 'We Undertake to Demolish Buildings', 'Suppliers of quality radiator cores' – and everywhere the shifting layers of price and progress were as visible as the geological ages in a cliff. Jute sacks and cadjan packing materials were giving way to fibreglass bags and plastic sheeting; bullock carts plodded on behind Morris and Austin, trailing in their turn behind Toyota and Hyundai; hand-painted cinema advertisements, where over-ripe women looked up breathlessly at warriors gazing into the far distance, were pasted over with printed posters advertising *Emmanuelle in America* or *Temptress of Seoul*. They had turned down a narrow street which appeared to specialise in office services, and here too the waves of change were pushing urgently through: 'D. R. Senanayake – Sellers of Fine Carbon Paper and Stencils' threatened by 'P. N. Perera - Photocopying in Minutes – Bulk a Pleasure'; 'Block-makers and letterpress printer' struggling on against 'Off-set litho and plate-maker', itself under siege from 'Computer typesetting – tomorrow here today'. And as they had forged their way back through the busy streets, Clara, perspiring in the back of the little Morris, had begun to see her own world from further and further away, looking back in wonder at its oblique slogans and contrived motifs, its coy corporate façades, its strange culture of suggestion and allusion, its relentless pretence that life was no longer a struggle. And among the motley of shops and work-places, where every enterprise showed its innards to the world and a million souls were struggling to make a living, she had found herself escaping for the first time, prised loose from herself for a few minutes by the preoccupations of others. In her own cities, the fit between herself and the activity around her had long ago worn itself smooth; but here she had felt the freshness of bewilderment, the rawness of life breaking through some invisible barrier that she had hardly known was there; and a crack, like birth, had opened for an interminable moment as, amid the unknown struggles of unknown people, she had come together for an instant with her own insignificance, and had felt the first aching possibility of relief.

Vijay Jayasinghe breathed in the pure morning air. He had not slept well, and had been vaguely aware that Chandra had been up for much of the night. Then the bus had broken down and he had had to walk the last mile and a half, feeling the damp earth of Galle Face Green through the spreading holes in his shoes. Now, his bare feet comfortable on the warm tiles, he attempted to calm his agitation and allow himself to be soothed by his verandah. Whether in the early morning, when the still innocent sun flattened its perspectives, or later, in the evening, when the soft lamps lent depth and sophistication to its arches and pillars, he knew that the scene corresponded to something within him, inviting him to reach out and make it part of himself. Sometimes, for a few moments, he was able to surrender himself, letting its perfections wash over him, calming his disorders and dissatisfactions as the waves cleanse and smooth the disturbed sands of the shore line. At other times, the same perfections hurt him, as if they had created some embryo which pushed and longed for birth and a life of its own that was always to be denied.

It was with a polite 'good morning' and a small inward grimace that he normally greeted the first guests. But today he had admitted the occupant of table ten with good grace onto his verandah. Usually, the customers obtruded into its tranquillity, but Clara Lane seemed already to be a part of it. Any moment now, others would begin to arrive, running their fingers against the nap of the morning, unappreciative, in a hurry to swim or to sunbathe, to pack or to unpack, rushing their food, scraping their chairs, the women wearing ostentatious jewellery, or clashing red lipstick, or tight shorts over plump legs, or sweatshirts emblazoned with slogans and brand-names, or arched eyebrows pencilled in where no eyebrow had ever been before. And when they wanted to sign their bills and be off they would lean over the backs of the cane chairs and seek him out with impatient eyes. But the woman at table ten was, for the moment, exempt. Elegant and restrained in an Indian print dress of a black and sandalwood colour which wisely covered her pale shoulders, she sipped her coffee discreetly and set her cup down silently. Vijay looked long at the lonely figure on the verandah until the lobby doors burst open and four blond children came running to table six, followed by the two families of Scandinavians.

By eleven o'clock the restaurant was restored to order and Vijay and the waiters were taking a break, sipping saucers of hot, milky tea in the stone cellar under the hotel. Lalith, about Vijay's age and the only member of the verandah staff whom he considered a friend, was on his feet speaking excitedly, as was not uncommon. The others were proving a poor audience for the local representative of the Hotel Workers' Union, but they were all he could command at that hour of the day.

'It is lot of nonsense, I am telling one and all,' he was declaiming, conscious that he had pitched his voice inappropriately for an audience of five. 'Troubles are excuse for everything, everything! Hours are too long. Pay is too low. Conditions of service . . . execrable.' He wondered why he could not stop himself from projecting his voice as if for the larger audience to whom he had addressed a not dissimilar speech the previous evening at Kollupitiya Hall. 'Ah, it is the *troubles*,' he mimicked, throwing his hands up, fingers splayed, pushing out his stomach and his lower lip in what he believed to be a wickedly humorous personification of capitalism. 'No tourists are there. Hotels losing crores of rupees. How can we be giving wage increase?' He ended the mimic, his face suddenly sober, and addressed the group with a long silence which had somehow seemed more dramatic under the lights of the Kollupitiya Hall. 'I am knowing how,' he nodded his head slowly, 'I am knowing how.' Another silence, during which he noticed a not wholly appropriate glint of amusement on the face of his friend Vijay Jayasinghe. 'By taking out of wages they are paying brothers and cousins, uncles and all, who are supposed to be working but in fact are putting in appearance only on pay-roll. That is how. By taking out of foreign bank accounts and tax write-offs. That is how. By taking out of profit column in books kept for self only. That is how. By utilising vast profits of multinationals and hotel chains with many tentacles. That is how.'

'But I am telling this,' he hurried on, holding up his hand to forestall the applause which he felt should have been forthcoming at this point. 'They are not giving up any of these things willingly and woluntarily. Bourgeoisie is never giving up anything willingly and woluntarily. Legitimate rights not being given, my friends. Rights are having to be taken!' There was a half suppressed explosion of mirth from one of the other waiters and instantly the audience of five collapsed into hysterical laughter. Lalith stared at them with a look more pitying than insulted; this was not the reception he had received at the Kollupitiya Hall, where no less a person than the Ward Secretary had told him that his speech had done great credit to the Galle Road Branch of the HWU.

None of his present audience, his own chapel members, had attended the meeting, being confident that they would be treated to the highlights at a later stage. Now they were staggering around the boot room or lying in an undignified fashion over its benches, laughing themselves to that uncontrollable point where the spirit of laughter itself sees that two or three are gathered in its name and comes rushing down to bless their paroxysms of prayer, cutting loose their devotion from the particular cause of mirth and setting it free to celebrate the absurdity of life itself. Lalith, who even as he had built to his peroration had become increasingly conscious of addressing his five friends in the boot room as if they had been a rally of thousands on Galle Face Green, was now grinning ruefully despite himself.

'Peasants!' he shouted over the laughter, roughing up Vijay's hair as he went to refill his tea from the battered urn. It had been ever thus with the leaders of the working classes. The cup was one of those too badly cracked and chipped to be used on the verandah.

Even old Gamini had joined in the laughter. And now, wiping his rheumy eyes, he led the way from the old boot room as the staff wandered off to resume their duties.

Vijay walked with the old man as far as the bottom of the stairs.

'I wonder what Comrade William is saying,' he said, knowing the direction the old man's thoughts would have taken.

'Not mentioning in same breath,' said Gamini emphatically.

Old Gamini would have liked to pursue the subject, but his companion had turned up the steps towards the light streaming down from the verandah, and he found himself alone in the corridor under the hotel. Slowly climbing the back stairs, he eventually turned onto the disused gallery that looked out over the old ballroom and threaded his way between the redundant furniture to his accustomed place. His station was the gloomy first floor landing, but there was nothing much for him to do there at this time of day unless it was to bow his head and say good morning to a late arising guest, or unlock a door if someone had forgotten a key. So it was that he often found his way to the little clearing he had made for himself amid the jumble of former days, the wardrobes with doors which wouldn't close and the chests of drawers which had long ago been surrendered to the woodworm. Here he had picked out an easy chair of the traditional kind with a curved cane seat and extending arms on which to rest his legs. Screened off from critical eyes by the tall wardrobes, his retreat looked down on the old ballroom and, on the other side, to the verandah and the lawns. Here he sat for a while, his thoughts still on Comrade William, who had shared his shift so long ago. William, he said to himself, had not been all talk like Lalith. In that long-ago summer he had brought out almost every waiter and room-boy in the city and closed down every hotel in the city except one. Gamini stared into the dusty piles of furniture. What a battle it had been for those weeks, right in the middle of the season. There had been just a dozen of them left, including R. G. Thompson himself, and somehow they had kept the place going. They had manned the reception desk and the verandah restaurant, they had served bed-tea and made up the rooms, they had cooked kedgeree and haddock for breakfast, they had washed the guests' clothes on rubbing boards and whitened them at dead of night with dolly-blues, and they had stayed up until the small hours polishing the shoes and the riding boots. One of the greatest memories of his life was the night he had spent in the old boot room with R. G. Thompson, just himself and the general manager, silently cleaning dozens of pairs of boots by lamplight. He had seen then what Englishmen were made of, and he had shown that he too was made of the same stuff. What a fight they had put up. The memory still stirred his blood, flooding him with a fierce nostalgia. What a time that had been. He had been a man then.

Absently, the old man traced the name of William in the dust on the top of a chest of drawers. Years later, he had gone on to become a Senator, even made an official visit to Moscow. Thinking about his old adversary with something that bordered on affection, he remembered how they had loathed each other at the time. A traitor to his class, William had called him. But Gamini too had fought for the order he believed in, and he had sensed that William had secretly respected him, and that this was somehow a part of the fierceness of their antagonism. But now, in the sepia tints of his memory, he saw William, proud in his white hall boy's uniform, not as the implacable enemy but as someone betrayed like himself, as if William, long since dead, were sitting there with him and they were looking back together, from the same side of a subtler but wider divide than that which had separated them at the time. They had shared stirring times. Believed in something. Fought for it. The old man wiped his hand impatiently across the top of the chest so that the dust rose to spangle the pure shafts of sunlight like a scattered universe. Squinting, he leaned forward to rest his elbows on the balustrade which looked down over the old ballroom. Its pitted mirrors and dusty pilasters stared back, unmoved by his memories. He saw Umberto Nazzari, the flamboyant Italian, mixing his martinis with a flourish behind the pink plaster walls of the Octagonal Bar, and heard again the far off strains of Sacha and his Melodists on the patio over the lawn. In his mind's eye he saw the name of the *Canberra* chalked up on the arrivals board, and heard again the excited first-night chatter mixing with the perfume and the tobacco smoke and the strains of the music floating up from the glittering ballroom where the men stood around the walls, immaculate in evening dress, and the women drifted in and out with busy fans in an aviary of silks and satins. The music had gone on until two in the morning and the guests, returning to their rooms, had had to step over the hall boys sleeping in the corridors. One memory leading to another, Gamini struggled to his feet and wandered across to the open archway, looking out over the verandah from where he could almost smell the cigar smoke as it drifted up over the years.

Down below, a few tourists were taking an early lunch. Vijay was standing by one of the white pillars, looking bored. At table seven, two young Japanese were each listening to their separate sounds on bright plastic headphones, drumming their fingers on the table top. From the lobby, two Indians in brown suits walked onto the verandah carrying bright red airline tote-bags. Vijay seated them at table nine. Gamini pushed out his lower lip and narrowed his eyes: tape recorders and bags on the verandah! Below him on the path, a fair-skinned girl and her boyfriend were returning from the pool and Gamini watched in disbelief as they sat down at table eight, the boy wearing only long flowery shorts and the girl still in her bikini. He drew in his lip and bit it gently as he thought of what R. G. Thompson would have said. Moving slowly to the next window, he looked out across the lawns to the black and white chessboard patio where so many evenings had been danced away. All gone. Gone the order in which he had known his place. Gone the times when men took pride in doing what they did well. Why couldn't life come and go in neat generations, he thought to himself, so that a man could die in the order in which he had lived rather than this anarchy of birth and death which leaves men stranded in an alien time. For he could not come to terms with the turbulence that had swept aside those clear-eyed days. No one knew if his life was the right way up any more, if his lights were the eternal stars or just fireworks in the night sky. Now everything was, as he had heard it said, up for grabs. No one knew his place, all was permanently disorientated, dissatisfied, restless. Looking down he saw Vijay speak politely to the pair at table eight who reluctantly got to their feet, their movements heavy with surly condescension, and went to change out of their swimsuits. Gamini had always had a soft spot for Vijay Jayasinghe. Before he had taken to spending his nights in the dormitory under the hotel, he had walked over the Maligawatta Bridge every morning on his way to work. He knew the boy had lifted his whole family out of the shanty and into a respectable home. But Gamini had caught the look more than once. Even Vijay was not satisfied. The boy was not settled in his place, not settled at all.

8

Chandra hovered in the kitchen, trying to decide if this was the moment. Premawathie was out on the verandah waiting for her afternoon cup of tea, and it would be at least half an hour before she would begin looking down the garden for Vijay's return.

Several times her resolution gathered momentum, but each time some essential catalyst of courage was missing and she had gone no further than the bedroom where the clothes had already been rearranged half a dozen times on the line. Now she stood in the dimness of the kitchen, telling herself that it was only sensible to wait. Premawathie was furious with Godfrey, and there was every chance that her anger would spill over to scald Chandra as well. The next moment she was chiding herself for always finding some good reason for postponement. The only sound was the first little vibration of the kettle coming to the boil as she stood in the middle of the floor, rooted in indecision. A beetle scuttled away from under the pile of firewood. Through the gap in the tiles, a single shaft of light fell onto the metal rim of the lamp. Chandra picked up the tray with the teacups. On the cake-stand were two rather stale butterfly buns which she hoped might soften the fierce old lady out on the verandah. She turned towards the door with the tray and caught sight of the bottle of coconut oil glinting at her in the gloom. She decided that she would speak if Godfrey left the verandah before Vijay returned.

There was no acknowledgement from her mother-in-law as the tray was placed before her, and Chandra retreated to her chores, listening for the creak of the chair and the heavy footsteps which would mean that Godfrey was escaping.

On the bench outside, Premawathie remained rigid with anger. Godfrey was sitting uncomfortably on the red plastic chair, looking up between the eaves of the houses to an untroubled sky. The previous evening, he and two or three of the other men had been celebrating a mild win on the horses, and had returned well after midnight, waking up half the garden with their noisy farewells. Premawathie had lain furiously silent on her bed-board as he had entered the front room, none too steadily, and begun to undress. Then, in case anybody were still asleep, he had sent Vijay's framed diploma flying from the top of the display cabinet, shattering the glass on the concrete floor. Gunatilleke had banged angrily on the planking next door, disturbing Susil who had begun to cry, waking Chandra. Premawathie herself had lain awake for two hours more. Godfrey had gone straight to sleep.

But now, on the confined verandah, he was being silently roasted on the spit of his wife's disapproval. He blew on his tea, another habit of which she strongly disapproved, and rested his gaze on his feet, well aware of the look that would be awaiting him should he be unwary enough to catch her eye.

Premawathie sat straight-backed on the bench, her arms folded and her hands gripping each elbow, pulling the cloak of her anger ever more tightly around her shoulders. She stared out, unseeing, across the alleyway while, a few feet away, her husband shifted in his seat in a little exploratory move to test the prospects of leaving without attracting any untoward attention. Catching the small movement, Premawathie turned to look at him with all the accumulated resentment of her married life. Godfrey slowly sank back in his seat, pretending that he had not been about to get up, avoiding her eyes, aware that her look fell some way short of tenderness.

Premawathie continued to stare, her bitterness only increased by the fact, which she was sure would not have troubled her husband's memory, that tomorrow would be the forty-second anniversary of her marriage to this man who had returned from Europe promising her the world. She had not known, all those years ago, how typical it was of him to pin his hopes on some vague promise rather than on any realistic plans or diligent effort. For a long time she had believed him when he had told her that it was only a matter of waiting until things settled down after the war, that they were going to England, that he was going to be a man. She had not even despaired when they had been evicted from the modest rented accommodation into which they had moved after her marriage. More embarrassed than depressed, she had helped erect their makeshift shack of bamboo poles and plaited palms on the banks of the St Sebastian Canal; it had been just a temporary shelter until word came from Luton.

She looked at him as he sat opposite her in his off-white vest, picking at a loose strand of plastic in the chair. There had been no particular moment when it had become apparent that casual employment and a makeshift home were to be the permanent reality of their lives. At first, every setback had been borne with an 'I expect we'll hear from England soon' or a 'We'll soon be going home anyway', for that was in the days when England was still home to millions who had never seen her shores. But gradually, as his bus journeys to the Fort Post Office had become less and less frequent and the cheerful references to home had become fewer and fewer, her hopes had faded with the colours of her two good saris and her illusions had become as threadbare as the sheets on her marriage bed. After a few more years, the subject of England had become as painful to them as a dead child, and had never been mentioned again.

Godfrey sipped his tea. Balancing the cup on the wall, he began to reach unobtrusively for one of the cakes on the stand but made the mistake of looking up and, at one searing glance, he withdrew his hand and scratched his knee. From inside the house came the sound of Chandra sweeping the kitchen floor.

Premawathie was forced to relax her lips a little in order to drink. In compensation, she glared over her teacup at Godfrey, who was wisely looking down at his feet again. Soon, her eyes left her husband and travelled down the garden, already searching for her son's return. For almost fifteen years, she had refused to have a child at all, hoping that the shame of it would force Godfrey into getting a proper job. But as she had gradually abandoned hope of her husband, so she had eventually reasoned that there was no sense in depriving herself of the son who might one day succeed where the father had failed. It was, she had resolved to herself, her one last, best hope of not dying in that wretched place. Thereafter, she had done the thousand-and-one unregarded women's jobs which hold home and family together, bringing up their child as best she could, scarcely knowing an hour not weighted down by necessity or obligation. And if her husband's losings at the card table had been taken into account as well as his winnings, a method of calculation which he had never quite grasped, the truth was that she had also earned most of their little income over the years.

She looked down at the pitted chromium cake-stand but could not bring herself to eat anything, teeth-clenched, thinking of the thousands of such cakes that she had made during the years when Vijay was growing up. Even in the poorest homes of the city, shop-bought cakes were essential for weddings and funerals, for *poya* days and family visits, for anniversaries of birth and death. But baking was a middle class skill that had never filtered down to the shanties and, in her plight, Premawathie had seized the opportunity. For the best part of twenty years, her cup cakes and butterfly buns, maids-of-honour and Victoria sponges, had been their only dependable income. But to Premawathie it had been much more; it had been a public declaration of her respectability, her statement to the world that she did not belong in such a place. For her cakes were acknowledged by all to be every bit as good as shop-bought and, at one time or another, most of the women of the shanties had sought out the mean lean-to kitchen where dainty tissue-wrapped delicacies were born out of the blackened womb of an oil drum, crudely set in clay and heated by all manner of combustibles scavenged from the shanty or dragged from the canal. As she stared now at the cakes that Chandra had for some reason seen fit to bring out with the tea, all the pride and defiance of those years rose within her. She had seen to it that her son was as well-fed and well-clothed as any child from the slum gardens, providing him with everything he had needed including a regular supply of kerosene for the magnificent steel tilly-lamp by which he did his homework in the evenings amid the moths and mosquitoes on the banks of the St Sebastian Canal.

At her side Godfrey shifted again, wondering whether he

might still slip out for an hour or so before supper. Reluctantly, he decided that he had probably not yet served his time and began to fiddle miserably with the dial of the radio. Premawathie looked at him with no slackening of her hostility, daring him to start trying to find the BBC. Going home, she thought bitterly, going to be a man. It had never mattered to her. It was not against some imagined life in another country that she had set her life on the banks of the canal; it was against the more modest hope of a proper, legally occupied home with solid walls, separate rooms for sleeping, a latrine instead of the river, and somewhere to wash herself, privately, in clean water. Transcending these things, she had craved the recognition of her respectability; for her sense of her own worth was as solid as the earth under her feet, and her inner status burned like an unseen fire at that earth's centre. In circumstances which break and demoralise, the pliers of poverty cruelly breaking the fingers' grip on the rungs of respectability, she had clung stubbornly to her standards. Even as the months stretched into years and the years into decades, she had never ceased to regard with horror the crude hut, indistinguishable from a thousand others, on the banks of the St Sebastian Canal. Nor had she ever ceased to loathe the filth and the stench and the heat, the interminable flies all day and the millions of insects scratching in the cadjan at night, the festering heaps of rotting refuse, the beaten earth floors which turned to mud in the rains, the burning corrugated iron roofs held down by stones and tyres that were constantly having to be replaced, the motley of cadjan and rough planks which formed her four walls, the shard of broken mirror wedged between the planks, the lean-to kitchen with room only to crouch over the sooty oil drum and the blackened stones of her fire. Beyond anything, she had hated having to choose between the public latrines across the bridge, with their maze of slimy, excrement-smeared walls and their almost unenterable smell, and the undignified bottomless hut built on bamboo poles over the river with its screens of flapping plastic torn from old cement sacks and filthy fertilizer bags. Twice a week she had arisen at two o'clock in the morning to walk the half mile to the public facilities on the Mihindu Mawa where she could wash herself in private, without crowds or queues. At other times, she had been forced to join the women of the shanty who gathered on the stone steps to bathe themselves and wash their clothes in the green waters of the canal, just upstream from their own latrine but downstream from the hundreds of other shanties and latrines that stretched back through the crowded suburbs of the city.

Sitting on the verandah of the slum garden, oblivious now to Godfrey, Premawathie's face had grown dark and fierce with her memories. There had been thousands of other women in the shanties who had entertained hopes for a better life, but they had gradually become reconciled to what was, ceasing to press their faces against the broken glass of earlier hopes. And as the years went by with no change in their circumstance, they had eased the pain, found a degree of contentment, even a brief happiness, through adjusting the axes of the graph, gradually and imperceptibly reducing the gap between expectation and reality. But such accommodation had not been Premawathie's way; she had never bowed her head one inch to life in the shanty, never compromised her contempt, never relaxed for one second the tension between her life as it was and her life as she thought it should be. For almost forty years she had regarded her home as temporary, keeping locked in an old tin trunk the framed photographs of her parents and grandparents, the china tea-service, and the other refined household items which had been part of her dowry; for to display such things would have been to subject herself to a daily mockery of her circumstance, a constant reminder of its permanence. Nor would she even allow herself to sip from the cup that was the one great solace of the shanties: the sense of solidarity with the other women, the shared hardships, the little scraps of gossip, the ritual complaints and mild conspiracies, the helping hands and the small mid-week loans, the little mutual insurance of friendship and sisterhood. This, too, she held herself from, for to accept it would have been to accept that she had become a part of it all; and while her contemporaries had turned plump-armed and soft-faced from starchy food and social surrender, Premawathie, tense-jawed and sharp-eyed, tight strung to every slight touch on her respectability, had remained wiry and thin from the fires of resentment which consumed her from within. Others might consider her to have ideas above her station, but she had never regarded her aspirations as anything other than modest and reasonable, being convinced that if her husband had only fulfilled his role as she had fulfilled hers, with a degree of diligence in the jobs he had held and a proper respect for his wife, then they would have been able to achieve what she had never ceased to desire. But instead, he had reconciled himself to their life as it was. And so, as she approached old age, her respect for him had curdled and she no longer treated him with the submissiveness of earlier years; she had become grim-mouthed and iron-haired, and gradually the sap of her love had withered until it was as dry and sere as the brittle palm leaves which she had plaited for the walls of their temporary home so long ago.

Premawathie's eyes, ever attuned to her son's comings and goings, picked out Vijay the moment he entered the garden. She was about to take the tray inside, not wanting to be seen sitting out taking tea and cake in the afternoon, when she saw him step up onto the verandah of C. J. Periera, who came from a good family in Kandy and who also had a proper job as a clerk in one of the old-established department stores. The fierce knot of resentment inside her dissolved into a sudden and intense exultation in her son and his position. She had always known that it would be through him that the day of her recognition would come, that it would be Vijay who would lift her out of the shameful life that she had been forced to live. She had always been sure that this boy, with his height and his looks and his English, was destined for greater things. She thought, too, of the diploma that she had taken to be re-framed that morning, the intertwined 'Cs' of the City Catering College embedded in the red wax of its seal, and then turned her look contemptuously towards her husband. If Godfrey's prized photograph of his old platoon had been anything like the same size, then she would gladly have removed the frame from that instead. But as she looked at the radio that was in danger of falling from his sleeping hands, a moment of truth appeared like a blister on the perfect surface of her resentment and she acknowledged that Godfrey, for all his betrayals, had made one essential contribution to the fortunes of the family Jayasinghe.

Premawathie herself had been able to speak adequate English before her marriage, but her husband had returned from the war in Europe speaking like a *sahib*, and he had taught Vijay to speak the language as well as any boy from St Thomas' College. There had never been any doubt that he would take the school English prize, and with it had come the place at the City Catering College. Three years later, when Vijay had emerged with the only distinction of his year on his Diploma of Catering and Allied Studies, Premawathie had expected him to be offered a position in one of the grand international hotels either in the city or down the coast. But after a year had passed, and then two, she had been forced to acknowledge that Godfrey had been right, that her son lacked the one qualification more essential than any diploma: he had no one of any influence, no one who owed his parents any favours, no uncles or aunts with jobs in their giving, no brothers who could lean on anyone, no in-laws who could breathe the right words in the right ears, no money for the *kappang* to oil the hinges of employment's gates. But after more than two years of casual labour and tireless job-seeking, returning home shaking his head without wanting to look into his mother's eyes, the tide had finally turned in Vijay's favour. All along the coast the cry had gone up for hotel staff who not only had diplomas certifying their proficiency in English but who could also speak a word or two of the language, and one day, despite his helpless shrug of the shoulders when asked about the two-thousand rupee sweetener, Vijay had been interviewed and hired as an under-waiter in a place which, even if a little down-at-heel, was unquestionably the oldest and most respectable hotel in the city.

Now the flame of his mother's ambitions had risen from the embers which she had kept glowing over the years in the iron grate of her will. Fierce and unsmiling, she had gloried even in the deductions from his pay-packet: the union dues, the medical insurance, the sick pay contributions, the provident fund. Even net of all these tributes to a regular job, the small brown envelope had contained more than eight hundred rupees. But as no one knew better than Premawathie, its real worth was many times more: her son had become a catch, and could command a dowry in sovereigns, in gemstones and jewellery, in china and cutlery, in bed linen and Manipuri for saris, and perhaps even a sewing machine or a TV set. The problem now was that after so many years in the shanty her acquaintance was not such as to furnish many potential brides to populate her dramatically expanded horizons, and the little shack on the banks of the St Sebastian Canal was not, in any case, the sort of place to which one invited suitable families to take tea strained from a china pot and eat dainty cakes served from paper doilies. For months she had worried about selecting a bride, finding satisfaction only in the contemptuous dismissal of many of the shanty women who had daughters and who had suddenly begun to treat her with a little respect.

Then had come the dreadful, sickening day when her son had returned home and announced, out of a clear blue sky, that he had made a proposal of marriage to an eighteen-year-old girl who lived in a shack on the opposite bank of the St Sebastian Canal.

'Vijay, she is black,' was the first thing that Premawathie had said, feeling a tightening chill on her skin which rapidly contracted to close like a cold cage around her heart. 'She has no family. There will be no dowry.'

But she had known, even as she had spoken the words, that she would not prevail. Her son was now the head of the household, with all their destinies in his hands, possessed of all her own stubbornness and unrestrained by any pressure from kinsfolk, any overwhelming obligation to the family name, any parental wealth to be disowned by, any real understanding, despite all she had done, of the importance of station. For the rest of that day she had pleaded with both words and silence. But that night, lying on her bed-board listening to the scratching of the insects in the darkness, Premawathie had come as close as she had ever come to admitting defeat. And after a week of concentrated acidity to which Vijay had proved impervious, she had wordlessly begun preparing for the wedding.

As the day approached, she had waited bitterly for him to ask her about 'the arrangements', already resenting the thought of moving out of the hut so that Vijay could be alone on his wedding night with the woman she referred to openly as his little black bride. Like all mothers in the shanties, she had long anticipated the day when she would have to arrange to stay the night with friends or relatives, boarding out other members of the family on feeble pretexts, making sure that no one would call, putting up with all the subtle hints and coy questions. But Vijay had not approached her about the arrangements; even this, she thought, I am to be denied.

As the wedding day neared, the atmosphere inside the little hut had been thick with fumes from the engine of disapproval revving furiously within Premawathie until, exactly one week before the appointed day, Vijay had come home unexpectedly in the middle of the afternoon. Finding his mother alone, he had calmly sipped his tea and told her that there was something he wanted to show her. Tight-lipped but curious, she had covered a batch of cakes with a cloth and followed her son back up the embankment. Reaching the top of the shanty, they had walked alongside the old wall to a point where a dozen or so bricks had recently been removed. Without the slightest circumspection, Vijay had stepped through the gap in the wall and reached back to help her.

It had been a quiet time of day in the garden. The decaying latrine blocks and washrooms were unoccupied, and there was no one at the stand pipe with its dripping brass tap and cracked concrete apron. Nearby, the blackened ashes of a rubbish pile were smouldering slowly. In the shade of the wall, a dog slept peacefully and chickens strutted about, pecking at the bare earth. Slowly they had walked down between the houses with their fretted wooden verandahs, sagging lines of washing making it impossible for them to see as far as the alleyway. Only P. D. Norman Stanley, sitting on his verandah listening to the radio, had seen them enter; but he had shown no surprise and merely smiled a toothless smile at Vijay, leading his mother by the hand down the narrow lane.

When he had persuaded his mother to step up onto the verandah of No. 29, Vijay had quietly told her that his regular wage had secured the loan for the year's rent in advance, with enough left over to pay the outgoings, and that the house she was now standing in was to be her home. Premawathie had listened numbly as he had asked if he and Chandra could move in first and stay there alone for their wedding night; and then she had let herself be taken by the hand and led slowly back into the depths of the house. With the silhouette of her son framed in the doorway behind her, she had walked through the two rooms to the dark, empty kitchen. There, under the blackened beams and the rough tiled roof, standing in the darkness touching a concrete wall, she had cried for the first time in forty years.

9

Miles Perera was in the habit of inviting those whom he considered the more presentable of the hotel's guests to take a little light luncheon with him in his private dining-room. It was the equivalent of an invitation to dine at the captain's table, a comparison which often presented itself to the General Manager, it being a matter of no small regret to him that he was not empowered to perform wedding ceremonies for his guests. He did, however, pride himself on his little luncheons, to which he usually also invited two or three of his acquaintance selected from the more influential layers of the city's life. On this particular Tuesday, there had been the editor of one of the Lake House newspapers, the new Minister for Tourism, and the General Manager of the Intercontinental Hotel.

After introducing Clara, Miles Perera had summoned a servant to chase away the jackdaws that were having the temerity to caw disrespectfully right outside the window. He explained to his guests, as they took the iced drinks which left dark rings on the damask tray-cloth, that he had explored all possible ways of ridding the hotel of these pests, even writing to the Royal Society for the Protection of Birds to offer a donation if they could come up with a method of replacing the harshly cawing jackdaws with softly cooing doves for which he would have built white wooden dovecotes, on tall poles, in keeping with the style of the hotel. But they had had nothing permanent to suggest, and so he had tried to add jackdaw-chasing to the duties of the security guards; but they were not birds to scare easily and the guards, standing all day under the heat in their dark uniforms and peaked caps, had not shared his enthusiasm for running about flapping their arms on the shadeless lawns.

Clara had answered politely, but not fulsomely, several questions about her position as Director of Planning at Boston International, leading to a predictable discussion about how few women held senior positions in the corporate world. After that the conversation had soon settled, as she had gathered it usually did, on 'the troubles' and their effects on business in general and the tourist trade in particular. Only the previous day, she had gathered, a land-mine had blown up another army bus somewhere near Kalutara. A lightly grilled fish was served. Reprisals were confidently expected within the week. Miles poured a chilled Frascati.

She escaped at precisely two o'clock, relieved to retreat to her sunlounger on the strip of sand overlooking the ocean where a long afternoon stretched emptily before her.

Clara, the girl in the bikini on the cover of the holiday brochure, long languid limbs stretched out under a thatched sunshade, ice floating in the fresh lime-soda at her side, a cloudless sky above and the temperature curving effortlessly towards the mid-eighties as the palm fronds stirred gently in the small breeze coming in off the sea.

She closed her eyes. She had decided to do nothing but relax and listen to the ocean, hearing each wave, willing it to soothe her as the heat built up under the shade and she wondered whether she might need more cream on the flat of her stomach. For a few more minutes the steady warmth substituted for a sense of well-being, but soon her habitual concerns were setting up camp, driving little tent pegs into her consciousness. She resolutely pulled them out and strained to hear only the sound of the waves.

For a while she managed to maintain her sea wall, but the effort was such that she soon found her arms stiff and tense by her sides. She applied more cream, telling herself not to try so hard, to lie back and let relaxation find her. Meaningless wave followed meaningless wave, thrown onto the shore with a roar that had sounded down the centuries, while in the empty sky a gull slipped sideways on the wind and answered with an insignificant cry.

She opened her eyes. From somewhere across the lawns came the slow clack of an old typewriter. A faint headache was threatening and she reached for her sunglasses. Lifting her wrist, she let her head fall to one side, a small glow of pleasure, as always, as she looked at her watch, elegant, understated, gold. A few moments later she looked at it again, having failed to register the time, and wondered whether she dared risk lying for a few minutes under the open sun. She sank back and listened again to the waves, restlessness struggling within, fighting for the air of consecutive thought, of plans and resolutions, as she attempted its suffocation.

'I think you can look forward to some good news when you eventually get back from your holiday.' The 'eventually' had been redundant, and the Chairman had deliberately pronounced the word 'holiday' in a slightly puzzled tone as if to emphasise that the concept was unfamiliar to him. She felt blindly for her drink. The ice had melted and the lime-soda was almost warm. It meant that she was being appointed to Strasbourg. Success there would take her to Boston as the first woman on the board of BI. A fly landed on her thigh and she slapped blindly. The ocean hushed into the shore. The gull was nearer now, balanced in the wind, calling forlornly.

Clara sat up on the sunlounger, impatient with herself, hunting through her bag for an Anadin and a novel. She washed the capsule down with the last of the soda and began to read. But the overwhelming brightness of the sun poured around the edges of the page, blinding her to the print. Lying back, she tried holding up the book to block out the brightest area of sky. After a while, the tops of her arms began to ache and she turned over and propped herself up on her elbows. She had read less than a page when she gently lowered her face down onto the open book. She felt she might be able to relax now. But she had no sun cream on her back.

The waiter appeared but she smiled and shook her head. It wasn't altogether a pleasant sound, she thought, the waves launching themselves ambitiously at the beach and being sucked greedily back into the ocean. She sat up and began pushing her fingers between her toes to dislodge the little wedges of sand, wondering if the perfection of the holiday brochure was as elusive for everyone. The last product brochure out of Strasbourg had been a disaster. That would have to be a priority. She stared out to sea and thought about the speech she would make at her first meeting with her new staff. A particularly strong wave thudded against the sea wall below and, a second later, she felt its fine spray on her legs. Thinking that music might work where the waves were failing, she disentangled the headphones from the contents of her bag and lay down again, arms stretched out over her head, trying to concentrate only on the deep strains of a cello concerto. But the headset could not quite shut out the waves which crashed carelessly across the music with a disturbingly fresh and uncontrived sound, setting up confused messages inside her head. She brought her arms forward again, covering the tops of her thighs with her palms. The problem in Europe was that virtually the entire product range was two years behind the competition. All her marketing skills could not alter that fact. Yet it would take years to bring a new range to market. Elgar had moved into the middle movement and become grating and tense; she lowered the volume, wondering whether to change the tape for something else. The waves seemed louder now, and she decided she should really listen to one or the other. In a minute or two she would order another lime-soda, with a second glass of ice on the side; then she would swim and see if she could improve on yesterday's time. She closed her eyes again. The music was now almost too soft to hear. It would be time for her to move on by the time a new product line-up was coming on-stream; it would be her successor that would reap the benefit. A pair of seagulls had joined in with the tetchy cello and the deep thud of the waves; the cacophony was too much and she snapped off the cassette-player, wondering if she should perhaps have gone sight-seeing after all. She lay back again, the tops of her thighs tingling. With what they had to offer in Europe at the moment, even a brilliant marketing operation would probably do no more than maintain market-share. That would not impress anyone in Boston. She decided to try her mother's old remedy, relaxing each set of muscles in turn, starting with her toes. The clacking of the typewriter had stopped. It was quite easy relaxing the legs. From behind her, she could hear the verandah staff preparing to serve afternoon tea. Somehow she needed to condense years into months and launch a new range by December. She closed her eyes while the bees of her concerns swarmed on and on without ever alighting, sometimes descending to buzz around impenetrable bushes before being borne aloft again by an unseen energy, their noise overpowering the sound of the sea as they visited the next bush before rising again in a storm of anxiety, until Clara opened her eyes to stare up into the dark, aged, thatch of the sunshade, telling herself that she might as well be back in her office.

She raised the back of the lounger and looked out from under the eaves of the thatch. The vastness of the ocean stared back at her. For long seconds, she attempted to commune not with herself but only with the glory of sea and sky and the gentle, unselfconscious sound of the waves. But consciousness mocked her efforts, easily retaining her, clasped in its pure, cold prison, withholding her from her surroundings, holding beauty at a safe distance, screening out its wordless message.

After a few more minutes, she walked the narrow strip of sand to the pool, struggling against dizziness born of heat and jet-lag and the blinding light. She smiled at the waiters standing in the shade of the pagoda, and lowered herself into the water. Releasing all the air from her lungs, she let herself sink slowly to the tiled floor of the pool, imagining her preoccupations floating away, left behind on the surface like so much flotsam. She pushed easily back to the surface and hung from the brass rail, watching the large clock on the changing-room wall. As soon as the second hand reached the vertical, she launched herself into the first length, determined to think of nothing but the effort of thrusting and gliding from end to end. The water, deliciously cool, tasted of salt, and she wondered if it had been treated or simply pumped in from the sea. It was good to stretch out so weightlessly, with less risk of a strain. Taking another deep breath as she turned, she pushed off hard, opening her eyes to see the tiles gliding silently by beneath her. Perhaps a licensing deal would be the answer. One of the Japanese or Korean companies, eager to establish a presence within Europe's walls.

She pushed her face back into the bright water, confident that two more strokes and a long glide would take her to the brass rail. She would need to go to the Board, and it would probably be opposed. Boston still had its dinosaurs who could only see the Japanese as the enemy. Turning again, unaware of the four poolside waiters who were intently following her progress, she forced herself to push harder into the last two lengths, heart pumping and thoughts racing. It might even give her a new product line-up inside six months. As she turned again, she blinked the water from her eyes and glanced at the clock. She was easily going to beat eighteen minutes.

Clara lay down without drying herself and let the small breeze cool the beads and rivulets of water on her suncreamed skin. She raised one arm and looked again at her watch. Four o'clock. She drank too much tea. She would give it up for the whole holiday. Or at least wait for another half-hour. She lay back again, feeling her skin begin to tighten as it dried. Every last little thing was choice, mother of anxiety. That was it: too much choice and too little necessity. She looked up at the underneath of the thatched umbrella with its spokes of thick bamboo, darkened by age. Behind her were the massed millennia of necessity, the whole human race being herded through history by the black dogs of need; and now she had arrived at the sea wall, poised before a new millennium of infinite choice, infinite anxiety, and herself among those brave souls who were the first to plunge or be pushed over the edge. She was reminded of the moments in the back of the taxi when she had felt as though she might be being taken out of herself, and the thought came to her like a distant hope that this was one thing she could do to break out of her self-absorption: she could get out and see ordinary people living ordinary lives, people with dirt under their fingernails, people who weren't afraid to handle naked, grubby money without hiding it in red leather folders, people who cared nothing for her own existence or concerns, people who were managing and coping with their own world as best they could. Her small foray into the city had evoked a response in her, and in an undefined way it had seemed to help. But as she thought about venturing once more outside the hotel, she saw again the face of the dark, intense little girl on Galle Face Green.

She decided to risk a few minutes under the unhindered sun, and began dragging the lounger sideways over the sand until it was clear of the elliptical pool of shade. Smearing on more cream, she lay down again, hoping that the heat would help her to relax. Some way to her left a young Asian girl had walked down to look at the sea, carrying a parasol against the sun. The girl smiled shyly and looked away.

Within seconds, a conscious heat was seeping through Clara's every pore, flooding her blood with warmth, caressing her bones, laying ardently across her stomach, pressing down on her breasts and the hollow of her shoulders with its fierce friendship, an orange universe of friendship, visible even through the veins of her tightly closed eyelids. And as the sun insisted on its brightness, so the truth began to softly demand its due. She thought of all that lay ahead, and watched the feeble dam of her enthusiasm breaking, seeing all that was important to her swirl away in a frightening wave of indifference, carried off in a sea of insipidity, an eternal, pale, underwater boredom, an ocean of vapid grey waters through which only a little yellow sunlight filtered as the waves passed gently overhead. She thought ahead to the next week, to all that awaited her on her return, in London, in Strasbourg, in Boston: new challenges, new colleagues, new home, new city, and the vapid sea became a desert of endlessly undulating dunes, dunes of soft sand which would absorb her strength, dunes whose crests held no promise but of more dunes beyond, dunes which held no possibility of relief and into which she would eventually fall and disappear without ever knowing why.

The sun burned her, fusing thought with feeling and removing all the normal denominators of her life as she clenched her eyes tight and fought to stay with the threatenings that she had long avoided. But as soon as she glimpsed the shape or the shadow of a truth she began thrashing in the water as if to escape, fighting to the surface, struggling to regain the conviction that all was tiredness, only tiredness, tiredness circling round to attack her from behind, tiredness disguising itself in all manner of ways in order to get past the sentinels of her willpower, her pride. Her earlier resolve had been right; the thing to do was to rest and unwind, restore herself, and all would be well. But the sun bore down upon her unmercifully, telling her that it would not do, forcing her back inside the bright mirror of her closed eyes, confronting her with what she knew but would not know: that there was an unignorable failing of the sap, a desiccation of some vital essence, leaving only a dusty void in the place from which the water of life should have been drawn. She covered the tops of her thighs with her book and attempted once more to submerge herself in the sunlight, trying to connect what she had glimpsed to what she was, to all that she had achieved, to all that lay ahead. For brief moments she held in her burning eyelids the knowledge that for months she had been dredging her motivation from others' expectations, concerned only with maintaining a reputation that defined and supported, driven only by securing the daily diet of approbation, a humming bird sipping nectar only to stay aloft, staying aloft only to sip nectar, wings vibrating at invisible speed, ever moving on, nectar to energy, blurring the wings, never looking down; and in a moment of certainty beyond recall, she knew that what had carried her to this place was the knowledge that she could not go on, that the wings would stop beating, and that she would fall, light and desiccated as a long-dead insect.

10

Even with the door open the heat and stench inside the latrine was making Chandra feel faint. As she bent to begin scraping the cracked squatting plate with the stiff *ekel*, her own body blocked most of the light from the doorway. Not breathing, she swayed with the rhythmic movement of the brush.

When she was sure that every centimetre of the plate had been scraped, she turned to face the open door. Taking several deep breaths before turning round again, she noticed two or three of the garden women watching her surreptitiously from just inside their verandahs. She blocked her nose with air and turned into the latrine, pouring the bucket of water slowly around the cracked concrete plate. This done, she stepped out of the cubicle and began again to fill the bucket from the standpipe. As always at this time of day, there was hardly any pressure in the tap and the water dribbled reluctantly into the bucket. She wondered whether she was doing the right thing. 'They will just be letting you do it', Vijay had said when she had mentioned it to him early that morning. 'Already, Amma says she is hearing Mrs Ranatanga saying it is job only for blacks.'

The bucket was still only half full. Until the beginning of the year every family in the garden had contributed five rupees a month for the Tamil coolie to come and clean the latrines; but the coolie's son had secured a job in the Middle East and the old man had immediately retired. No one else could be found to take on the work, and eventually a new system had been agreed upon at the Garden Council: every house had been put on a duty roster assigning a different pair of women to clean the latrines every day so that no one had to do the job more than once a month. At first all had gone well. But over the last few days the system had begun to break down. Two or three of the women had refused when their turn had come around, arguing that latrine-cleaning was unsuitable to their status. Within a day or two, those who had been willing to take their turn were announcing that they were no longer prepared to do so if others were going to declare themselves above the job. Soon no one was cleaning the latrines at all, and as the smell had arisen so had the familiar sounds of resentment and recrimination. In a week the situation had become so bad that people had begun walking the half mile to the public latrines on the Mihindu Mawa. But the filth and stench in the public toilets were nearly as bad, and it had not been long before the search for a usable latrine had shifted to the junior school just across the bridge. This had quickly brought a complaint from the school authorities who had sent a note home with all pupils, and even prompted a visit from a bored policeman whose attempts to investigate provoked only angry outbursts as neighbour blamed neighbour and recrimination flew from verandah to verandah long after the policeman had retreated on account of the stench. The community had known nothing like it since the days of the great wall-breaching dispute.

The smell was worst in the heat of the day, but it was at night, when silence had descended on the gardens, that Chandra, lying awake on her bed-board with the smell of the latrines coming and going in waves through the wood-smoke and the night air, had decided that something would have to be done. With the sound of Susil's gentle breathing on the floor beside her, she had worked the problem round and round in her mind and eventually a plan had begun to form.

The water had slowed to less than a dribble now and the bucket was still not full. Impatient to get the job done, Chandra turned off the tap and prepared to open the door of the second latrine. She took another deep breath and stepped inside.

Ten minutes later, as she stood in the confined space of the garden washroom, pouring cold water onto her body in the darkness, she went over the rest of the plan. There were three or four young mothers in the garden whom she knew she could rely on. She had persuaded them to go with her to the classes at the clinic and, following one particular lesson, they had started a garden playgroup and a shopping pool. Rita, Merlin, and Dhanawathie would certainly clean the latrines with her if she asked. But she knew it would not be long before the other women of the garden brought themselves to accept this arrangement, and even to think of it as natural that the job should be done by the younger wives, especially if they happened to be darker-skinned.

In the dimness of the washing cubicle, she decided to lather herself all over again with the tiny bar of perfumed soap from the hotel. As she slowly rinsed off, the water glistened and shone on her limbs in the little light that filtered in from the letterbox-size opening in the door. Her plan depended entirely on the visit she was about to make.

Normally, Chandra would have been on no more than nodding terms with Mrs C. J. Periera, a tall, fair-skinned Burgher woman of good family who had fallen on hard times but who was still, without doubt, the first lady of the slum garden. Although she had not known the family herself, Chandra had been pleasantly surprised to find that there had been no objection to Susil playing with the Periera children and even entering their home. Trying not to scrape her elbows on the rough concrete walls as she dried herself, she built up her courage. She had made the acquaintance the previous January. On the Saturday, Mrs Periera and her oldest boy had taken the bus to Kandy to visit her ailing father, leaving her three-year-old son in the charge of her husband. On the Sunday afternoon, while the father was out for an hour, the boy had drunk from a glass of *Pulli* insecticide which was waiting to be painted into the cracks of the kitchen walls. It had been Susil who had discovered his friend crying and vomiting in the darkness. Chandra had carried the boy in her arms through the gap in the garden wall and along the back of the shanty to the traffic lights at the bridge where she had stood in front of the first car and directed the driver to take them to the Co-operative Hospital. By the time Mrs Periera had returned from Kandy that evening the crisis had passed, though her son was still in the hospital. Some women of good family, Chandra knew, would have resented the help she had given, mortified at being under an obligation to a person such as herself. But Mrs C. J. Periera had visited Chandra in her own home, thanked her profusely, and complimented her mother-in-law on the lightness of her cakes.

Chandra, dressed and feeling clean again, allowed all of this to run through her mind, charging her confidence, as she passed by her own verandah and continued on down the garden.

She had not herself been inside No. 7, and she looked around curiously when Mrs Periera had retreated into the kitchen to make tea. The walls were made of concrete and planks like her own, but the floor was tiled and smooth. On top of an intricately carved teak display cabinet stood what Chandra knew to be a television set, covered in a muslin cloth. Beside it stood an old but still working National Panasonic cassette-player, softly playing traditional music. On the wall was an antique clock with a fine walnut case in which a heavy brass pendulum swung to and fro in a dignified manner. The house was legally connected to the electricity line on the main road, and a light bulb hung from the centre of the ceiling. On the floor a fan whirred as it swung menacingly towards Chandra. Tea, when it came, was served in china cups, taken casually from the display cabinet.

At first Mrs C. J. Periera had been speechless at the suggestion, but Chandra had kept on talking in order to forestall an outright refusal and, after reflecting for a few moments, while pouring them both a second cup of tea, the older woman had begun to see the point: if she and Chandra began cleaning the latrines together, then the social pressure on the others would be almost irresistible and the rota system might be reinstated. After the initial shock, the idea began to grow in appeal as she saw that, in an upside-down kind of way, it would in fact be an underlining of her status in the community. Chandra, sitting up very straight, sipped her tea and spoke in Sinhala.

'I have already cleaned both latrines thoroughly this morning. The job would not be very unpleasant tomorrow.'

Delighted by her own daring, Mrs C. J. Periera had agreed to secure her husband's permission and join Chandra in the latrine cleaning. Any little difficulty with her husband, she knew, could be overcome by alluding to the unfortunate circumstances which had placed her under an obligation to the young woman from No. 29.

'Why don't you speak up more at meetings, Chandra?' said Mrs Periera, changing the subject. She was the only woman on the Committee of the Garden Council, and frequently made what Chandra considered to be the only sensible contributions. 'And can't you persuade your husband to come too? We won't get anywhere you know if people like Vijay Jayasinghe don't get involved.'

Chandra said something about Vijay's shifts and Mrs Periera shook her head and admitted that she couldn't get C. J. interested either. C. J. Periera had a job in the accounts department at Harrison Lester's, the old established department store in Fort, and was the only other man in the garden who was paid by the month. Mrs Periera seemed to be implying, extraordinary as it was, that this gave the two women something in common and Chandra, eager to respond to the gesture of friendship, promised to speak up at the next Garden Council meeting when an official from the town hall was supposed to be coming to discuss the possibility of additional latrines.

'I have been meaning to ask you,' said Chandra, nervously, 'about the loans for women in the gardens, for starting small businesses.'

Mrs Periera shook her head.

'Apparently all you have to do is fill in the forms and get them stamped by the President of whatever garden you're in. Then they go off to the Town Hall. Munyandi should know all about it, but he never reads anything they send him you know.'

'Have you heard of anyone getting such a loan?' asked Chandra.

'I've heard that hardly anyone has applied. Two women in one of the gardens on the other side of Grandpass have got loans for coir making, though where they'll sell the stuff no one knows. And Connie de Silva was telling me that a woman in Bloemendhal has started a small book-binding thing, just for school note-books and the like. If you're interested, Chandra, why don't you just go and see Munyandi. He'll jump at the chance to stamp anything you know.'

❊

No home in the slums is complete without one of the low wooden cabinets with sliding glass doors in which is kept everything that can be considered a luxury. Standing always in the front room of the house, it is the inventory of status, the focal point of rivalries and snobberies, the place where any new prosperity is revealed and any decline in fortunes first becomes evident. Although second-hand, the cabinet before which Premawathie Jayasinghe now knelt was a fine example, with a prim chromium lock for the glass doors and a mirror fitted across the back to double the depth of the display. On most days, Premawathie found a few minutes to rearrange the contents, even if they had not been disturbed, but this afternoon she had decided to empty out the cabinet in order to dust its three glass shelves.

Most of the treasures had come from the blue tin trunk which had stood, padlocked, for over thirty years in a corner of her hut in the shanty, and to see its contents properly displayed was a pleasure that had never palled. She gently dusted the few items standing on top of the cabinet, including the fading portrait of her own father in a stiff white collar. The blue trunk still stood in the corner of the room, but now it contained only bleach and insecticide, and a few medicines. On the day that she had carried it through into the slum garden, she had refused all offers of help; with her head held high and her mouth set firm, she had passed between the ranks of the curious and lifted the trunk up onto the verandah of No. 29. There had been very little hostility to their arrival in the garden; some of the younger women, seeing the way their husband's heads turn to follow Chandra whenever she walked down the garden, had been heard to describe her as a 'little black wall-jumper', but many of the women had been surprised to find that their husbands already seemed to know Godfrey Jayasinghe, and had laughed and jeered good humouredly as he had come through the wall carrying his rickety old table with the torn green-baize top.

The seal had been set on their acceptance by the satisfactory furbishment of the display cabinet, a task which Premawathie had approached with all the reverence of a moment for which she had waited all her married life. With the trunk on the floor beside her, she had arranged a patterned china tea service in the

sponges, four or five different kinds, to the shops in Grandpass. There are so many of them now, you know. It would be a small business for you and me, Amma, to help Vijay.'

Premawathie was about to defend Vijay but Chandra hurried on to forestall her. 'I know he doesn't need our help, Amma, but if we could just help him to save the advance so he doesn't have to take the loan . . .'

Premawathie turned away and looked down the garden. The family's finances were none of Chandra's business. Vijay did not even discuss such things with her, let alone with Chandra. But as the moments passed her leaning towards an outright rejection of the idea was slowly hauled to the upright. She would like to think that she could still be of use to Vijay, that he still depended on her for something. And she was almost certain that he was not managing to save very much, and would need to borrow most of next year's rent all over again. She had heard people saying that they were wanting more than five per cent per month in Kochchikade. She began immediately to consider what the other families in the garden might think, and decided that there would be no loss of status providing there was no scavenging.

'What we are doing for fuel?' she asked, sceptically, switching to English.

'We are having calor gas stove,' Chandra repeated, elated at Premawathie's use of 'we'. 'Changing heat just only with dial, Amma. No mess at all. Not even smoke is there. It is proper baker's oven we are having.'

Premawathie looked away down the garden. With calor gas, it would not be too much work. Chandra had picked up baking remarkably well for someone of her background. And in any case, Chandra would just be doing the fetching and carrying.

'Shops are selling?' asked Premawathie, in a tone which, though still sceptical, betrayed a rising interest.

Chandra, her enthusiasm bursting her restraint, replied in Sinhala.

'Oh, Amma, I am sure they'll take them. Even Mrs Periera, when she gave me tea. "Have some cake Chandra," she said, "though it is not as good as your mother's."'

After a long silence, Premawathie had promised to think about it, though nothing was to be said to Vijay for the present. There had even been talk of a trial run, with Chandra taking some of Premawathie's cakes to the shop at the corner of Messenger Street. Chandra went to collect Susil from the top of the garden, burning still with the lie.

11

The verandah was at its most perfect in the evenings when the parchment lamps glowed gently on the whitewashed walls, contrasting with the deep rhythms of the shadowed arches, lending an intimacy to the scene, dissolving its imperfections, drawing its occupants together in identical pools of light while across the dark lawns the careless night winds blew in from India and the ocean murmured to the shore.

Vijay stood by the antique desk, his fixed place for the evening shift. The first diners were perusing the menus and ordering aperitifs, their low voices strangely insubstantial against the vast, stirring wind under a star-filled sky. He looked down the groups of guests huddled in the yellow light of the lamps and thought how feeble and vulnerable it all was compared to the universe of night and ocean out across the lawns. There was still no sign of the English woman. He had been aware of her down by the beach all afternoon, wondering if she would be red and burnt when she came to her table. The half-dozen Germans in the bar were pushing their chairs back noisily, standing and waiting for each other, stretching and looking bored. Eventually they sauntered into the verandah restaurant.

He returned to his place and stood waiting to be summoned, telling himself that he must somehow find a way to unpick the knots of his dissatisfactions. But the night was warm, and he soon wandered away onto less strenuous paths of thought, knowing only that his periods of restlessness assaulted him in sudden forays, with no obvious pattern or cause, coming and going according to some inconstant chemistry beyond his control. He looked at the empty tables in his own sector, drawing pleasure from the one contribution he had made to the verandah's perfections: some months ago, on an impulse, he had replaced the scratchy dried flowers on his eight tables with tender white temple flowers bought for a few cents on the Kollupitiya Road. The act had afforded limitless amusement to Lalith, but the General Manager had happened to take lunch on the verandah that day and, liking the effect, had ordered temple flowers for all tables during the season.

Sometimes he could gaze down the row of softly glowing table lamps and find contentment in being part of it all, carried along by its harmonies, comfortable with his sarong, knowing that both he and it had a place in the order which made possible its civilised beauty. But there were other times when he felt himself overwhelmed by his surges of discontent, pushing against the cloth of his sarong, fighting against being nothing more than one of the slim white pillars in the colonnade. It was at such times that he engaged in the most wounding encounters with himself, the endless self-absorbed questionings, finding respite only in a temporary certainty that the self he questioned was circumscribed by waiterdom, that it was useless to chafe against such irons. But more often he was dragged down by a weightier certainty that the problem had to do not with what he was but who he was, that it was ultimately a question not of his waiterdom but of some inner lack, a lack of that unselfconscious self-confidence, that maturity and manhood, that ease of presence and personality, that assured sense of equality, lightly worn. That this must be true was evident to him from the demeanour of the other members of the verandah staff. They were not, he supposed, constantly writhing and wrestling with such problems. He looked up at the day captain and saw that, for all his unctuous vanity, he was a man who was all of a piece, someone for whom the inner self and the outer self were in touch with each other, standing on the common ground of a sure personality. Vijay stared at the captain, certain in his own mind that such a man did not suffer from this separation of powers, this acute, intense, persecution from a personality-less observer at his centre, constantly and critically monitoring every nuance of his behaviour, certain too that he did not squirm under every human contact, raw to every insult and abrasion, racked by panics, doubts, humiliations, comparisons, that absorbed most of his energies in a constant, feverish inquisition in some dark dungeon under the mind. For a brief and steady second, Vijay knew that it was this which brought him to the verandah each perfect morning with a new and tender hope: the quest to be of a piece with himself, to find a place on which to stand, neither mounting parapets of pretentiousness nor tumbling into the dungeons of self doubt, but standing at ease on his own personal ground. This was what summoned him to each shift with an eagerness, a trepidation, making every trivial encounter into a personal battle in which his fortunes rose and fell by criteria known only to himself. At the times when he felt he was succeeding, the beauty of the colonnade seemed to become a part of him, its lamps glowing with a present nostalgia, the tiles cool beneath his feet, the familiar sounds convivial, the guests equal spirits, buoying his sense of self and leaving him at peace with his world, at one with his verandah. But when he was failing, the same surroundings became his hall of humiliation where he could only shuffle awkwardly, walking barefoot on the coals of his self-consciousness, unworthy to be there, he alone spoiling its perfections. At such times the guests became monsters of rebuke to his inadequacies, their smiles a leering mockery of his failures, each burst of inconsequential laughter a chorus of derision at his exclusion, their politenesses a condescension to the vanquished, their rudeness a confirmation of his own inadequacy.

Vijay watched the wine waiter taking an order from table six; Ananda had never tasted wine in his life and always asked the guests if they would be kind enough to order by number. He was due for retirement soon. Vijay himself had taken a course in the selection, storage and serving of wine at catering college, and he supposed there was a chance he might get the red stripe round his sleeve and the ten per cent off the top of the tips. Vijay watched Ananda shuffle away to the wine cellar. It was also rumoured that the captain might take early retirement to go and live with his daughter when she came home from the Middle East. It was even possible that he might one day be made captain, if he showed a little diligence and kept reminding the Food and Beverage Manager of his qualifications.

He served soup to the Germans at table twelve, feeling his

tensions rise to the indifferent provocations of those who looked elsewhere when they spoke to him, ordered their food without a serif of civility, used him like an ashtray, a napkin, a tooth pick, without any acknowledgement of a fellow human being. There were times when he responded by asserting himself, emerging from the furniture, starting little conversations, using his very best English. Sometimes he would go for a whole day concentrating on not letting the first syllable of his speech stretch out at such yawning, leisurely length that it lasted longer than all the rest of the sentence put together, rigorously avoiding expressions like 'fellow' and 'one fine day' which the others took to be hallmarks of familiarity with colloquial English but which he knew to be quaint. And he was especially careful, whenever engaged in any conversation with a guest, to restrain himself from the national habit of giving a little wag of the head and uttering a small guttural sound in the throat to indicate his attentive agreement. Since the day he had seen the Frenchman at table nine woodenly imitating this sideways rocking of the head to the amusement of his whole party, he had vowed to keep a still head on his shoulders. Yet after each small, insignificant assertion, he would experience a reaction, not needing Lalith to point out to him that he was only asserting himself as a sahib; he knew that he was saying in a false voice 'I am a person in your terms', and that he was no nearer to saying, without need of words or obtrusiveness, 'I am a person in my own terms'. He knew this was true, and he knew that it was the door he must enter; but he could not cross its threshold, for he knew not what his own terms were.

He wished the hotel were busier. Keeping track of twenty constantly changing tables would have left him little time to indulge his oscillations of tense and calm. But the tourist tide had ebbed, turned by the pictures of the blown up aircraft on the runway, the contents of charred suitcases scattered on the tarmac: the bikinis and the beach wear; the shrivelled plastic bottles of sun lotion; the pitiful collections of cosmetics and insect repellents; the broken spectacles and half-burnt guidebooks. Nowadays the city's hotels had nearly as many waiters as customers, and Vijay spent most of his time standing at the end of the verandah gazing for long minutes out over the ocean, often having to be brought back to earth by the captain's cough.

A movement above caught his eye and he looked up to see the white-haired figure who had now appeared at one of the windows of the first-floor balcony. Despite the difference in their ages, he suspected that old Gamini knew something of his discontent. It had been Gamini who had shown him the ropes when he had first come to the hotel, and it had been Gamini's address he had given to avoid revealing to his employers that his home was in the Maligawatta shanty. In the years since, he had spent hours listening to the old man's memories, his aching nostalgia for an order that was gone, shattered as completely as the chandelier which had fallen to the ballroom floor and of which Gamini still kept a single piece – a pear shaped earring of cut glass – wrapped in tissue paper at the back of his locker. There was nothing the old man enjoyed more than to reminisce about more glorious days, and Vijay had become intimately acquainted with Gamini's certainties. But even as he dismissed it all as ancient history he knew that the old order was present still, like the part of the splinter that is left beneath the skin. The human weakness for certainty, the given order, the set place, permeated Gamini's every utterance, and he recognised that it was this that had insidiously secured the tacit complicity, the inner acquiescence that had allowed such an order to survive for so long, and even to win acceptance for the absurd notion of its own naturalness. But as he linked the weakness and the power he knew, too, that the pretence that such an order was unalterable, God-given, had meant that the subtle exercise of status and control, malevolent or benign, had reduced other abrasions, eased other tensions. Gamini did not feel humiliated by a life as a servant because he believed that this was his pre-ordained place in the natural order rather than a result of his own personality, abilities, actions. And so he had been able to find in it a satisfaction and a self-respect, even a pride, which might have been denied to him in an order which decreed that his position in the world, servant or master, rich or poor, looked up to or looked down upon, was entirely his own responsibility. But Vijay had been born into a different order, deprived of the unquestioned and the pre-ordained, so that each day brought the challenge of taking responsibility for one's own position, of defining who and what you were, of arming oneself for this permanent confrontation of the personality.

He looked up once more; Gamini was slowly walking along the first-floor balcony, disappearing and reappearing in the galleried windows, finally losing himself in the darkness of the landing. Vijay stared at the last empty window, knowing that the fragments of the shattered chandelier were somehow still embedded in his own life, still causing him pain. But he had no response, knowing only that he had to face forwards into the anxieties of the new rather than backwards to the comforting nostalgia of the old. For him there was to be no contentment, no place to know, and however mountainous the barriers might still be between the rich and the poor, the influential and the powerless, the prestigious and the despised, the free man and the slave, and however strictly stratified life still might be, however practised the eyes of the doormen in reading the secret language, the important thing was that the idea of place itself lay shattered; its elaborate moral bluff had been called. The revolution Lalith dreamed of had not occurred; but the more fundamental change had already come upon them. The notion of place had fallen from the plaster ceiling of the preordained to the whorehouse floor of negotiation. It had become the game and not the rules. And each day now, men must find themselves anew.

At the other end of the verandah, Lal was pretending not to be leaning against the pillar. He saw Vijay watching him and assumed a look of long-suffering boredom, exaggerated so that it would travel the whole length of the restaurant. Vijay grimaced a response. Lalith, for one, had found a place to stand in the struggle to remake the rules, in the politics and the union work that gave him a sense of self which was separate and secure from the trials of his days at the hotel. But the two had different souls; for Vijay lived only on his verandah, his raw and undefined self exposed and buffeted by every wind that blew, lacking all shelter.

A vapour trail crossed a cloudless sky towards the horizon, breaking up into a wake of pure gold in the setting sun. On the narrow beach, he could hear seagulls fighting over some relic from the sea. Occasionally he thought of the story he had heard earlier that week about the waiter at the Capricorn Hotel who had been offered a job by a guest and was going to the George V in Paris. It was not the first time it had happened. Two years ago an under-waiter at the Intercontinental had also been recruited by a guest and sent for training at a hotel in Switzerland. Vijay looked down his verandah. Such guests usually stayed only at the larger, more modern hotels, or at the Mount Lavinia down the Galle Road.

At that moment, he saw one or two of the diners looking up towards the entrance and he too turned to watch the English-woman walk the length of the verandah, fluid, balanced, sure of her ground. His sarong stretched against his shins as he moved to her table.

'Good evening, Miss.'

She smiled at him without reserve as she said good evening, looking him in the eyes for a full second, and waited for her chair to be withdrawn from the table. She was wearing a pale blue dress in the finest of cottons, bare shouldered and high necked, her hair glowing more deeply than the gold of her earrings. Vijay offered her the menu.

'Special tonight, Miss, is lobster bisque followed by lasagna al forno.' She assented to the bisque but rejected the lasagna in favour of a grilled seer fish.

'Do you serve wine by the glass?' she asked, her eyes taking on the colour from the pale blue dress.

'Yes, Miss, but I am not recommending house wine. It is better to be choosing from wine list. We are keeping in fridge until you are needing.'

'That sounds like a good idea.' She showed appreciation in her glance and handed him back the menu. Vijay retreated, nodding the wine waiter towards her.

Several of the other guests had also preferred the grilled seer, but as Vijay carried the dish to his tables he felt less than happy with its presentation. It was covered in a greyish sauce which had the aspect of elderly frog spawn and which should, at the least, have been left decently to one side to expose the fine, flaky symmetry of the seer steak. In his early days at the hotel he had once ventured a suggestion in the kitchen but had unfortunately made the mistake of beginning with the words

'At catering college . . .', a phrase with which he had been mercilessly belaboured in the following months. Eventually, he had grown resigned to the antics of the two chefs, one of whom had trained in Lyons and gave his creations elaborate French names while the other defended himself with an aggressive gastronomic nationalism so that the same dishes would appear as 'Entrecôte à la Béarnaise' or 'Steak Sigiriya', 'Langoustines Château Bouscat' or 'Trinco Treat', depending on which of the two happened to be on duty at the time.

Clara looked down the narrow row of table lamps and wished she had ordered Asian food. From tomorrow, she decided, she would work her way through the local menu, asking advice and paying particular attention to the names of the dishes and their proper deployment in the meal.

'Your English is excellent,' she said rather abruptly to Vijay as he came to place a soup spoon before her.

'Thank you, Miss'.

'Where did you learn?' The blue eyes were seeing him. Vijay began to reply, but he felt the captain's touch on his arm and politely withdrew.

'Good evening, Miss Lane,' he heard the captain say, confident in his smart white trousers and full jacket with the gold epaulettes.

'Good evening,' she smiled. 'As you know my name may I also ask yours?'

'My name is Chulaprasad Wanigasundara, Miss, but they are calling me Bertie. I am captain. Anything you are wanting, I am here.'

Exulting inordinately in his gallantry, his ample glossy face shining in the lamplight, the captain withdrew with a small bow.

Vijay watched him serve the soup to the Englishwoman and guessed that he would personally wait on her table for the rest of the evening. But when the helper arrived and stood waiting in the inner gangway, the captain motioned Vijay forward to collect the tray.

Silently, Vijay placed the fish steak before Clara.

'It must be quite a big fish.' The smile.

'Seer fish can be six feet, Miss'.

'Is it eaten by everybody here?'

'No, Miss. It is too costly. It is mainly for tourists and business people. Ordinary people . . . once a year it may be taken only.'

The wine waiter was hovering.

'What fish do you eat yourself?' said Clara boldly.

'Usually we take a little fish just with chilli, Miss.'

The captain coughed lightly.

'Do you always wait on this table?'

'When I am on shift, Miss.'

'Can I ask your name too?'

'I am Jayasinghe. People call me Vijay, Miss. Excuse me, Miss.'

He stepped back down the verandah to make way for the captain who immediately moved in with some new gallantry.

Arriving now at table nine were the honeymoon couple, much talked of in the boot room. The man was a middle-aged Japanese aid-worker and his bride was said to be a teenager from one of the Maldive Islands; Lalith insisted that neither could speak a word of the other's language. Behind them, a mixed group of young Swedes straggled onto the verandah, looking pleasantly bored. After taking their order, Lalith came to stand by Vijay and imparted the information, speaking quite unnecessarily out of the side of his mouth, that the Australians on table four had ordered a bottle of Montrachet which, at more than three weeks' wages, was the most expensive wine on the list. Vijay moved off to greet the American foursome who were arriving on the verandah, the men arguing loudly, their voices grating and arms gesticulating even as they walked to their table. Vijay seated them with his normal 'good evening'. The two women gave him small smiles but the men ignored him, carrying on arguing, carelessly scraping their chairs. 'I hear you, Carl,' one of them was saying. 'I read you all right, I see where you're coming from.' He took the proffered menu without a glance at Vijay and looked around him critically, frowning with his nose and slightly puckering his lips, as if suspicious of the fragrant evening air.

12

Vijay breathed in the familiar smell of the slums, a hundred years of heat on a hundred years of dirt and urine, and put his bare feet up on the verandah wall. At least the latrines were not singing out tonight. In front of him, a chain of small children, each with one foot on either side of the drain, rocked from side to side, moving up towards the washhouses where two of the older boys were also straddling the concrete gully, their arms gripped around each other, seeing who could force the other to put a foot into the slime. Radios blared from the verandahs on both sides as more children ran screaming to join the chain rocking its way towards the top of the garden. Vijay shifted his position. At No. 18, relatives were arriving with little leaf-wrapped parcels of rice and sweetmeats, paying their last visits to the dying Weerakone. Tearfully ushering them inside, Mrs Weerakone shooed away the children, but it was a losing battle against the cacophony of the garden. Even the jackdaws, clinging to the gutters, called and scolded unheeded, as if trying to make themselves heard above the clamour.

He looked at his watch. In another ten minutes things would quieten down and he would have his smoke. He picked up the magazine that had been left by the American couple. It was mostly advertisements: in one, a beautiful girl with a strange expression urged him to fall in love with Spain this summer; in another, a softly photographed air-hostess invited him to fly with her; over the page a man in a loose-draped jacket with immense shoulders dared him to take up the challenge of personal style; opposite, a discreet script announced that there had never been a quartz Blancpain watch and never would be.

He flipped more pages, invoking him to enjoy the future now, enter the world of Calvin Klein, join the comfort revolution, steep himself in tradition, diversify his assets, come on down to Marlboro County, and never to settle for second best. He closed the magazine as Premawathie appeared on the verandah. Just in front of him, the midges were gathering in clouds over the open drain.

'Smell is OK tonight.'

'You can ask that girl of yours why,' said Premawathie, tilting her head towards Chandra who was leaning out from the wooden verandah post trying to catch sight of Susil. As Chandra told the story, he glanced at his mother. He had never thought to see such a look on her face; it could easily have been mistaken for pride.

'But I cannot be asking Mrs Periera to go into latrine like that,' Chandra was concluding matter-of-factly. 'So I am also cleaning today.'

Vijay looked out across the alleyway, gauging the social pressure which his wife was about to bring to bear on the women of the slum garden. Of late, he thought, Chandra seemed to be coming out of herself after living for so long in her own shadow. And for an instant, sitting on his verandah, he seemed to see his wife with new eyes, looking beyond her beauty to the woman she had become. It came as a surprise to him, the kind of surprise that he would have received if Chandra had suddenly walked onto the verandah of his hotel and seated herself at one of the lamp-lit tables. Vaguely he realised that Chandra, his own wife, seemed to be making the kind of advance which was eluding him, that she too was becoming a person who was all of a piece, the different facets balanced like a cut gem, with an integrity that united them all and was the one transparent source of all that she said and did. The secret, he recognised fleetingly, was Chandra's steady unselfishness, her yearning to go out to other people, put herself in their place, see through their eyes, hear through their ears, feel upon her own pulse their satisfactions and their sorrows. He looked at Chandra as she strained out over the verandah calling for Susil, and held on to her for a second or two in his mind. She exchanged a few words with the Tamil girl opposite and it occurred to him that there had been quite a few instances recently of the younger women in the garden appearing to take their lead from his wife. She seemed able, in an inconspicuous way, to draw out the best in those around her, exerting some subtle influence which tended to subdue the mean and shameful, reaching out to what there was to respect so that the virtue in others came halfway to meet her. He had seen it first of all with his father. Chandra had quickly seen what Premawathie had not realised over all the years – that Godfrey brought a rounded, uncensorial human understanding, and more than a little wisdom and compassion, to the resolution of the disputes which were increasingly brought to him from the shanties; she had seen that these were real qualities, and that they had earned him his reputation among those who had no other means that they could trust or afford for the settling of their conflicts. He smiled inwardly as he remembered Godfrey's reaction when he had first brought Chandra home; the old soldier had stood up and simply surrendered, handing over his sword at the first shy glance from the jet and diamond eyes which flashed with an unjaded clarity that gave both pleasure and pain to eyes more clouded with the residue of the years.

Premawathie set a tray of vegetables on the bench and the two women began preparing the evening meal. Vijay lit his cigarette. His mother had remained unmoved by the girl's eyes, beyond eventually conceding that she would be tolerably presentable were it not for her unfortunate colour. For weeks after the wedding she had remained as stone towards his bride, and even with the move to the slum garden she had not been able to bring herself to forgive the girl whom she saw as only a little black upstart who had somehow managed to trap her son. She had remained stiff and watchful, and whenever she had Vijay to herself she would find some excuse for an oblique remark on Chandra's inadequacies, accompanied always by a veiled reference to the absence of dowry. If Vijay mentioned in passing that perhaps they could afford some new sheets to replace the darned and threadbare coverings stretched over the bed-boards, his mother had quickly pointed out that of course that was just the kind of thing they might have expected when he married. When he had talked of saving for a kerosene ring instead of the three-stone fire, she had commented that this was the sort of little luxury she had thought they would be able to afford after his wedding. One evening, about three weeks after the move to the slum garden, Premawathie had sent Chandra to fetch water with a sneer of cold command such as would have been resented by the most weathered servant. Vijay, who had been sitting on the verandah, followed his mother back into the kitchen. Speaking in their own language he had said, simply, 'Amma, I will not have Chandra spoken to like that.' His mother had turned, devastation on her face at being addressed in such a manner by her son.

'If she cannot bring a dowry she can at least know her place,' she had hissed into the darkness.

'I can pay our way without a dowry, Amma,' Vijay had said firmly, raising his voice to dominate his mother's protests, 'and I am telling you now the word dowry is not to be mentioned again in my house.' His mother had looked into her son's eyes, and then something had snapped and she had bowed her head tearfully and stood in silent, remorseful, defeat. Vijay had put his hands on her shoulders and spoken to her more gently. 'Amma', he had told her softly, 'Chandra is my wife. What I want most of all is that you should love her like you have always loved me.' For the second time in a month Premawathie had wept in the dark little kitchen of her new home and, nodding her head slowly, she had turned to tend the fire.

After a few days of awkward overtures and shy responses, Premawathie had asked Chandra if she would like to learn how to bake cakes. Within a week, she had taken her as a daughter. The relief, he sensed, had been as much his mother's as Chandra's. In the months that followed, she had begun to find pleasure in showing the girl how to shop and cook, for most women didn't really know, and had more than once reported to Vijay that the girl showed no trace of stubbornness and would soon let go of her shanty ways. Slowly, through apprenticeship, a kind of friendship had come and his mother, who had for years denied herself the company of other women, had begun to find ordinary enjoyments filtering into her grim existence. Her ferocious pride had enabled her to sustain life in the shanty, but it had also denied her all joy; and in opening herself just a little to her daughter-in-law, she who had for so long held herself rigid now began to unbend, to allow something of the daughter's spirit to restore the sap of her life. And as she had slowly surrendered some of her stiffness, so she had begun to get to know some of the older women in the garden and occasionally to take tea on one of the other verandahs. Before long, she had attached herself firmly to the rump of the wall-builders' party which always used the proper entrance to the garden and still found it necessary to frown on those walking past in the wrong direction. Even now, her most frequent criticism of her daughter-in-law was the girl's habit of slipping through the gap at least once every day to visit her mother and an altogether unsuitable childhood friend in the shanty on the opposite bank of the St Sebastian Canal. But mostly she managed to contain herself on this point, being content with just a few minutes of her old tight-lipped formality whenever Chandra returned through the wall.

Vijay wished he had saved his cigarette and was on the verge of taking another from the packet of ten in his shirt pocket. Two a day was not extravagant for a man with a salaried position. He folded his arms instead, staring at his toes protruding into the indigo sky over the garden wall and thinking how little he had managed to save. Soon, the next year's rent would have to be found, and this time it would be more. He would have no choice but to borrow almost two thousand four hundred rupees all over again, about the same sum as before. Each year he had thought that he would be able to save up the next year's rent as well as repaying the loan. But at five per cent on the arrears, he was paying well over three thousand a year into the pockets of K. W. Matthew. He knew now that it was too much. He could not save up as well. And after five years of trying, he was facing up to the fact that he was locked into his debts. He looked at the broken brickwork of the garden wall and told himself for the thousandth time that he should have waited, saved up the rent before making the move. He had borrowed only because he had had a tip-off about the house in Garden 178; he had known that houses hardly ever became available in the slums, almost always being passed on between kin, and that they were always let before the vacancy became public knowledge. Garden 178 had also happened to be close by, near to Chandra's mother and to all the people and places they knew. He had known, too, how much it would mean to his mother, and how impossible his marriage would have been had the four of them remained in a one-room hut in the shanty. It had been his desperate attempt to compensate, to ease his mother's pain at his choice of wife which he had thought would break her heart. He had worked it out at the time, confident that the tips would cover the loan and that his salary would enable him to save up the next year's rent. But the tips had dwindled as the troubles had grown, each new bombing seeming to close another corridor of the hotel.

He looked at the little piles of foodstuffs on the tray that his mother had just set down on the bench, at the chopped green chillies, manioc, onion, lime, shredded leaves, coconut, powdered fish, and the small heaps of salt and pepper. They could no longer buy their food and vegetables from the Tamil head-load carriers who had come daily through the shanty selling the jackfruit, the cheap two-rupee bundles of leafy vegetables grown around the city, and the sprats and left-over pieces of fish which were not whole or fresh enough to be sold in the shops. Instead, they now had to buy all their food at the market where prices were high and where, as his mother insisted, it was appropriate to his position that they should buy only up-country vegetables. Firewood was also reaching astronomical prices; kerosene was even dearer; nor could they scavenge for fuel in the shanty as they had always done. And his mother had made it clear that his wife could not be seen walking up the garden to the standpipe carrying two rusty paint cans. Then there was the water-rate, the garbage collection levy, the weekly contribution to the Garden Council, and the bus fares to the hotel and back six days a week. And soon the *bhikku* would be coming round the garden with his bowl again, taking advantage of having to visit old Weerakone. He smiled grimly to himself as he thought how his money worries had seemed less when they were poor, how life had seemed almost carefree before they had moved to the garden, memory carelessly softening the edges of shanty life. He took his feet down from the wall and battled between another cigarette and thoughts of all the responsibilities he had taken on with his job: his wife and child, the house in the garden and all its outgoings, the payments of the loan and the interest, the regular support for Chandra's mother in the shanty.

Suddenly, a beam of white light cut through the noise of the slum and illuminated the concrete wall of the latrine block. It was the signal for noisy gravitation to the top end of the garden.

'What is programme?' said Vijay, as his father came up the alleyway.

'Olympic highlight. It is colour,' said Godfrey. 'They will be coming from other gardens.'

Vijay's eyes turned to Chandra, now framed in the doorway. She suppressed a small smile and looked down at the floor. The traffic outside the verandah increased as the population of the garden began crowding towards the latrines, the pace of the procession quickening as a burst of stirring music heralded the arrival of the Olympic torch in Garden 178. As the crowds settled to watch the film show, Vijay and Chandra slipped unnoticed into the darkness of their own home.

Godfrey wandered amongst the men standing at the back of the crowd. He had seen this particular curtain-raiser before and was hoping to remember the winners and raise a few bets on the track and field events. He had also seen the look pass between Vijay and Chandra, and had persuaded Premawathie to go and stand with Mrs C. J. Periera and the other women so as not to appear stand-offish.

It was the first time in months that Vijay and Chandra had been alone together. Smiling, Chandra moved quickly to put one of the battered aluminium water pots just in front of the dark living-room doorway where anyone entering could not fail to fall over it. Then she crept back into the bedroom, loosening her sari, and slid down beside Vijay on the narrow bed-board. Making an effort not to rush, Vijay touched his wife's cheek and gently ran his finger down the side of her face. He could see only her shining eyes looking up at him in the darkness. Slowly he pushed aside the *palu* and unbuttoned her bodice as Chandra luxuriously stretched her arms out over her head. He reached up for her hands and slowly drew the tips of his fingers down, barely touching the warm, smooth skin. Kissing her gently, he loosened sarong and sari and pulled her towards him in the darkness.

Outside in the garden the jackdaws, having the garden unexpectedly to themselves, descended freely to pick over the refuse in the drains. At No. 14, the radio was playing to an empty house. Down the length of the slum, the row of posted verandahs stood dark and vacant under the strip of indigo sky as from thousands of miles away in Montreal the dull roar of a crowd washed over the latrine-block wall and a black American came off the last bend with a surge of power which left the opposition in his wake, dipping his trunk to the tape.

In the darkness of No. 29, Vijay and Chandra were lying side by side, staring at the last fragment of purple sky where the tiles above them were broken. They spoke in their native language.

'We'd better move.'

'They'll be two more minutes.'

'I went to mother's today. Amma pretended she didn't notice.'

'I don't think she minds so much now.'

'She thinks if we give her money that should be enough.'

Vijay was silent.

'I went to see Sithie as well. That's much worse than going to see mother.'

'Is she OK?'

'I've been wanting to tell you. He's left her'.

'Eustace?'

'You know he had a woman while she was in Middle East?'

'Yes'.

'He's gone to live with her, in Dematagoda.'

Vijay was silent.

'He took all the money. Everything. All she earned from two years in Middle East. She has just her clothes.'

'We'll have to do something.' Chandra reached out to touch his arm in the darkness.

The music rose and the credits rolled over the close-up of a gold medal superimposed on a stars and stripes that billowed on the latrine-block wall. As the light died, the health warden hurried to change the reel to the black and white film on ringworm prevention that was the point of the evening, but even as he struggled to load the reel his audience was melting away into the dusk and, by the time the wall had flickered into life again, most of the population of the garden were already safely back on their own verandahs.

❋

Vijay sat looking down the garden, his mouth in a set line and his teeth lightly clenched. Making love to Chandra usually restored his sense of well-being, but tonight his tensions had quickly returned. He looked at his wife, sitting out for the last few minutes of the day. He could see that she was content, and he struggled to know why he too could not feel any commonplace satisfaction, any unanxious sense that all the pieces of his life were in place, why he had this feeling of being alone in the garden, as if he were perched there temporarily, instead of being settled, engrossed, as Chandra and his mother were. The thought crossed his mind that perhaps he had expected too much. The religion of his childhood had been his mother's serrated consciousness of the indignities of the shanty and her fixed longing for the respectable life. Now that this nirvana had been achieved, there seemed to be nothing left. A neighbour came up the garden wearily, spitting beetle-juice into the drain where his dog had stopped to pee. Moths and mosquitoes hovered over the drain, occasionally straying to visit the oil lamps which were being relit on the verandahs all down the garden. Two doors up, the radio was turned to full volume as old Senanayake, long since deaf, struggled to hear the racing results from Nuwara Eliya over the sound of children crying. And through it all the jackdaws screamed from the gutters, overriding the cawing of car horns on the road outside. Vijay took his feet down from the wall. He longed to be able to hear only the sound of the sea. Had there always been this ceaseless noise in the shanty? He could not remember. All he knew was that the edges of life in the garden seemed to cut daily into his sensitivities; for it was not the opposition of slum and shanty which now formed the axes of his graph and against which he measured the rise and fall of his joys and disappointments; it was the opposition, rather, of where he spent his days and where he spent his nights. Wood smoke stung his eyes as he looked down the garden to where the *bhikku* was taking his bowl up the steps of No. 12. A smaller movement at his feet drew him back to his own verandah; two cockroaches were wandering out from the living-room, as though they had finished their chores and were coming out onto the verandah to take the evening air.

Vijay raised one leather *chapal* and struck twice. The compressed roaches sailed out over the verandah into the drain.

'That is teaching them limits of Buddhism,' said Godfrey, looking enquiringly at Vijay.

'Vijay said nothing. A starch-fed girl with dark eyes walked past with her bucket and another radio started up two doors down. Godfrey roared as Susil came running out of the house and grabbed Vijay's knees, shrieking with delight as Chandra caught up with him and whisked him up in her arms. She carried him, protesting, up the garden to the wash-tap. Vijay's eyes followed her as she joined the queue. Three or four other mothers were ahead of her, and a temper snapped as one of them poured what the one behind considered one bowl of water too many over her child. Vijay sat down again and shoved his feet deep into his *chapals*. A corner of his vague dissatisfaction broke the surface as he looked around him; he wanted his wife to have her own tap, her own latrine, her own place to get washed; he wanted a room where he and Chandra could sleep alone and talk alone and make love alone; he wanted to be rid of the ceaseless dogs and jackdaws; he wanted to have only his own radio to listen to; he wanted his wife to have tranquil and tasteful surroundings for her life, a table-cloth, a bowl for flowers, an existence a little more ordered, graceful, without foul smells, or clouds of insects around every light, or armies of roaches scratching across the floor, and with no open drain running through the middle of their lives. He didn't want this seedy, stale-aired, dog-eared sort of life where the squalid guts of everything spilled out into the street and people queued to breathe and grew not to care.

Godfrey reached for the radio. The noise was beginning to die down as Vijay looked at his watch and lit a second cigarette.

13 ∫

Another long afternoon was ending as the sun sank in state towards the ocean. From the hotel, one or two of the guests drifted down over the lawns to watch its setting, rediscovering their souls in an ancient rite. Clara stirred at the sound of their footsteps on the gravel path, conscious of the five or six others standing silently along the little strip of sand. To her left, a woman of about her own age and an older, larger lady were lying out on the wooden loungers. She looked at the younger woman: slim, but her legs were shapeless; probably on holiday with her mother to convalesce after a divorce. Clara lay back as somewhere below her a large wave threw itself desperately onto the shore and was dragged reluctantly back, its fingernails scrabbling at the pebbles and the coarse sand. In the lull, a faint, familiar sound made her head fall to the left again. The young woman's mother, sitting under the sun shade in a large one-piece maroon bathing costume, had begun knitting.

All day her thoughts had wandered without finding any path which did not eventually either dwindle out or return her only to well travelled roads. Her books lay open and unread on a table littered with teacups and the remains of a pineapple. The only firm decision she had come to all day was that tea did not really go with pineapple.

The faint bitt-bitting of needles came to her again on the slight breeze and she thought idly of her own mother. It occurred to her in a dull way that she had always seen her mother as belonging to a lesser realm; cosy, was how she thought of her, unambitious, unconcerned about being taken for granted, completely unaware of things outside her own small circle. But as Clara lay bathed in the warm afternoon sun she wondered if there wasn't perhaps something to envy in her mother's life. It was a shocking thought, envy, coming from this unexpected source, like a monster suddenly surfacing in a garden pond. Could it be that, despite all, her mother knew something, had something, that Clara did not? Her thoughts stalled at the question, trying and succeeding only momentarily to see the person who was Mrs Lane, over sixty years old and still eternally enthusiastic, still exuding a great heaving sense of contentment and pleasure over everything and everybody. Whenever Clara phoned, somebody had always just called in for a coffee, or she was just about to go and do something for somebody, or somebody was just about to do something for her, or she was planning an outing with Pauline, or she was just popping across to check on Mrs Knight, or she had just got home from the Belseys', or there was something on at the church, or she was just finishing knitting something for somebody's baby. They had spoken by phone on the night that Clara had left, but all that she could remember of the conversation was that her mother had gone on about a coach trip to see the crocuses at Harrogate. Clara lifted her chin so that her throat could catch the last of the sunlight and considered simple things that had never before merited her attention. Her mother went every year to Harrogate; she looked forward to it; it took an hour to get there and an hour to get back; and when she was there she strolled with her friends along the aimless paths across The Stray, pointing out virtually identical clumps of flowers to each other and ending up at a little outdoor café where they drank stewed tea and shivered in their coats and cardigans as a chill spring wind stirred the still-bare trees in the Valley Gardens. Where did the enthusiasm come from? What sustained it?

Clara glanced down at herself, but the glare was coming in at a low angle and seemed to make everything silver and sepia, so that it was impossible to tell if her tan had deepened. Was there, perhaps, a slight thickening of the waist? Was the tummy quite as flat? She sank back again. Thirty-four. A good age. But not everything was possible any more. She peered down the dimly lit corridor ahead, hearing the slamming of all the doors which would close in the years to come until the noise gradually became a drumming in her head and she came out of her doze with the startling thought that perhaps she hadn't yet made the mental shift from her twenties, or even from her days at college, when everything had been a preparation for life. This is no longer preparation, she articulated to herself as the sun flooded in under the eaves of the thatched shade: this is it.

Along the strip of sand, mother and daughter were packing up the debris of their day and preparing to return to their rooms. Clara closed her eyes again and thought idly about children, seeming to hear a voice that she half-recognised: 'It comes to them all sooner or later,' said the voice, 'they're all so full of their independence and their careers and all that, but when they get to thirty-three, thirty-four, thirty-five, that's when they start to wonder. Oh yes,' said the voice, filled with a petty satisfaction, 'it doesn't matter who they are, they all start to wonder then.' Soon, she had slipped into a half-doze, thinking or dreaming of the Leonardo exhibition she had seen at the Hayward, the detailed studies of pregnant women, women in childbirth, women breastfeeding, and then the drawings of animals, the wombs, the organs, the sinews. Sometimes, she thought she could remember being born.

When she awoke, the dying sun had turned the sea to ripples of pale metallic turquoise, its last crimson reflections playing delicately in the waves as they slowly advanced towards her. She watched, conscious of a silent bond with the strangers around her, as the moment neared when the sun would reach down to fill in the space above the horizon and make its blissful contact with the sea. But at the last, a treacherous cloud, hidden in invisible ambush, began to nibble at the lower edges of its glow, spoiling the magnificent geometry of its descent into the ocean.

As soon as the sun had gone, Clara packed her beach bag and strolled back across the lawns to the hotel. Those who remained by the ocean front witnessed a spectacular few minutes of fading daylight in which, from below the steel horizon, the sun tinged broken banks of cloud with every hue of evening from the deepest reds to palest amber, until the light drained from the sky and night came down over a purple sea.

❀

From the deck of the verandah where the pools of lamplight were just beginning to show through the dusk, Vijay watched Clara crossing the lawns. The first guests had not yet descended from their rooms, the beauty of the verandah was unsullied, and Vijay was at peace with his world.

By the time she came down to dinner, several of the tables were occupied and the row of lamps was struggling bravely against a vast darkness. Vijay took her order and reminded the wine waiter about the Chablis in the fridge. An hour later, when all was cleared away, he approached her table to ask if she would like coffee. But it was Clara who spoke first.

'Is it always as quiet as this, Vijay?'

'Since nineteen eighty-three, Miss.' He was startled that she had remembered his name.

'That's when the troubles began?'

'Yes, Miss.'

The captain joined them and took over the conversation.

'Yes, Miss, it is July nineteen eighty-three when it is all beginning.' He stood there, hands behind his back, waiting for Vijay to retreat to his place.

'Yes, you see, Miss, after that date the tourists are being cut in half and cut in half again, so now it is very few that are coming at all.'

Clara suppressed a smile but caught Vijay's look as he took up his position by the little desk. She politely enquired whether she might have coffee.

It was Vijay who brought the tray to the table.

'You are seeing much of city, Miss?' He poured the thick black liquid.

'Just a short drive around.' The smile.

'What you have thought, Miss?'

'Fascinating. But I couldn't work out where all the houses were. It was all stalls and markets, and little workshops and a few large homes with walls and gates and guards, but there were no, what you would call, small, ordinary houses. Where do all the ordinary people live?'

Vijay pushed the heavy sugar bowl with the red hotel crest a little closer to Clara.

'Poor people are living out of city, Miss. They are also living in small garden houses that are not being seen at all unless living there. Even shanties not always being seen. When Queen is visiting, Miss, Elizabeth Second I am meaning, shanty is having visit from bulldozer. Even billboards they are putting on airport road so visitors not seeing shanty.'

'When the Queen came?' repeated Clara.

The Australians on table eight were looking round impatiently.

'Excuse me, Miss.'

Clara sipped her coffee and stared out over the dimly lit lawns towards the ocean and the night. The top of her thatched umbrella could just be made out between the palm trees and she tried to recapture the thoughts that had seemed to germinate under the full heat of the sun. Soon the verandah was empty save for herself and the three waiters. The wind was strengthening, blowing in over thousands of miles of darkness, guttering the candles on the verandah. Vijay came to replenish her cup.

'What kind of house do you live in yourself, Vijay?'

'Excuse me, Miss, just small little house in Maligawatta.'

'Does it have electricity?'

'No, Miss, electricity not there.' He smiled.

'Water?'

'Yes, Miss, standpipe is there.' Another smile.

'Toilets?' Clara was smiling now.

'Yes of course, Miss. Latrines are there.' Vijay was embarrassed.

'For how many people?'

'Miss?'

'How many people, for the latrines and the standpipe?'

'Two hundred and fifty, three hundred, Miss. But two of each we are having.'

The Captain was lifting his ample chin out of his tunic collar.

'Excuse me, Miss.'

Clara looked down the verandah at the white saronged figures, romantic and characterful against the white arches and the sepia woodwork. No scene could have held more charm, or offered such peace, were it not for the picture struggling unsuccessfully to establish itself in her mind of hundreds of people, one of whom she knew, living with no electricity or water or toilets, sharing two latrines and a tap.

She drank her coffee with both hands. The night wind blustered over the lawns. By one of the pillars the waiters were standing in a group and she realised she was keeping them from going off duty. She caught Vijay's eye and he came towards her with the leather folder enclosing her bill.

'Vijay,' she said brightly, her hair curtaining her face as she signed the slip, 'I would like to know more about the city. Not just the tourist things, I mean. Would it be possible to talk to you some time when you're not on duty, so we don't keep on getting interrupted?' She glanced towards the captain at the far end of the verandah as she finished signing her name and turned to look up.

'Miss, I can tell you all what I know.'

'What time do you start work tomorrow?'

'Thursday I am working late shift, Miss. Coming at twelve o'clock only.'

'Could we talk before that, in the morning, say, ten o'clock?'

Vijay hesitated only for a moment.

'Ten o'clock is no problem, but where we are doing talking, Miss?' He too looked down the verandah towards the captain's desk.

Clara knew only one other place.

'The Oberoi Hotel?'

'Oberoi? Galle Road?'

'Yes, there's a kind of raised bar area in the middle, right in front of the main door when you go in. You can't miss it.'

'Oberoi I am knowing.'

'Good, then I'll see you there at ten tomorrow? You're sure that's OK?' Clara was fingering her room key.

'Yes, Miss. No problem.'

The captain approached softly.

'Everything is quite OK, Miss Lane?'

'Yes, thank you. I think I'll just take a last look at the ocean before I go up.'

The captain inclined his head graciously. Clara walked down the three steps from the verandah and strolled along the path between the dimly lit lawns.

There was no moon and the dark fronds of the palm trees, moving restlessly, were just visible against the sky as she approached the bare wooden lounger where she had spent her day. She perched for a moment on its damp edge and looked out to sea, surrounded only by the night. Why did she feel much closer to the elements here than anywhere else she had known? Was it the tropics? Was it Asia? Was it the palm trees swaying in the night? Or was it just being far away from the familiar? She did not know; but from all sides a sense not exactly of danger but of significance, of greater potential, reached out to her from the darkness.

After looking out into the night for a full minute, she found that she could just distinguish between sea and sky, a dark horizon broken only by what she guessed to be an oil tanker standing a few miles off-shore, its shape picked out by the isolated lamps spaced at intervals along its deck, culminating in a superstructure of a hundred tiny lights. Along the strip of sand, the hotel's night watchman stood watching her at a discreet distance. Below her, the shifting edge of the ocean surged to the sea wall while, fifty yards out into the darkness, it was just possible to see the gentle, menacing swell of a wave beginning to summon its momentum, rippling its muscles, steadying itself, glinting in the darkness, preparing to throw its full weight on the shore.

The night watchman was now about ten feet away.

'Sea is vast area, Miss,' he said.

Clara smiled at him in a tired way, and rose to go.

In the quiet room on the first floor, she turned off the parchment lamp. Her day on the lounger had exhausted her, and her body-clock was still awry. She had been sure that she would sleep, but for hours she had seemed to be suspended in the kind of unrestful half-sleep which would neither drag her down into oblivion nor let her surface into consciousness, an elastic cocoon which stretched as she strained for sleep or waking but would not let her go. She dreamed dreams enough for a lifetime, but the one that eventually returned her to wakefulness was a confused affair in which she found herself dancing across a broad swathe of grass, dressed in a navy skirt and jacket of the kind she usually wore to the office. Her feet were bare. Slowly she realised that she was playing a thin, reedy pipe as she danced, and that she was playing the music of money; notes of all denominations, torn notes, worn notes, floating up from the pipe and fluttering to the ground behind her as she danced from side to side over the threadbare grass. She was not conscious of them having been there before, but now there appeared to be hundreds of children all around her, tearing at her skirt and jacket and blouse, making her fall and grazing her knees so that she was soon ragged, dirty, sweating, but still struggling forwards, still piping notes over the grass. Looking up, she recognised that the road ahead was Park Lane. Directly ahead were the blazing lights of The Dorchester, but as she stumbled towards it, falling to her knees again and again, still pathetically piping, she saw that there was a furious traffic jam on the road. Reaching the edge of the grass, she could see that there was not even a centimetre of space between the cars and taxis, and to escape from the park she would have to crawl on her hands and knees over burning bonnets, feeling the throbbing engines, breathing in exhaust fumes, still trying to play her pipe. With oil on her face and traffic dust in her hair, she finally reached the far side of the road and staggered gratefully towards the glass doors of the hotel. Inside she could see cool fountains and a string quartet playing silently on a small dais as immaculate waiters brought what she imagined would be cucumber sandwiches to glass-topped wrought-iron tables under graceful palm trees. She drew herself up to her full height before the great glass plates and assumed her most authoritative manner, but the automatic doors remained closed. She looked aghast at her reflection. Behind her, in the park, she could hear small explosions. She stared into the cool and calm of the Dorchester. Only because of her reflection did she know that she was crying.

She awoke in a hotel room, five thousand miles away, weighted to her bed. Only the soft explosions continued as from outside her open window the ocean rolled steadily in to the shore. Perspiring in the single damp sheet, she struggled to sit up, reaching for the lamp. It was three a.m. After a few moments sitting on the edge of the bed, she closed all the windows, worked out how to turn the air-conditioning up to high, and took a bottle of table water from the tiny fridge. She swallowed a sleeping pill and quickly made the bed again, propping herself up on the pillows to read. Again she opened the teachings of Buddha that was still at her bedside, but long before sleep came she had given up on the Noble Eightfold Path and was absorbed in the magazine she had bought at the airport.

14

Vijay sat on the verandah of No. 29 smoking his late shift cigarette and leafing through a copy of a French magazine. He had already resolved to buy a new pair of slacks; the only newish pair he owned were flared at the bottoms and he knew that they would look ridiculous to Clara Lane. Turning the pages, he wondered whether he should also buy a new shirt; the problem was that the baggier, looser-fitting style, pouched slightly at the waist, would look ridiculous in Maligawatta where shirts were still worn tight, pulled straight down into the belt, showing every rib.

He leafed through advertisement after advertisement. Women like Clara Lane looked out at him from every page. He drew fiercely on his cigarette, intimidated by their disdainful expressions. Staring at a hard-eyed beauty wearing a fur coat and apparently nothing else, his mind raced ahead to the Oberoi, circling around what he would talk about, wondering what was expected of him. Several times he tried to forget all about the meeting, but the mixture of excitement and dread lay like a cold weight in the pit of his stomach, and he could not stir far without it lurching alarmingly within.

In the gathering gloom he saw the figure of his wife returning down the garden, passing through the light and shadow of oil lamps, her head modestly lowered as she passed between the men who sat and smoked on the verandahs. She was holding what looked like a newspaper in her hand, and her only jewellery, a plain gold bangle on the fragile, dark wrist, caught the light from the garden lamps as she approached. Aching with a sudden tenderness for her, he dropped the magazine and reached for his packet of cigarettes.

❋

Chandra had only glanced at the set of green forms she had collected from the President of the Garden Council, but her eye had immediately been drawn to a notice in heavy black type in both languages announcing that loan applications must be received by the end of the month, now only two days away.

After disappearing inside for a few moments, she came out onto the verandah. Usually Vijay liked to be left to smoke his cigarette in peace, but tonight he smiled at her and, sensing that he would not mind, she sat down on the low wall opposite her husband. Quickly she told him about her plan, giving him the facts and ending by asking his permission to apply for the loan. His face betrayed no reaction and, fearful that he was about to refuse, she did what she had earlier decided not to do by telling him that it might mean an income of three hundred rupees a month.

Vijay looked critically at the remaining half inch of his cigarette. 'How you are knowing if they are buying cakes?' he asked, picking up the magazine again from the floor.

'We are having small trial first,' said Chandra apprehensively.

There was a silence as Vijay began turning the pages, noticing that every single one of the men was wearing a loose-fitting shirt.

'So it is OK if I am filling in form for getting loan? For oven? Calor gas.'

'I am knowing all about loans,' said Vijay, with a smile that was a mixture of patience and bitterness. 'It is big mistake, I am telling. Anything you are getting is only paying interest. Loan itself is never going away.'

Chandra realised that he had not been listening, and simply pointed to the title at the top of the first green form which announced that all loans were interest-free.

'Interest not there at all?'

'It is saying here, no interest at all. That is whole point. It is to help just little business getting started.'

Vijay raised an eyebrow.

'But repayment is there. Capital sum is there. When it is being paid?'

'Capital sum after five years only. Repayment beginning after one year only.'

'I myself am needing this kind of loan.'

'Loan is just for small women's business only.'

'What is Amma saying?'

'She is saying OK.'

Vijay turned the page of his magazine to see a perfect air-hostess smiling down solicitously at a distinguished looking businessman reclining in an enormous soft seat. He looked at his quartz watch, wondering if he should take it off for the meeting at the Oberoi. The hostess was handing the man a glass of what he imagined must be champagne. He wondered what would be the right drink to order at ten o'clock in the morning.

'If you are saying OK, then tomorrow Amma is doing baking. It is for trial run.'

Vijay closed the magazine and took a last pull on the cigarette.

'If you are getting definite order, then that is little bit OK.'

He looked at Chandra for the first time since she had come to sit on the wall and suddenly saw how much what she was saying meant to her. And with a small shock he realised that his wife was quite capable of making such a plan, and of carrying it through. His mind caught at the three hundred rupees a month, and he felt the first tug of tension between the difference it would make and the threat that it represented.

'I am also needing little bit of help with this,' said Chandra, offering him the printed green papers. Vijay glanced down the long questionnaire.

'Tomorrow is better. Soon I am having to be going out.'

'Application must be reaching town hall day after tomorrow. Pilot scheme loans all finishing then. Also they must be having official stamp from Garden President.'

'Munyandi is putting stamp on anything,' said Vijay, smiling at her. 'Maybe I am doing later on.'

'Many people are also wanting you to be sitting on Garden Council, Vijay,' said Chandra. 'You are only one who is knowing how to talk to officials and all. You will be getting things done.'

'It is waste of time, I am telling. They are only talking, talking, talking. Three months now and they are not even fixing broken tap. Only having meetings to be talking about fixing.'

'Mrs Periera says if you and C.J. would be there, then it would not be all talking.'

'C.J. and myself are having real job. We are not having time for meeting and talking and all.'

Chandra left Vijay on the verandah to finish the last of his cigarette in peace. After a few moments he flicked the stub into the drain and left the verandah, heading for the garden wall and the two or three new boutiques which had recently opened up in Messenger Street.

When Godfrey stepped up onto the verandah, Chandra was sitting on the bench with Susil on her knee, trying to read the first page of the green form.

'Two stoves I am finding today only,' he said, lowering himself gently into the red plastic chair.

'How much?' Chandra asked.

Godfrey smiled fondly at her excitement and shrugged, a man of the world.

'I am opening negotiations by telling they are entirely wrong kind of stove and we are not wanting even if they are giving.'

'But how much you are thinking?'

'Eventually I am taking one of them off hands for, maybe, thousand five hundred roops, maybe little bit more, maybe little bit less.'

'Maximum loan is two thousand rupees.'

'Maximum is good. Then you are having contingency.'

'What is contingency?'

'Contingency is what I am telling after bringing tea.'

In the darkness of the kitchen Premawathie could hear what sounded like conspiratorial voices out on the verandah and she imagined that Godfrey was embarking on some unseemly subject under the guise of an English lesson. Chandra could speak the language as well as any of them now, but the lessons continued; it was an excuse for Chandra to sit for half an hour during the day. Premawathie did not begrudge the girl that. Not everyone had her own stamina. She frowned in the darkness as a burst of suppressed laughter floated through from the verandah. If Chandra had had Godfrey for a husband, then she would not be continually smiling at the old man and listening to his absurd stories. But though she had no intention of forgiving him or treating him any differently, Premawathie was forced to acknowledge that there was some small improvement in her husband. He had somehow revived in spirit. He did not take so long to get up in the mornings; he shaved more often; he often whistled tunelessly at odd times during the day; he appeared more interested in what was going on around him; he no longer sat for hours on end with a vacant expression camped on his face; and his hearing seemed to have improved. In her conscious thoughts, Premawathie put all of this down to his undeserved change of fortune, and to having a respectable home at last. But she dimly suspected that there was more to it than this. Godfrey had always seemed to wear almost any circumstance as comfortably as his old *chapals*, and in some vague way she suspected that it had not been so much the move to the garden which had stimulated his revival as the entry into his life of the girl who was now sitting beside him on the verandah. It had been with mixed feelings that she had watched the surrender of her husband to what she had at first seen only as the wiles of her daughter-in-law. She approved, albeit with more than a touch of cynicism, of the fact that her husband had begun to wear a shirt again over his vest, and even to shave occasionally in the middle of the week. But the image of roguish wisdom which he had cultivated for the girl's benefit made her mouth turn down at the corners. She had always been mortified by her husband's ability to get on with everyone, even with people who ought to have known better. She had despaired of his constant involvement in other people's disputes, his little adjudications as he had taken to calling them, and had often lain awake terrified and humiliated by the uncouth voices outside her hut in the middle of the night. On the rare occasions when she went anywhere with her husband, she was appalled at his being constantly greeted in the street and saturated in bonhomie and alcoholic breath by every low and shiftless character from Grandpass to the Maradana Station. Catching up with the local gambling news outside Price Park was not her conception of a proper social life, and she particularly objected to her husband being hailed as 'Judge Godfrey' and to herself being familiarly asked by his various acquaintances if she would care to take a cool drink at some unspeakable place around the corner.

From the verandah she heard him break off his conversation with Chandra to greet one or other of their neighbours returning from work. She inspected the floor to see if it had been properly swept and began filtering the cooking oil into the bottle. It had also irked her that he had taken so easily to life in the garden, that the change had been of no moral significance for him, that the transformation of their lives was shorn of all the associations of the life-long struggle for respectability which for her had weighted the move through the wall with such momentous significance. She resented the fact that he could so openly enjoy life in the slum garden without feeling a shred of guilt that he had done nothing himself to bring it about, as if the move from the shanty had been just another of life's unfathomable vicissitudes, as if he had simply been dealt a better hand by what he liked to call the great shuffler in the sky. She waited a long time for the last drops of oil to drip into the bottle, wondering if the baking business was really going to work. And in a private moment she admitted to herself again that she had been wrong about Chandra Jayasinghe.

Later, when Vijay had not returned, Godfrey had helped Chandra tackle the forms. Details of proposed business, amount of loan required, proposed book-keeping procedures, expected yield on capital invested, proposed accountancy period. Eventually, Godfrey came up with something for all of them, bluffing his way through the denser thickets of bureaucracy until they came to the last item. Chandra read out the question: 'List reasons for expected success of venture.' Godfrey thought for a moment and lit a cigarette from a newly acquired plastic lighter. 'Aforesaid Premawathie Jayasinghe,' he dictated, narrowing his eyes and releasing the smoke, 'is making most beautiful cakes.' Although true, this did not seem to Chandra to be quite businesslike, and she amended 'most beautiful' to 'shop-bought standard', hoping that Godfrey would not want to read it through.

When Susil had been read to and put to bed, she had sat up

at the kitchen table making three copies of the completed form under the light of the broad-brimmed lamp. Vijay had not yet returned when she slipped out of the house to pay a visit to the Garden President who had, after some time, found his wire-framed spectacles and begun running his fingers down the various boxes on the green forms.

'Everything seems in order, my dear,' he said, reaching for his best ballpoint and the official stamp which was used to approve the minutes of each meeting and which he kept permanently on display in the glass-fronted cabinet.

15

Vijay's first thought had been to try the staff entrance. But just as he was turning into the narrow lane that led around the whitewashed walls to the back of the Oberoi Hotel, he realised that he would need a pass. He would have a better chance, he decided, at the main door. He emerged from the alleyway again and turned back down the Galle Road. At the white pillars he hesitated; there was no footpath; the curved drive was meant only for cars. He turned in, walking quickly, conscious of the playing fountains as he neared the glass doors from which a low white portico reached out to shade the hotel's guests as they alighted. The two red-liveried doorman eyed him as he approached the entrance.

'Yes, sir,' said the nearer of the two, addressing him in English, unsmiling, his hands still behind his back, making no move to open the glass doors.

'I am meeting someone inside.'

'A guest, sir?'

'Yes,' lied Vijay.

The doorman eyed him with a pronounced lack of deference and opened the door, raising an eyebrow to the dark-suited lobby manager sitting behind a teak desk just inside the entrance.

Vijay passed through into the cold. 'Yes, sir?' The lobby manager did not stand up, and the 'sir' was pronounced in an unpleasant way.

'I am meeting someone . . . here in bar.'

'Guest of hotel?'

'I am not sure if staying here. She is one Miss Clara Lane of UK.'

His English, as always, was his passport. The lobby manager resumed his examination of the important papers on his desk.

Passing into the cool central well of the hotel, Vijay saw that the sitting area which Clara had described was a raised and rose-carpeted dais that occupied most of the inner quadrangle. It was empty. For several seconds he stared at the desert of opulence in front of him, unable to bring himself to mount the carpeted steps or seat himself in such prominence. Wishing that he had not arrived early, he decided that he would be less conspicuous if he browsed in the boutiques around the edges of the great quadrangle. It was just after ten minutes to ten.

After two circuits of the dais, feeling the lobby manager's eyes constantly upon him, he retreated to the men's room, hoping that this would buy him another three or four minutes. It was as he was looking around for a towel that he saw the machine on the wall that Lalith had spoken of. There was no one else in the washroom. Tentatively he prodded at the button with the heel of his hand. The gush of noisy air made him step back. Slowly he advanced his hands under the nozzle. It was hardly hotter than the air outside. Rubbing his hands together as instructed, he read the metal plate advising him that the device was made by World Drier Corporation, a subdivision of Beatrice Foods, which sounded like a cake shop in Maligawatta but was in fact located in Chicago, Illinois. He smiled to himself as he remembered Lalith's speech in the boot room: 'Towel changer losing job, van driver losing job, dhobi losing job, cotton spinner losing job, weaver also losing job. Why? Why? So we can be having electrical machine to make hot air. In this country I can be getting hot air for free! But no! No! We must be getting electrical machine so we can be having energy crisis, so we can be having power-cut, so we can be damming Mahaveli and flooding villages and all, so we can be pouring crores and crores of rupees into power stations. Why? Why? So we can be having hot air in toilets only for visitors! What is more, it is not even drying hands. I am hearing afterwards I am having to dry hands on trousers!' More important to Vijay at that moment was the fact that the machine would not dry his face.

He emerged at three minutes to ten. The raised area of seats was still empty. For five more minutes he wandered the air-conditioned corridors, looking at velvet cards of the island's gem-stones and trying to muster the confidence to mount the dais. By now two or three groups of tourists and a few local businessmen were knotted about in the maze of chairs and sofas, and he tried to affect their easy nonchalance as he ascended the four steps. Slowing his walk, he headed for an arrangement of seats that were out of sight of the lobby manager's desk. But as he sat down on the rose-pink settee, he found his knees rising into the air and his bottom sinking towards the floor so that he had to struggle to regain the front edge of the seat, looking around desperately to see if his alarming experience had been observed. Slowly he lowered himself back again, wondering if there were some special technique for getting in and out of such chairs. Recovering himself slightly, he locked his fingers together and tried to affect a bored look as he surveyed the comings and goings in the hotel lobby. Several locals walked freely in through the great glass doors, unchallenged by doormen or lobby managers. His mind jumped. What was it that identified him as someone who did not belong? He had on a pair of brand new straight-sided trousers and a clean white shirt which he had tucked as loosely as he could into his black plastic belt. He wore socks and well-polished shoes; both shoes were lined with newspaper to block up the holes in the soles, but this was a detail which could not be noticed so long as he kept his feet on the ground. He was clean-shaven, and his hair was neat and dressed with coconut oil. Coconut oil! Perhaps that was it. He anxiously scanned the heads of the other men on the dais. No. Others were wearing oil too. The signs had to be subtler. After a few moments he had decided that it was purely a question of manner, of how one looked and held oneself, of the attitude given off, of the confidence in the eyes; it was a hidden language, spoken and understood only in such places as this, a language of confidence which instantly communicated one's status, cowing all those beneath, presenting one's credentials to all those above, as inexorable as a chemical reaction, seeking out who you were, locating you in the table of the elements.

A waiter approached.

'Sir?'

'I am waiting,' said Vijay, in the tone which he hoped was

confident but which he suspected was merely aggressive. The waiter withdrew. Vijay kept the soles of his feet on the carpet. He knew that it was only a matter of time now before the lobby manager was summoned and he would be asked to leave.

He opened the leather-bound menu on the glass-topped table in front of him. The amounts that visitors were charged for drinks and snacks had never been real to him before. His unopened pay packet lay flat in his shirt pocket. A sudden panic struck him. Why hadn't he emptied it? If he did not do it now then he would have to produce the brown paper pay-packet when the time came. Surreptitiously he slid the notes out and buttoned them in his shirt pocket, pushing the empty packet into the earth at the base of one of the tall trees which grew around the dais. Table water was twenty rupees; tea, twenty-five rupees.

The glass doors were opened the moment Clara stepped from the taxi. Both doormen saluted as she passed through into the air-conditioned well. The lobby manager rose to his feet and made an elaborate gesture of standing to one side.

He saw her ascend the dais, like a goddess, every head turning to look at her as she crossed the rose-coloured carpet, her perfect skin glowing against a pale cream dress of finest cotton, the discreet spotlights of the Oberoi gleaming softly from the gold earrings and the watch at her wrist. Vijay exulted in his heart as he struggled to rise from the sofa, hoping they were all watching, every one of them, the doormen, the lobby manager, the condescending little waiter.

Approaching the seating area, Clara suddenly realised that she might not be able to recognise Vijay without his sarong and tunic. Her gaze swept round the little groups of settees and armchairs. There was only one young man on his own, and she recognised him by his recognition of her. The waiter was there even before she had sat down. She ordered tea and Vijay followed suit.

After commenting on the heat outside, Clara leaned back into the depths of the sofa and looked around her appraisingly. Determined not to be tongue-tied, Vijay began telling her about the hot air machine and Lalith's views on same. Clara responded with the idea that she would pass all this on to a friend of hers who was in line for the top job in the hotels group which was managed by her company. It was a strange, detailed subject to launch into so quickly and it soon died, rootless, from nervous exhaustion. The silence was broken by the pianist who had arrived on the dais and launched into 'Once I had a secret love', rendered a little too passionately for the hour of the morning.

'Tell me about what you were saying last night, Vijay. About the Queen's visit,' said Clara, leaning forward slightly and resting her face in her hands as if to encourage him.

'Nothing to tell, Miss,' said Vijay, who was sitting on the front edge of his seat. 'All along airport road, shanties were there. One fine day bulldozer is coming. It is so Majesty is not seeing anything of shanty when she is passing. Also they are putting up wooden boards with advertisement and all. After putting up, no one is seeing shanties at all from road.'

'What happened to the people?'

'All are having to be leaving, Miss. They are going somewhere, on canal or in Summitpura. Some of it very bad land, Miss, wet, leeches, fevers, everything.' Clara thought about what he was saying. She looked intently at him. She was somehow surprised by him, and she had no sooner recognised the fact than, to her shame, she realised why: she had come to talk with a waiter, and instead she was talking with a man. It was not just the change from the sarong and tunic of the verandah to the slacks and shirt of the dais in the centre of the Oberoi; it was also that he seemed much larger here, and somehow more of a force. He was tall, with rather classic looks, and had it not been for his acute nervousness she might have recognised, across all the differences in nuance of expression, a certain look which she was not unfamiliar with.

Vijay saw that Clara was inspecting him rather than listening, and he desperately carried on talking. He was still perched on the edge of the sofa, keeping his feet firmly on the carpeted floor.

'It is always same, Miss, even when we are having socialism. Even in time of Mrs Bandaranaike, it is same. When we are having non-aligned summit in nineteen hundred and seventy-six, Miss, all must be coming down airport road from Katunayake. Presidents, Prime Ministers, big people from all countries. Those days also, shanties being bulldozed. All people going to Summitpura. Before summit, small shanty only. Nowadays, very big shanty is there. That is why people are calling Summitpura. It is meaning summit city.'

The waiter poured the tea in what Vijay considered an obtrusive manner. Clara smiled briefly at him and sat back in her chair with the cup and saucer. Vijay glared as the young man filled his cup.

'I would like to see Summitpura,' said Clara.

'Summitpura is not place for tourist, Miss,' said Vijay, smiling.

'Is it dangerous?'

'No, Miss, no danger is there. Just not good place, that is all. We are having beautiful places for tourist, but unfortunately nowadays tourist is not coming.'

'This hotel is almost empty as well,' said Clara, looking round at the vast emptiness of the Oberoi.

'All hotels, it is same, Miss, Oberoi, Hilton, Intercon, Meridian, Capricorn, Ramada . . . all empty, even though rooms are half price only.'

'They must be making huge losses on a place like this,' said Clara, looking around at the balconies which rose around them on all sides.

'Hotel companies not having loss, Miss. Only government is having loss.'

Clara looked uncomprehending.

'How can the government be making a loss?' she asked.

'Miss, it is like this. Before even building hotel, Intercon, Hilton, etcetera, are having talks and all with government. They are saying if Intercon or Hilton is there then that is big signal that country is little bit OK. They are telling that such hotels are key to lock. Sometimes they are also telling it is trigger as well as key. Also sometimes green light. When Hilton is there, tourists are knowing everything hunky-dory. Tourists coming from everywhere, they are saying. Thousands are coming, Englishmen, Americans, German people, Swedish people, Japan people, everyone is coming once they are knowing that Intercon is there. Millions of dollars they are spending on eating and drinking. Also excursion, Miss. Also souvenirs, wood-carving and all, batiks, everything. So they are saying of course only fair for government to be paying for building up of hotel itself. Government must be putting up seventy per cent, even eighty per cent of cost for hotel. That is why government is now having huge loss. Tens of crores. Dollars I am meaning, Miss.'

Clara looked up into the vastness of the air-conditioned hotel all around her, her eyes tracing the tiered balconies where softly lit rosewood doors gave discreet access to the guest suites. She was thinking of a conversation she was going to have over dinner with her newly appointed colleague. Her eyes came back to Vijay, determined not to misunderstand by pretending to know.

'So the hotel companies are only taking a small share of the loss?'

Vijay felt able to be benignly impatient.

'No, Miss, I am telling. Some are making profit, even now. It is because they are having management fee.'

Absurdly conscious of her masters degree in business studies, Clara tried to stop herself from looking too incredulous.

'You see, Miss, Intercon, Hilton, etcetera are saying hotels must be having certain standard. It is because of name they are having. It is matter of reputation they are saying. If hotel is having name of Hilton or Intercontinental, then they must be saying how hotel is being run and doing supervising and all. That is why they must be having management fee from government. Fixed fee or percentage of turnover, not percentage of profit. Profit is big if turnover big, small if turnover small. But always profit is there.'

'So they are making profits without even putting up any real risk capital. If anything goes wrong, someone else takes the loss?'

'Government taking loss, Miss. People taking loss.'

Vijay was filled with relief at finding himself on home ground. Clara noticed that he had stopped looking quite so uncomfortable.

'Please call me Clara, Vijay,' she smiled. 'You're not on duty until twelve o'clock.'

Vijay looked alarmed and edged back a little into the sofa.

'How do you come to know so much about the hotel business, Vijay?'

'I am graduate of City Catering College, Miss. But that is here nor there.'

The waiter glided over. Vijay ignored him. Overhead the softly lit red and gold batiks hung down into the vastness. On one corner of the dais, the Indian pianist was playing 'Ol' Man River' with what Clara thought was unnecessary mawkishness.

For an hour or more they talked, with only a few silences, about the city and the troubles, about Vijay's work at the hotel, about Clara's life in London. Clara asked about the things she had seen in the old town, and an indefinite arrangement was made for a taxi to be hired so that she could look round the city again with Vijay as her guide.

The approaching waiter unhesitatingly presented the bill to Clara, and Vijay felt humiliation tinging his relief. She waved down his attempt to pay.

As they got up to leave, Clara turned to him, a more playful expression on her face.

'I bet I can tell you something about this hotel that you don't know.'

Vijay's eyes looked wary, suspecting he was being teased.

'What kind of trees do you think these are?' she asked, gesturing to the graceful foliage around them.

Vijay looked at them inexpertly. He was a city boy.

'They are just only rubber trees,' he suggested, 'all over island there are such trees.'

'Not rubber, Vijay, plastic.'

Wonderingly, Vijay reached out to touch first the leaves and then the bark of the tree behind the sofa.

'They're made in Singapore,' said Clara. 'One lakh rupees each.' Vijay rapidly translated. Twelve years' wages for a plastic tree. There were eight of them around the dais. A century of wages. He struggled to his feet, savouring every step of the way as they strolled together across the carpet, totally ignoring both the lobby manager and the two doormen, conversing with Clara, speaking their language.

Once outside, Clara sensed his reluctance to walk down the Galle Road and arrive back at his own hotel in her company. She stepped into a waiting taxi, explaining that she wasn't used to walking in such heat, knowing that Vijay would refuse the ride.

16

Chandra watched her mother-in-law arranging the samples on the grease-proof paper: four each of the butterfly buns, maids-of-honour, iced fancies, and Victoria sponges. An hour earlier, she had slid the cakes out of the battered old oven, light and perfect, and placed them before Chandra without a word. Chandra had been instructed to stand and watch as Premawathie completed the cutting, filling, layering, icing and powdering. Now, all was ready. In her good sari, her hair scraped back and oiled so that it rejoiced with the blackness of life, she left the kitchen, carefully carrying the tray which Premawathie had covered with a spotless muslin cloth. As she emerged onto the verandah, Godfrey half rose to his feet, stricken anew by her beauty as she stopped for his final word of advice.

'Remember it is game of poker, that is all,' he said enthusiastically. 'Everything little bit OK if you are doing what I am telling. If they are bluffing and you are calling bluff, then you are winning. If they are not bluffing and you are calling bluff, then you are losing. If you are bluffing and they are calling bluff, then they are winning. If you are not bluffing then they are losing. Only rules are these. But you are not knowing whether they are bluffing or not. Old soldier is knowing, but you are not knowing. That is not important thing. Important thing is you must be knowing if *you* are bluffing.' He was stopped by the appearance of Premawathie in the doorway.

'When you are finishing huffing and bluffing, cakes are going stale,' she said sternly, and sent Chandra off down the garden with a look.

Emerging from the alleyway into the raw light of the street,

Chandra felt suddenly exposed, as if she were carrying something precious and vulnerable out into a polluted world, like the time she had left the Co-op maternity after giving birth. Surrounded by the dust and fumes and noise of the city, she negotiated Messenger Street, carrying the little tin tray before her, pregnant with her hopes. What Godfrey had said had in fact made perfect sense to her, though only because they had gone over the tactics together, step-by-step, the previous evening. Her advance intelligence was sound; she had researched all the prices in the shops; and Godfrey had had no difficulty in finding out the wholesale rate. But her trepidation grew as she neared the Grandpass Road. On every street, shops and boutiques pressed shoulder to shoulder so that they were almost indistinguishable: greengrocers and fruiterers, cotton and silk emporia, outfitters and shoe shops, lighting and electrical suppliers, household goods and hardware stores spilling their aluminium pans onto the pavements. And in front of every shop were spread the humbler wares of street traders, the sellers of scraps of food and single cigarettes, the roast-nut vendors and the hawkers of cheap plastic goods, their offerings flowing into each other along the sidewalks so that Chandra despaired at the sight. What space could there be for her here, where every niche in the market was filled?

As she turned into the Grandpass Road, all other concerns fell silent, giving way to the dread of entering the Sweet Tooth. Losing her nerve for a moment, she crumpled inwardly with misery and shame as she leaped ahead to see Premawathie's face when she heard that the shops were not interested in the cakes. She had persuaded her mother-in-law to the trial by praising her baking, arguing that her cakes were better than any that could be bought in the shops. Flattered despite herself, and not reluctant to show off her skill in this preserve of the refined, Premawathie had agreed. But her solidarity was brittle. It would not suffer a rebuff. If the shops rejected the cakes at the first attempt, then that would be the end of it; the subject would never be mentioned again. She rehearsed again Godfrey's strategy. It all came down to one rule that she repeated to herself as she struggled to protect the tray, swinging and twisting her way through the throng on the Grandpass Road: down to one hundred and ten, you are bluffing; below one hundred and ten, you are leaving.

As she neared the Sweet Tooth cake shop, she was suddenly seized by the thought that they would not buy from her because she was black. With a sinking heart she glanced at herself in the plate glass window of the Hyundai Emporium. After a second she lowered her eyes again to the tray and walked on, feeling a small flush of guilt at her immodest thoughts. Her unstable spirits sank again as she saw the cakes on display in the window of the Sweet Tooth. Why did they look so different from the humble, home-made samples under her cloth? Why were they so much more shop-bought? She looked again. They were not different, she decided bravely; it was just that they were set out under a light. That was what made them look more professional, more glamorous. Once inside, she must be sure to stand near an electric light. She held the tray tightly and stepped up into the shop.

'I have come to see Mr Punchihewa,' she said to the figure behind the counter.

Wary because the boss had been asked for by name, the young assistant at the Sweet Tooth called through to the back of the shop. He stared boldly at Chandra, picking his teeth with a match.

After a few moments, a very fat man in an immaculate white sarong and fine cotton vest appeared in the doorway and looked at Chandra through the strong glass wall of his spectacles, chin lifted, mouth slightly open, stained teeth bared as if this might help him to see who had called. Chandra stepped forward and addressed him in dialect.

'I am starting a small business, Mr Punchihewa. Making cakes. I have brought these samples.' She carefully removed the muslin cloth while holding the tray steady in front of her with one hand. Mr Punchihewa, seeming to give up the attempt to locate Chandra, bent down close to the tray and poked about among the delicate cakes. Without a word, he picked up one of the iced fancies, peered at it from two inches away, and ate it in two mouthfuls. He looked round, screwing up his eyes as the young man put a mug of dark orange tea into his hand. Mr Punchihewa drank deeply. Chandra stood in the dim centre of the shop, stranded far away from the electric light. Empty shelves lined the walls. The floor, she noticed, was grooved in a diamond pattern like her own. The young man at the wooden counter was openly leering at her. Mr Punchihewa swallowed his tea noisily and peered again into the tray. He chose one of the butterfly buns, bit half of it off, and threw the other half back into the tray, chewing loudly. Another swig of tea. He destroyed three other cakes in similar manner. The tray was now a battlefield of discarded cakes and yellow crumbs. There were still two more shops she had been intending to try.

The light from the shop window reflected in the thick glass of Punchihewa's spectacles so that she could not see his eyes. He had moved on to the Victoria sponges and was about to throw away the half that was not in his mouth when he appeared to think better of it. Breathing through his nose, he stuffed the remaining half in and stood, full cheeked, rocking slightly on his heels, eyes bulging through the pebble glasses, chewing up towards the ceiling and making an ugly noise with his teeth. He smiled and swallowed the last morsels, as his eyes cast about again for Chandra.

'Not interested,' he said, and turned towards the door at the back of the shop.

Chandra too turned to go, feeling as if she had been struck in the face. All she could see was the bright oblong of light at the door and she moved towards it, knowing that humiliation and disappointment were waiting in the street outside.

'Unless of course,' said a voice from far away in the doorway behind her, 'they are coming very, very cheap.'

Chandra turned and walked back into the centre of the little room. Her blood rose, heart pounding, and she seemed to feel Godfrey standing there by her side. Her nervousness fell to the floor as she opened the bidding.

'They are not coming cheap, Mr Punchihewa,' she said, 'they are a higher class of cake than you are selling. You can sell for more.'

Mr Punchihewa bent his neck forward, his fat hands resting comfortably on his vest. A quick little smile came and went.

'Good morning,' he said, and turned once more towards the little door at the back of the shop.

'And they are coming just a little bit less than you are pay-ing now.'

Her voice stopped him, as he stooped slightly in the doorway. After a second, he came back into the middle of the room, screwing up his eyes. Having found her again, he lifted the muslin cloth and slowly ate half of another butterfly bun.

'No better, no worse,' he said, giving a quick smile and licking a crumb or two from his lip.

He turned and retreated, quickly for one of his bulk, and this time he disappeared completely through the door at the back of the shop. Chandra was left standing in the middle of the room with the devastated tray. After a minute, she decided that she had better leave; somewhere she had gone wrong. As she was pulling the cloth over the remains of the cakes, Punchihewa reappeared, peering intently at a worn black notebook.

'How much?' he asked abruptly.

'I can come twice a week with four trays. The price is one hun-dred and forty rupees for four trays. Mixed. Twenty-four of each.

The little smile became a laugh. Mr Punchihewa rocked back on his heels and then forward again, thrusting his spectacles towards Chandra.

'That is twice what I am now paying. I am wishing you good morning.'

'It is almost the same as you are now paying,' said Chandra, giving him her first smile, desperate not to lose him.

Punchihewa had been a street trader for twenty years before he had bought the little shop in Grandpass. His mind worked like lightning behind the opaque pebble-glasses. Black. Beautiful. Knows more than she should. The card game in TN's bar. The old rogue Godfrey, pressing a conversation about the difference between a fair profit and a shake-down. His son, the shanty boy with the regular job and the beautiful wife. The little smile appeared again.

'You were saying they would be less.'

'One hundred and thirty for four trays. So you are getting better cakes for less money.'

'One hundred bucks. Best I can do. Final offer.'

Chandra knew she would have been lost now without Godfrey's advice.

'One hundred and twenty-five is the lowest I can go.'

Mr Punchihewa gave her the quick little smile, shook his head, and turned to go.

'Mr Punchihewa,' she called him back as he filled the little doorway. He turned, still stooped, and the pebble glasses groped for her.

'One twenty I can do, but you are pushing me too hard. Even though it is farther away, I am going somewhere else.'

Mr Punchihewa came back into the arena.

'One hundred five,' he said. 'Absolutely final offer.'

'I am sorry. Thank you for your time.' Without any hint of hesitation, she turned and walked briskly to the door.

'One ten.' Punchihewa tried to sound bored.

Chandra turned. 'One fifteen,' she said solemnly, wondering at herself.

Punchihewa stood in the middle of the room, shaking his head slowly and with great finality.

'I can start only next month,' said Chandra.

'At one ten?' he said, lowering his chin and thrusting forward his lower lip.

'At one ten,' she smiled.

'Tuesdays and Fridays? Before seven a.m. Fresh-made mind you.'

Mr Punchihewa's little smile appeared and remained. Squinting, he sought out one of the last few cakes on Chandra's tray and pushed it into his mouth almost in one go. He smiled in the middle of eating, wanting to be friendly.

'What is name?' he said, suddenly, in English, through the last mouthful of cake.

'I am Chandra Jayasinghe.'

'I am seeing you Tuesdays and Fridays, Chandra Jayasinghe.'

She smiled once more and turned to go. As she reached the door, elation mounting inside her, she heard his voice call out once more from the recesses of the little shop.

'My compliments to the judge.'

Vijay exulted. For minutes on end he had been able to focus himself into one person, frayed edges sewn tight, his mind engaged cleanly into the cogs of conversation, managing to suppress his feverish absorption in the impression he might be making. And now, as he made his way back down the Galle Road, his soul soared with his achievement: he had talked for more than an hour with Clara Lane, sitting in a sofa on the raised dais, with scarcely a scream from the dungeons. There had just been the one time when he had leaned back on the settee and she had glimpsed, he was sure, the newspaper through the hole in his shoe, but this was as nothing compared to the heady relief of his acceptance. It had been as if he had burst through some wall, stood on new ground, breathed new air. Smiling at the surly guard on duty at the staff entrance, he showed his pass and crossed the cobbled courtyard in just a few strides. There would be time to take a cup of real tea before the start of the afternoon shift.

'Good for you, Vijay!' shrieked Lalith as soon as he showed his face in the boot room. Before he had time to wonder how the news about his meeting with Clara had got back before him, Lalith was roughly grasping his shoulders and kissing him on both cheeks. 'I am saluting noble act of true revolutionary, Comrade Vijay Jayasinghe.' Old Gamini, sitting on a bench in the gloom sipping tea from a saucer, said nothing, the look on his face suggesting that the world had come to an end but that it was only what he had expected.

'She is just wanting to be finding out city, that is all.'

'No, Vijay,' said Lalith mounting his soap box. 'This is it. This is true beginning of independence struggle. And I am there . . . I am knowing him . . .' He performed his stock mimic of the frail, bent old man. '"Those days comrade Vijay and me pulling on same oar."'

'It is beginning of trouble all right,' said Gamini sourly. He shook his head and turned to go. 'I am thinking you are having more sense Vijay Jayasinghe.'

'Nonsense!' whooped Lalith. 'Why it must always be us down-stairs and them upstairs? It is still colonialism I am telling. They are still and always up there being served and we are still and always down here doing only serving. Why should Vijay not be sipping tea with sexy English lady on pink chair in Oberoi? This is what struggling is for. This is true meaning of independence!'

'You are not doing struggling,' sneered Gamini.

'Always it is same,' said Lalith, ignoring him. 'Look at Middle East. All our women in Saudi doing domestic servant for Arab lady. Why we must always be servant? Why, never once in my life, is white man bringing me bed-tea?' He grinned at the look on Gamini's face and began asking Vijay about Clara.

Soon Lalith was standing on a chair, over-excited by the dialectical significance of Vijay's visit to the Oberoi, preparing once more to address a rally of thousands, and forestalled only by the arrival of the day captain who held out one arm in the direction of the stairs and ushered them up into the sunlight for the start of the afternoon shift.

Vijay laid his hand for a moment on old Gamini's shoulder as the two of them left the boot room, then he turned up the stairs, leaving the old man to climb to the first floor landing, still shaking his head.

Taking up his station on the verandah, Vijay fixed his eyes on the upstairs window. Eventually the white-haired figure arrived in his position, straightaway looking down to meet his eye. It was a look of such sad censure that Vijay turned away.

Later, when the captain had disappeared for his two-o'clock cigarette and the verandah was deserted, Lalith wandered over to join him and the two of them leant with their backs against the broad white pillar. At a suitable break in the oratory, Vijay gave him the details about the machine in the washrooms of the Oberoi.

'You mean you cannot be drying fucking face in it?' said Lalith.

It was twelve thirty. All the guests had left their rooms, and Gamini was free to make his way to the little clearing amid the discarded furniture. He sat for a moment, perched on the edge of his chair. He would have a strong word with Vijay. Vijay was not Lalith. He would get himself into trouble. He had seen it all before. It was against the rules to fraternise. It always led to trouble. He remembered the colonel's daughter in '44. A socialist she had called herself, out East to visit her father. The hotel had been full of officers, captains and above, so many of them that some had even been living in tents on the lawns. All those fine young Englishmen around her and she had danced and talked all night with a plantation supervisor's son who shouldn't even have been allowed in to the Governor's Ball. The boy had been banned from the hotel, but the next day they had brazenly walked out together on Galle Face Green. The plantation supervisor had eventually lost his job over the matter and the girl had gone back to England, to stand for parliament, so it was said.

Gamini leaned forward on the little balustrade overlooking the old ballroom and stared down at the past. The blank, peeling walls stared back, remembering nothing. In front of him, the capitals of the pilasters had mostly crumbled and there was still a gaping dusty hole in the plaster ceiling from which the great chandelier had hung. Unobserved, he watched the hotel receptionist cross through the empty ballroom below on his way to the cold-store. A poor specimen thought Gamini, remembering the first of the receptionists he had known, the immaculate Shelton, dressed all in white even to his boots. One night long ago, when Gamini had been drawn to the landing by some disturbance, he had seen him approach two Englishmen who had drunk a little too much and were making a nuisance of themselves on the staircase. 'Good evening, gentlemen,' was all that Shelton had said, but his look had told the two men all that he wanted them to know. 'You are English gentlemen, and

I am a native,' said the look, 'I play my part in this little game only if you play yours.' One of the two men had blushed deeply, and both had retired quietly to their rooms.

A shaft of sunlight now streamed across the balcony and Gamini got to his feet and wandered back to the gloom of the wooden landing, taking up his accustomed position by the pillar at the top of the staircase. To his left he heard heavy, hurried footsteps bouncing along the wooden corridor and inclined his head as a long-term guest, an Indian businessman who tipped well and wore an expensive gold watch, turned the corner and passed down the stairs to the fountains and tiled floors of the lobby below. As he disappeared from view, Gamini seemed to see again the young Maharaja of Baroda who had regularly stayed for three or four weeks a year and who had once tipped a room-boy more than a year's wages. He looked at the broad staircase curving down to the cool of the lobby, his thoughts back in that long gone springtime when the Rolls Royce waited under the white portico as the Maharaja prepared to leave. The entire staff had been lined up down the staircase to see him off that day. And just before descending the steps to his car, he had flamboyantly flung a shower of gold sovereigns into the sunlight streaming in through the portico so that the coins chinked and bounced on the tiled floors and rolled under the plants, dithering to a silence by the antique tables. Not a man had moved. And all these years later, the pride of it rose again in Gamini's mind. In the silence, the Maharaja had given an exaggerated look of surprise, eyes open wide, before being swept off to the races at Nuwara Eliya. Only when the magnificent car had disappeared from view had Shelton turned around to face the lobby in his immaculate white suit: 'Carolis and Chandrasekere picking up Maharaja's generous gratuity,' he had said. 'Rest of you returning to duties.'

Gamini stared at the exact point on the curve of the stairs where he had stood as a young man to witness what he still thought of as the hotel's finest hour. It did not seem to him to be all that long ago. He retreated now a little as a young Scandinavian couple began to climb the stairs. A tinny, disembodied sound escaped from the young man's earphones. He was eating an ice-cream as he strode up the stairs two at a time. The bright pink girl beside him obviously had nothing on under the thinnest of cotton T-shirts. The two tourists grinned familiarly at Gamini, who imperceptibly inclined his head.

The landing was empty again. On one side the great double doors of the old Governor's Suite stood open to air the huge rooms. Gamini wandered in. The balcony windows had also been opened and, stepping out for a moment, he could see spread below him the bright expanse of Galle Face Green. It was not watered now and the grass was yellow, with patches of bare earth where once the officers' ponies had grazed. There had been no more polo matches after the war, only a charred crater where the goal-posts had stood. They had all been told to crawl under their beds with pencils clenched between their teeth, but when the last explosions had died away and the eerie silence had given way to a growing tumult of excited voices, he had joined the crowds descending onto the Green to see the wreck of the Japanese bomber brought down to the everlasting glory of the Garrison Artillery. Next day, the government had issued the order for wide fire breaks to be driven through the most crowded parts of the city and, on his way to work, he had seen the raw wounds being scored across Pettah and Kotahena. Gradually, as no more planes had come, the tin and cadjan houses of the poor had begun encroaching onto the fire breaks, reclaiming them for their own as the jungle reclaims a disused path. But the polo had never returned, and all that remained was a slight indentation that could still be seen in the grass if one knew where to look.

Now, instead of planes, fifty kites were flying bravely on the wind over Galle Face Green, while on the tired grass small boys leaned against invisible lines. But these were not the home-made balsam and cotton kites which Gamini had made and repaired in his youth: they were plastic, streamered versions, disposable, bought from the sides of barrows at weekends. He imagined they were easier to fly, but even so some of the children and their fathers were struggling, running to and fro, trying in vain to catch the fickle breezes and eventually stopping, exhausted in the heat and blinding sunshine as the kites fluttered clumsily to earth behind them. The more successful were sailing majestically on lines stretched to their limits, occasionally flapping in frustration and falling a few feet and then stretching out again, yearning out over the ocean. And in a moment of doubt, Gamini wondered if he had really been as certain as he now believed he had been. Had he ever been unsettled, like Vijay? He looked back over the years but the time was too long ago and the answer too far away. He had had the offer of a job once, in Egypt. 'Oh yes,' he had often told himself, 'I could have been a man as well.' Had he really been so sure? Had he agonised over that decision forty years ago? He could not remember. All he could be certain of was the explanation with which he had justified his decision over the years. 'I knew my place.' But had he known at the time? Or had he gradually bonded himself to that comfortable certainty as the years had passed? He did not know. The gust of opportunity had passed him by, and he had stayed to become encrusted to the idea of his own contentment.

The old man wandered back to his station at the back of the first-floor landing and stood in the gloom where he had stood, off and on, for most of his life. The other hall boys sat on the steps or leaned on the pillars during the day, only coming to their feet when a guest approached. But Gamini could stand all day on his landing. And it was only because he was not often required that he sometimes went to find his own place amid the disused furniture and dusty memories of the ballroom gallery.

18

The sepia tones of evening had descended again on the verandah. Four waiters were on duty, including the captain, immaculate in his white tunic, hands behind his back, thumbs crossed, surveying his deck of diners. It was Thursday, and in addition to the hotel guests there were several families from the city's upper classes among whom the habit of eating out was just beginning to become fashionable. Under the soft pools of light, the groups of seated figures seemed all of one complexion.

Vijay served the entrées at table six.

'What is this?'

'Sir, it is goujon of fish'

'I ordered lobster. I'm not having this.'

'Very sorry, sir. I am taking back.'

'Well make it quick will you? I like to eat with my party, not after them.' The American pointed to the bottle of white wine. 'You can take that back as well, it's warm. Bring me a cold beer.'

Vijay retreated. The captain moved in to soothe table six with the emollient of his practised apologies.

Vijay passed on the chitty for the lobster and took up his position again. He was untouched by the man's rudeness, for tonight he was in a protected world where all of his being was waiting and straining in a state of pure expectation in which nothing else can happen, like the space between lightning's flash and thunder's slow roll. He looked at his watch.

She came onto the verandah soon after half past eight, wearing an almost black navy cotton dress and the lightest of heeled sandals, moving gracefully between the tables as though no one were looking at her. The captain withdrew her chair from table ten, one of the smaller tables set in an archway through which she could see out across the lawns to the ocean. It was reserved for her by a small notice, painted by hand on a block of polished teak.

'Good evening, Miss,' beamed the captain. He raised one hand to summon Vijay who was already on his way. As the captain solicitously advised her of the day's specials, he presented Clara with the menu and withdrew a step or two. Vijay stood behind and slightly to one side. It had seemed appropriate for only a small and formal 'Good evening' to pass between himself and Clara. She ordered the fish of the day and the captain remained by her, raising his arm again for the wine waiter. The distraction allowed Clara and Vijay to exchange a warmer smile as Clara silently mouthed the word 'hello', and gave a quick glance of mock fear at the captain.

Vijay retreated, ashamed in his sarong, exultant in his heart.

Clara took in her surroundings. It was strange, eating alone, no business to discuss, nothing to plan or to do, just waiting for food. Normally, at such times she itched for pen and paper, or something to read, but she felt that tonight she might be able to just sit and be content. The wine waiter arrived. It pleased her to know that he was called Ananda, that he was teetotal, that he received ten per cent of the total tips before they were divided up among the rest of the waiters, that his wife was working as a housemaid in the Middle East, and that he usually slept in the dormitory under the hotel with five or six of the other staff. She sipped the Chablis, and was aware of feeling a little calmer, a little more optimistic, than on the previous evening. Her solace on the sunlounger, all that long afternoon, had been the knowledge that she had enjoyed her morning, and was looking forward to another tour of the city. Her stay seemed to have acquired a little edge, to have begun to lose the bland purposelessness which she had found so disturbing. It was a strange feeling of relief, she thought as she looked out into the darkness, to be able to say simply and truthfully that she had enjoyed talking with someone, that she was looking forward to doing something, that she had been genuinely interested. It was a small thing, perhaps, but Clara clung to it; it showed that capacity was still there, that all was not indifference, that there was something more in the void than the effort of pretending. All afternoon, she had dwelt on the dreadfulness of the admissions she had made to herself. Was it normal, she had wondered, for such ordinary pleasures as these to be denied to so successful a life?

She turned to look down the verandah and was almost surprised to see Vijay standing there in his white sarong, lit by the lamp at the little desk; he had been only a waiter, and now he was not a waiter at all. She sipped the wine, pleasantly aware of the bond of a shared secret, the faintest tingle of conspiracy born in the space between the relationship of the verandah and the relationship of the Oberoi. It gave a little spice to the evening warmth as she looked out, content for an hour, across the grass to where the black fronds of palm trees slowly stirred against a silver sky.

It was at the opposite end of the verandah, in the pool of lamplight by the antique desk, that the genie of conspiracy was practising its arts to the full, massaging the sinews of the imagination, using the flat surface of boredom to exaggerate its own relief, exploiting the licence of secrecy to loosen reality's ropes. And pride, too, joined in the game; Vijay had seen them all looking at Clara as she had walked the length of the restaurant; if only they knew, he thought, the American at table six who had definitely ordered the goujons of fish, the Germans who never so much as looked at him, the local businessman who had just summoned him to pick up a napkin, the captain who thought that only he knew how to talk to the guests. But no one knew, save Clara and himself. And under the comforting lights of his verandah, Vijay Jayasinghe, born into the new order, thrilled to conspiracy's rites, its smoky illusions, its heightened sensitivities, its little edge of danger. He had no thought for any outcome of the little drama in which he was so suddenly on the stage; he released himself to this evening as if all time were present, and abandoned himself to the verandah as if all the world were pressed into its span. Feeling a surge of a new strength within him, he looked again down the row of tables and believed

that he might at last struggle free of the dross. For on this
night he felt the lamp-lit beauty glow within, and each time
he attended at Clara's table and exchanged a word or a smile
he returned as if with a renewed shot of a drug. No matter that
the conspiracy was so small, the deception so unimportant, the
secret so innocent; it was unbounded by any existence in the
real world of other people, and therefore knew no sense of
proportion, pulled at no moorings in the mundane. And as
the hour grew late, so the genie worked on this small potential
with a treacherous alchemy in Vijay's mind, metamorphosing
secrecy into intimacy, intimacy into an acceptance in which he
was investing his innermost hopes, eroding normality, holding
before him the undefined possibility of relief, of triumph over his
obscure oppression. He surveyed the long perspective of lamp-lit
tables and softly glowing arches. Never had the familiar scene
been as it was this evening; for to its calm beauty was added
a personal dimension which had lifted it into another realm.
Compared with this, all of its former attractions had been but as
a dead stage set; and now, as the lights in the world outside were
dimming and the spotlights were glowing down on his verandah,
he allowed himself another look towards table ten. The lamplight
gleamed on the gold and deepened the heavy fall of her hair as
she turned to look across the lawns to the ocean where a pale
moon lit the stones of the chessboard and caught the breaking
edges of invisible waves as they approached the shore. It was as
if every last gleaning of glamour in every left-behind magazine
he had ever seen, every fine and beautiful thing he had ever
felt upon his pulse, every particle of romance, every image of
the utterly desirable, was distilled and presented to him in one
unbearable moment. His verandah was at peace, and overhead
the fans turned slowly, redundantly, in the small breeze which
stirred the leaves of the plants and lifted the low edges of the
table-cloths.

Part Two

19

Clara looked out at the vast merging brightness of sea and sky, screwing up her eyes to count the specks of distant ships from left to right across the horizon. Over breakfast, she had arranged with Vijay that they would tour the city at the end of his afternoon shift. Until then she would do nothing but relax, read her book, swim her lengths.

An isolated breeze blew in from the sea. Moments later she felt the sting of the fine salt sand which had coated the sun oil down her right side. The taste of strong coffee lingered still in her mouth as the small wind died, leaving her at the centre of a stillness, listening for the voice of the Clara within that she knew only as an insubstantial presence. Yesterday, there had been long moments when she had glimpsed what was surely at the heart of it all; but what she had seen was not of that order of things which can be kept until next needed, and this morning her conscious efforts had brought nothing that she could hold on to.

The heat was building up again under the thatch and she closed her eyes, listening to the tired falling of the waves and the arbitrary cries of gulls, the aimless orchestra of the ocean, warmth and drowsiness contending with a consciousness pulling at the frayed edges of her thought. And then from the soft anarchy of the sea arose a gentle, rhythmic percussion. She lifted her head; a slender young man who had been sweeping the strip of sand had now stopped to rest, his fingers interlocked over the top of the broom handle, gazing out to sea. She lay back on the lounger, strangely moved by the immensity of her separation from the young man standing only five metres away.

She reached blindly for one of the books in her bag and pulled out the thoughts of the Buddha which she had removed from her bedside table. She was about to discard it in favour of a novel when it occurred to her to open it at random, as her mother sometimes did with the Bible.

'Hard is the hearing of the Sublime Truth, Hard is the appearance of a Buddha.'

A cooler breeze blew in from the ocean, causing her almost to shiver under the shade until the wind died and the warmth began to steal through her. She sat up on the lounger, pulling her feet out of the direct sunlight, and riffled through to another page.

'Be on guard against thinking of Enlightenment as a "thing" to be grasped at, lest it, too, should become an obstruction.'

There might be something there perhaps. She needed to move the lounger to keep the tops of her feet out of the sun. The alarm went on her radio, a spiky, mean little sound against the vast, dull hushing of the sea. She flipped over a few more pages.

'Though he should conquer a thousand men on the battle field a thousand times, yet he who would conquer himself is the noblest victor.'

The Bible was better at this, she thought; unless you just happened to hit upon one of the bits where people begat people for page after page. She let her head sink back to relieve her neck muscles. It was like the Bible though; nothing but a series of take-it-or-leave-it assertions, unsupported, thrown at her like the waves launching themselves on the unmoved rocks below. What did any of it mean? Words heard through the wall of a room with no door; a footfall in a corridor with no entrance; as inaccessible as the thoughts of the young man as he swept along the strip of sand. She pulled out one of the novels, struggling to find a comfortable position. But the perceptions and sensations of others entered her only to be attacked and overwhelmed by the antibodies of her own concerns, and she soon let the book fall on the flat of her stomach. Over breakfast, she had resolved not to eat in the middle of the day; but now she looked towards lunch as to a landfall.

Clara came out of her doze. She could drink no more coffee or soda, and neither music nor reading appealed. Under the eyes of the poolside waiters, she swam her twenty lengths in seventeen minutes and twenty-five seconds, physical effort almost succeeding in staying her thoughts. Breathing hard, she reapplied her sun lotion and tip-toed back across the burning sand.

Cooler now, she decided to risk a few minutes under the unhindered sun. The pool attendant rushed to help as she manoeuvred the lounger out from under the shade. She lay down once more, and her exertions fed the pleasure of letting her muscles relax. But immediately she knew the harshness of the sun, and wished she had showered away the salt. She shut her eyes tight and tried to find herself against the still bright world flooding in. But unprompted by any effort of her own, the tender, violent warmth seemed to overwhelm her, carrying her gently to the edge of some awful truth, like the gradual facing up to a dread disease, passing through the pretence that the symptoms do not exist, that they are imaginary or temporary or insignificant, bringing her to the brink of acceptance. Through her closed eyes she stared at what had been held at bay for so long, and one by one she admitted them, the unwelcome guests who had been kept waiting out in the cold: the huddled symptoms of absent joys, passions, eagernesses, the empty shells of love and solidarity. Here were none of life's lusts, none of its spontaneous joys; it was an entrance parade of negatives, of those who had fled, of ghosts of what had been, returning to mock the impostors who had taken their place, contemptuously putting them to flight, filling with emptiness the great hall that had once accommodated such feasts. Clara gazed into its fearful emptiness, entertaining the ghosts at last in the inner sanctum, aghast as she looked on the exodus of all enthusiasms, the diaspora of all delights, feeling the cold embrace of knowing that there was no life in the present, no prospects anticipated with any eagerness, no people whom she relished being with, no experiences savoured or relived, nothing in that silent, empty hall that was not draped in the undisturbed dust-cloths of her own indifference.

She opened her eyes for a brief second and was blinded by a sun which seemed to occupy the whole sky. She clenched them again, warm sweat mingling with the salt from the pool as she returned to the empty hall, tugging desperately at the dust-sheets, revealing only routines, obligations, things to be endured and achieved. And she knew then that she had come to this place to listen to the voice that could not be listened to. Under the burning sun it whispered its unspoken words, and a river of cold panic began to flow through the Clara she had created, its chill stealing over all she had worked for, all she had committed herself to. The voice made its claims known, and immediately the garrisons of her accustomed life began to rise against this feeble, impertinent usurper. But they were not enough, and the usurper marched on, its anthems telling her that all that awaited her on her return was not what it seemed, that she would be following no steady star of purpose but only the bright, brief spark of reputation, that she would be journeying only under the goad of expectation, sustained only by the drip of approbation, that in place of the eager surge there would now be only the dread draining of energy, of will, leaving only a tiring pride to hold in place the glinting mosaic of images, the little tesserae of accomplishments and abilities that she had become. Panic flowed again like a trickle of ice water as, with a lurch of the heart, she acknowledged the fatal faltering within. The heat, like the weight of the world, pressed her to her wooden bed, bearing down on her thighs, on her stomach, on the hollows of her shoulders. She cried for help from within and was answered only by emptiness. She sought for herself urgently in the dark corners, knowing that she had long been in hiding, watching the battle from a distance, leaving the struggle to the Clara of the mosaic, the Clara whom she knew so much better than herself. But there could be no succour from such a self as this, a cowering, insubstantial, long neglected thing, an intimate stranger, scarce recognised, scarcely there at all.

20

In the gloom of the old boot room, Vijay was sipping sweet tea with Lalith and two or three of the other staff.

'Take to pot-arrack parlour,' Lalith was saying, 'or I am thinking maybe Henamulla, Summitpura. All such places. Then eyes will be opening.'

Vijay refused the rare offer of a cigarette and, for the third time that morning, checked the rupees in his shirt pocket. A new white shirt was in his locker, still in its cellophane bag, and his shoes had been furtively polished on the guests' machine on the second-floor landing.

'Then you are also showing Cinnamon Gardens. Also St Thomas' College, where she will be thinking she is at home, even hearing willow on leather and 'jolly fine knock old chap' and all such things.'

Vijay smiled but composed his face again as the Food and Beverage Manager came hurrying down the stairs, picking out his target in the dim light. Vijay rose to his feet.

'I am coming straight to point,' he said, raising his voice to silence the chatter in the boot room. He pointed a finger towards Vijay. 'What is nonsense I am hearing about Vijay Jayasinghe going all around fraternising here there everywhere with hotel guests?'

In the silence before Vijay could answer, Lalith interjected.

'Why not fraternising?' he asked shrilly. 'We are having apartheid here now? We are still in state of subjugation?'

'This is not having anything to do with Lalith Surasena,' said the Food and Beverage Manager, turning to him angrily. 'This is not any of union business. Staff rules stating categorically – fraternising with guests not allowed. That is rule. Vijay Jayasinghe is breaking rule. That is all needing to be said.'

He drew breath to address Vijay again, but Lalith, conscious of the other waiters standing around in the gloom, moved to stand shoulder to shoulder with his friend.

'Why we are having Independence if not for getting rid of such rule?' he said, quick as always to relate small to large.

The Food and Beverage Manager, a weary man of about fifty with oiled, iron-grey hair and such large brown irises that there were hardly any whites to his eyes, was wishing he had found Vijay alone. But Lalith was entering into his element now, thriving on conflict with authority and sensing that he would be able to stand on the hard ground of principle while his opponent wallowed in the mire of bureaucratic rules.

'Is brown man not to speak to white except only when waiting hand and foot? That is what Independence is meaning?'

'This is not having anything to do with Independence,' snapped the Food and Beverage Manager, unwillingly being drawn into addressing Lalith. 'Staff rule is staff rule. And I am here and now giving Vijay Jayasinghe one official warning for breaking said rule.'

He turned his back on Lalith, incensed at seeming to be out-argued in front of the verandah staff, and spoke sternly to Vijay. 'Official warning. You are hearing, Vijay? I am thinking you are having more sense.'

He strode towards the stairs, but Lalith, the scent of political blood in his nostrils, intercepted him.

'Staff rule-book one hundred years old if a day, I am thinking. Any case, rule only there when we are doing work. Only there when slave wages being paid. Out of station, all are free men. Also all brothers. In own time I am speaking to Queen Elizabeth Second if I am wanting.' There was a small pause and, to cover the silence, he added lamely, 'And if she is also wanting.'

The other waiters in the boot room collapsed with mirth, and even the Food and Beverage Manager could not remove all amusement from his exasperated look as Lalith, provoked, plunged on.

'Nothing of hotel business at all. This is meaning of Inde-pendence, democracy, United Nations, Rights of Man, all such things. I am wanting to know if hotel is repealing Rights of Man?'

The Food and Beverage Manager was not a natural tyrant, but being harangued by Lalith in front of the other staff was not something to be tolerated if discipline and order were to be maintained.

'Persistent insolence to superior,' he said slowly, 'is also firing matter. Lalith Surasena is also having one official warning. I am telling Mr Miles Perera this very morning. I am telling him Lalith Surasena wanting to be discussing hotel rules with him. He will then be giving me job of firing same Surasena which I am doing without having heavy heart.'

With that the Food and Beverage Manager proceeded in a dignified manner up the stone stairs and Lalith, waiting until he was out of earshot, put on a show of bravado for his small audience in the boot room, hinting at vague but dire reaction from the Hotel Workers' Union should the Food and Beverage Manager be foolish enough to carry out his threats.

Soon, old Gamini was pouring scorn on Lalith's posturing. But Vijay was not listening. He stared at his locker. He could not now take Clara on a tour of the city. He would have to speak to her at lunchtime. He would have to tell her he had most unfortunately to remain on duty below stairs. He went to the battered tea urn, resentment and disappointment mingling in the empty thing his day had become.

'I am hoping you are still meeting English lady, comrade?' said Lalith, approaching him with a cup held out, his eyes still bright with conflict.

Vijay shrugged.

'Of course going,' said Lalith confidently. 'It is not business of hotel to be telling what to be doing in time that is ours only. Hotel is not owning Vijay. Out of station Vijay is equal, free, having rights of association same as Mr Perera himself. Why you are not visiting city with Miss Clara Lane? She is inviting. If guest is having brown face management is not kicking up big fuss. It is only on account of meeting white lady, that is all. It is petty apartheid we are having here, and management is lackey. If you are not going, Vijay, I am asking this lady if I can be showing city myself. I am very much serious, Vijay.'

The call came down the stone stairs for the verandah staff to resume their stations, but old Gamini insisted on taking Vijay's arm and leading him along the corridor under the hotel. Vijay knew what was coming but consented to accompany the old man up the disused staircase to his post on the first-floor landing.

'Vijay, I am also thinking you are having more sense.'

'It is OK, Gamini,' said Vijay. 'They are not doing anything.'

The two of them started up the creaking wooden stairs.

'I am seeing it all before, Vijay,' said the old man, pausing for breath on the landing. 'It is certain that very much of trouble is coming.'

'Nothing is coming,' said Vijay reassuringly, taking the old man's elbow for the second flight of stairs. He would be in more trouble if he were not back on the verandah soon.

'But I am also knowing something you are not knowing,' said Gamini stopping again after only three steps. 'This week only, brother-in-law of Mr Miles Perera is asking jobs for cousins. Same time, word is coming from big bosses, from London I am telling. No hiring at all is word, cost-cutting and all.'

Vijay pondered this information. Gamini might be old, but there wasn't much that went on in the hotel that he didn't know about.

'Still he will not be giving sack,' said Vijay, taking the old man's arm more firmly and continuing up the stairs.

'It is Minister who is brother-in-law. He is getting young Mr Miles job in first place. He cannot be refusing. Cannot Vijay. Cannot. That is why I am telling you these secrets.'

Vijay smiled fondly at the old man and steered him onto the long west corridor overlooking the verandah. There might be some truth in what Gamini was telling him: Miles Perera could not refuse a request from the man who had been the Minister responsible for signing the contract with Stateline Hotels and who had been kind enough to suggest the name of Miles Perera for the post of General Manager.

'Vijay is not Lalith,' said the old man, speaking more softly as if to a loved son. 'I know you will be doing all what is right.'

Vijay gave the old man's arm a small squeeze as he left him on the corner of the first landing.

21

Chandra shuffled forward a few steps and put the two buckets down on the concrete apron. After twenty minutes queuing she was now third in line for the dribbling tap. But on this particular afternoon she had plenty to occupy her mind. Even Premawathie had been caught up by her success at the Sweet Tooth. Before Vijay had returned home, she had taken her mother-in-law slowly through all the figures and accepted numerous small corrections. The ingredients for four trays of cakes would not cost more than twenty rupees even at shop prices. That left them about ninety rupees, every Tuesday and Friday. When she had finished, Premawathie herself had commented that there were also bound to be special orders for *poya* days, *wesak* ceremonies, weddings, births, funerals, and Chandra's own excitement had mounted as she had seen her mother-in-law being drawn in. Assuming they could get the loan for the oven, all now depended on how much the fuel was going to cost, an item of information that Godfrey was supposed to be finding out this very afternoon from a contact in Aluthkade.

Chandra inched the buckets forward in the queue with her foot, her mind racing ahead; if the gas was not too expensive then they would be able to save the next year's rent. She trembled inwardly at what she was embarked upon. It would mean that Vijay would not have to pay a quarter of his salary to K. W. Matthew. She restrained herself, forcing down her anticipations. She would say little about it to Vijay, letting it sink in gradually, glad that if it were to happen then it would happen slowly, almost without it being noticed. She called to Susil to stop him poking about with something suspicious lying on the ground by the washrooms.

It had been late when Vijay had returned from the hotel, and he had not seemed very excited about the Sweet Tooth. She was next in line now, impatient to get back and see if Godfrey had returned, but the tap had slowed to a dribble and the surly woman from No. 12 had three buckets to fill. She went over the figures again, sure that she must have missed something, delving down every dark alleyway of doubt but returning always to the same broad avenue of hope. The Sweet Tooth was not the only shop; if Punchihewa would buy, why not others? She tried to hold her imagination, but it jumped out of the grasp of caution and raced to the future; if they were supplying two or three shops they might need help with the fetching and carrying; maybe in time she could take Sithie in; maybe she would be able to do more for her own mother without always having to ask Vijay. She came down to earth as she moved to the front of the queue, Susil shouting excitedly as the water spattered into the first of the empty buckets.

She straightened her back and began the long wait. The tap should have been installed somewhere in the shade but they never thought of things like that at the Town Hall. She called out again to Susil to tell him not to play near the latrine and frowned as he set off after one of the garden dogs. The water ran thoughtlessly into the bucket as her blood pounded with possibilities. And underneath it all she could feel the heavy undertow of anxiety, the something larger that was disturbing her, telling her that she should not be taking on such responsibilities, inviting people to talk about her, stepping out of her place. The pressure on the tap seemed to be returning and soon she had lifted the first bucket aside and pushed the second into its place. Was she really doing it all only for Vijay, to help them get out of debt, to help her mother and Sithie? Or was she straying from her place because of some unseemly desire of her own? A longing for some sense of achievement, of stimulus, of the possibility of one day not being exactly like the next? She did not know, and her anxieties grew as she picked up the two buckets and began to struggle back down the garden, calling for Susil to follow and catching sight of Premawathie who was just emerging from the alleyway.

Godfrey was rousing from his nap when he saw the two women stepping up onto the verandah. Sleepiness blurred the inessential and he registered only the glow of his daughter-in-law's indulgent smile and the stab of his wife's disapproving stare. After they had passed through into the house, he struggled to his feet and retied his sarong, rubbing his hand over a grizzled face and wondering whether he might shave tomorrow.

Soon afterwards, Chandra reappeared on the verandah with his tea. He smiled at her teasingly and looked idly up the garden as though she had nothing to ask and he had nothing to tell.

'Well?' said Chandra expectantly.

'What?'

'What you are finding out,' said Chandra in exasperation.

Godfrey took Susil onto his knee and relinquished his pretence.

'Stove we are getting for twelve hundred roops.'

'Working order?'

'Working order. It is little bit old, but not being used.'

Susil had begun rubbing his hands over Godfrey's unshaven face.

'Gas?'

'Cylinder is coming in at six hundred bucks, but I am buying for three twenty on account of knowing fellow who is delivering all such cylinders to places in Kandy and all. It is very old truck he is telling, and road to Kandy very bad even in dry season. Also he is not wanting deposit on cylinder. Doubtless because he is not wanting cylinder back. I am thinking we are also having small business of selling empties.'

'How we are knowing how long cylinder is lasting?' said Chandra, not wishing to hear any more about the state of the roads to Kandy. Susil had struggled down from his grandfather's knee and was swinging out from the verandah post, looking up the garden to where the older boys were playing.

'Already knowing,' said Godfrey, sitting back contentedly on the plastic chair.

'If you are knowing then please be telling,' she said, looking at her father-in-law with exaggerated resignation. Susil had negotiated himself backwards down the two steps from the verandah. Chandra watched as he set off on his own to the top end of the garden.

'One cylinder is doing heating minimum eight times. *Minimum* I am hearing.'

Chandra rapidly fitted the final piece into place. The cost of gas for four trays would be about forty rupees, leaving a profit of about fifty rupees every Tuesday and Friday. More than four hundred a month. Enough, if it could be sustained, to pay back all of the loan and the interest so that Vijay could save the next year's rent; they would be out of the trap in a year. She glanced up the garden to where Susil was being shown how to hold a cricket bat by one of the Periera boys.

When Godfrey saw that she had finished her calculations, he leaned forward in his chair and delivered his final triumph in a low voice.

'Also I am getting all flours and eggs and sugary things, wholesale, whenever we are wanting.'

The old soldier rocked back in his chair, equally delighted with himself and with the expression on his daughter-in-law's face.

At ten minutes to three o'clock, the arguments for keeping the arrangement with Clara were still sweeping through Vijay's mind, each one seeming to carry its case with a surging momentum until it began to run out of confidence as reality's beach steepened and his resolve was slowly pulled back into a sea of doubts. But even as his conscious thoughts scoured back and forth, some separate process was already seeing him into his new white shirt and slacks in the locker room under the hotel.

Once out in the blinding sunlight he realised that, in his turmoil, he had given no thought to where he might take her. He had meant to plan an exact itinerary, and to store away intelligent, informative things to say. At five minutes to three he was still wondering whether to go or to stay, as he stood looking at two tailor's dummies in an otherwise empty shop window and wishing he had arranged to meet Clara further away from the hotel.

At two minutes past three he saw the taxi he had booked for the afternoon pull out of the road at the end of the Green. Hurriedly turning to the shop window, he ran a comb through his hair and pouched out his shirt. One part of his mind told him that this was his last chance to disappear into the crowds and go back to Maligawatta where he belonged, but a more anonymous force fixed him at the kerbside until the blunt nose of the vehicle was almost upon him. The next moment the safe world of the Galle Road was gone and he found himself in the cracked-leather intimacy of a taxi, sitting next to Clara Lane. He smiled back at her greeting and his senses rioted with each detail of her closeness, her delicate perfume mingling with the smell of heat and engine oil, the perfection of her arms resting against the scuffed seat-backs, the fineness of her cotton dress next to the cheapness of his new shirt. For a few moments everything in the interior of the little car, the pitted chrome catches on the windows, the overflowing ashtrays on the backs of the seats, the worn lino on the floor, seemed to have taken on an extra dimension of reality while the world outside had become impossibly remote. He realised that he was almost huddling up against the door of the cab, and fought to regain composure, forcing himself to lean back into the seat. Immediately he began to worry about whether he was sitting too close or too far away; on his verandah he knew instinctively at what distance he should place himself; but now the board on which the game was being played had been changed, and he could not be at ease with only a hand's width of leather seat between himself and Clara Lane.

'Where to first?' said Clara, smiling as if she were looking forward to the trip.

'Where you would like to go?' he replied hoarsely, and turned towards the window to cough.

'You're my guide,' smiled Clara.

'Fort,' Vijay said peremptorily to the driver who was staring with interest at the couple through a rear-view mirror festooned with a garland of white flowers.

Gradually, the feeling that the universe had been compressed into the back of the little cab began to fade and the world outside, the noise of the traffic and the blinding heat of the city, reasserted itself. Vijay pushed one elbow through the open window, trying to deflect the rush of air onto his face as they sped past Galle Face Green towards the downtown area of the city.

'I didn't know there was a fort,' said Clara.

'You are right, Miss. Those days there was fort. It is being razed to be making space for buildings and all that. But all people still calling it Fort, Miss.'

'Call me Clara, Vijay. You're off duty now,' she smiled.

'Yes, Miss, off duty until six thirty.'

Vijay cursed himself and stared at the black and white photograph of a plump lady and two frightened-looking children sellotaped to the dashboard of the taxi.

They were passing the end of the Beira Lake now, and from deep inside the bolt-hole of his anxieties he answered Clara's questions as best he could. But the composure he had somehow managed to maintain at the Oberoi seemed irrecoverably scattered, so that each sentence that escaped his lips was ruthlessly pursued and dragged back into the dungeons underneath his mind where the merciless inquisitors of self-doubt interrogated it until every nuance of word and tone had been exposed, scourged, and returned to him bleeding as a lesson in his pitiful inadequacy. He looked out of the open window as they drove past the army parade ground, trying to think of something to say that could possibly interest her, but he was soon lost in the thought that the chief of his acuities were occupied in the dungeons and that it was only the veneer of him that was riding in the taxi with Clara Lane. He could see that she was engrossed by the scenes that flew chaotically by and wondered why he too could not also reach out to the city and to her, why he must be absorbed instead in groping for some vestige of ease and assurance, scrabbling frantically on his knees to pull together some unscattered sense of a dignified, unembarrassed, unashamed self. He commented from time to time on the scenes outside the window, but he knew his words were not calmly chosen in response to what she saw but rather seized on as he might seize on anything to cover his nakedness. Worst of all, he knew that his eyes were giving him away, that he was failing miserably to speak that secret language of which the eyes are the voice. Fiercely he lectured himself as the cab proceeded slowly past the Intercontinental Hotel; he had thought he could be something else, someone else, if it were not for the sarong sheathed tightly around his legs. If he could not be different, equal, himself, now, here, in the back of this taxi, then he would never again be able to pretend that it was his circumstance and not his self that explained his crippled state. He looked at Clara as she turned her face away to the window, and Lalith's brave words came back to mock him. It was well after three o'clock, but his own lights had dimmed to nothing in the glare of her presence. Even when she was silently looking out at the passing streets of the city her unanxious confidence, the solidity of her assurance, seemed to destroy him, scattering any sense of a respectable self that he might have managed to bring together. Madly he cast around for pieces of his own identity, for a vestige of presence or personality he could call his own; but as the cab crawled by the grim brown pile of the former parliament building he could assemble no such substance, nor find any piece of ground on which to stand.

Soon they had turned into the commercial heart of the capital and Vijay began lamely pointing out the main stores. Clara peered dutifully at the dingy entrances of Miller's and Cargill's.

'Can we walk just a little way, Vijay?'

'Can,' said Vijay with a dry throat.

With a glance at the meter, the driver agreed to wait for them in the shade at the other side of the road.

Clara and Vijay infiltrated their way into the flood of people, pushing through the traders who clogged the colonnades, the beggars who encrusted the base of the pillars, the ragged, black-skinned women with dulled children in their arms who pitifully mimed the act of putting food in their babies' mouths while all around the hoarse voices and outstretched arms were imploring her to stop and take notice of their produce or their plight. She paused, confused about how to press on against the tide of people. At her feet an old man was thrusting an enamel mug towards her. He had no legs. Vijay ushered her forward and the man followed, scooting himself on a scarred, yellow skateboard with blue plastic wheels, very like one she had seen only a month ago, on Boston Common, ridden by a black teenager in an extravagant display of youth and fitness. The noise of the streets rose on all sides as the begging and the bargaining competed with the car horns and the throbbing engines while, above it all, a thousand jackdaws cawed angrily from the roof-tops.

Vijay looked at her, his face expressing concern.

'I am calling taxi now?' She nodded, smiling. Vijay waved urgently for the cab which had just succeeded in reaching the shade outside the main post office. As she stood in the heat, waiting for the taxi to battle back across the traffic, Clara's eyes travelled across the traders' stalls, taking in the wares which crowded every centimetre: hairslides and brooches, brushes and toothpastes, soaps and scents, torches and batteries, balloons and lollipops, belts and shoelaces, lighters and matches, scissors and spanner sets, light bulbs and hurricane lamps, shoe polishes and dyes, tin bowls and cutlery, penknives and twine, dice and playing cards, spices and sweets, purses and wallets, locks and bolts, sunglasses and identity-bracelets, wicker baskets and leather handbags, brushes and pans, note papers and envelopes, pencils and paints, candles and joss-sticks, picture frames and lockets, safety pins and needles, paper clips and rubber stamps. And in the heat and the clamour of the street corner, she recognised that what was displayed in front of her probably represented every last opportunity open to someone with little or no capital and whose entire stock must be carried each morning onto the street. The taxi nosed in to the kerb. An old man purchased a single cigarette from one of the discoloured plastic tubs on the side of a cart. As he slowly lit it from a smouldering rope, she opened her bag and purchased a shrink-wrapped set of batteries from the young man who presided over the stall.

Cocooned once more in the back of the old and solid Austin Cambridge, Clara quickly recovered and turned to smile at Vijay. He had been staring at her but, sensing that she was about to return his look, he immediately shifted his gaze an all important fraction to stare past her out of the window.

'Where to now?' she asked.

'Where you like?'

'I'd like to see something of the more ordinary suburbs now,' she smiled.

'Havelock Town,' Vijay almost shouted to the driver.

The cab was stifling and Clara pushed herself up against the window to catch as much of the rushing air as she could. She wished Vijay could relax. Whenever she looked at him he smiled, but far beneath the smile, at the very core of him, she saw the permanently scared light of his impalement. And as they passed again by the Beira Lake, she reflected on how acutely she was feeling another's pain.

❄

'This, Cinnamon Gardens.'

Clara looked around her, wondering why Vijay had brought them to this quarter of the city. On both sides, large private houses were set back from the roadside. Here and there, bored security guards in dusty uniforms crouched under the shade of garden walls. As the taxi passed between the avenues of jacaranda trees, Vijay began pointing out the houses of the locally famous. Through Clara's polite responses he sensed her lack of interest and a note of desperation crept into his voice. His city, he saw, was the dullest place on earth, and he lapsed into an anguished silence as they passed a cricket ground where an old wooden notice board announced a limited-over match between Reckitt & Coleman and a Combined Armed Forces eleven.

'This is Havelock Town,' he said, knowing that the afternoon was already a disappointment to Clara. 'That house is where famous cinema director Lester Pieris is living.'

By now the driver had entered into the spirit of it all and was meandering around aimlessly, awaiting further instructions and casting an occasional satisfied eye on the meter.

They turned into Havelock Road, lined with becalmed embassies, and Clara sank back in her seat, scarcely bothering to look out of the window. They were forced to stop as a chauffeur-driven car emerged from a leafy driveway. Vijay peered out of his window. The man in the back of the limousine looked at him impassively, utterly unperturbed, until Vijay averted his eyes and looked again at the scared-looking children in the photograph on the dashboard of the cab. What was it, he wondered, that determined who should belong to that superior order of those whom he felt the need to impress but who felt no need to impress him? Why could he not be as they? Why could he not be indifferent? And why could he not translate the city for Clara instead of so pathetically trying to translate himself? He told himself that he had always known that it had nothing to do with waiterdom, that there was an uncrossable divide between the great unassured, whose feet are planted not on the firm ground of a sure self but in the shifting sands of attempted impressions and effects, and those like Clara, the great assured, those whose sense of self is such that they do not need to concern themselves with the impression they might be creating on others, but instead succeed effortlessly in making others feel that concern. It was only from the commanding heights of assurance, he realised now, that the secret language could be spoken, that all ends could be achieved, all lands conquered, all peoples subjugated, all standards set. It was only the unassured who could take the full measure of that great divide, and for a few seconds Vijay saw that he must more modestly find himself if he were to find his place to stand. It was a small shaft of light cast across the dungeon as the door opened and Vijay emerged, blinking into the bright ocean at the end of Dickman's Road.

'What I'd really like to see, Vijay,' said Clara, turning to face him across the bench seat, 'is just an ordinary part of the city. Just where ordinary, poor people live. Can we do that?'

'Can go to Wanathamulla, also Pettah itself, Miss'.

'What is Pettah?'

'Actually, Pettah is meaning city outside of wall. In Sinhala it is also being called Pita Kottuwa, which is exactly same.'

'I'd like to go there.'

Vijay gave fresh instructions to the driver who performed a patient U-turn and headed back down the Galle Road towards the city.

Soon, they were heading inland again and Clara had begun a more energetic questioning, seizing fragments of the city that flew past her window and dropping them in Vijay's lap for an explanation. Gradually, he came to understand that the things she was interested in were the ordinary things, the things he knew about but which he had assumed were beneath her notice: the loin-clothed bullock-cart drivers, the head-load carriers and *watti* baskets, the fish-sellers with their *pingo* scales, the string-hopper sellers and the street hawkers, the burnt-out Tamil houses, the cool-shops and one-stop buys, the ration stores and the food-stamp queues, the barrow boys and street urchins, the monks with their shaven heads and tightly rolled umbrellas. On such topics Vijay's expertise flowed, and by the time they had reached Borella a little confidence had begun to flood back into the veins of his conversation.

'This is Wanathamulla, Miss, but now it is being called Borella because no babies are being born there.' He watched her puzzled expression for a second or two before continuing.

'Those days, Miss, pregnant ladies are travelling for clinic in different ward to be having babies. It is so children will not be having to give Wanathamulla as place of birth.'

'What's wrong with Wanathamulla?'

'Nothing is very wrong. It is having name for worst slums in city, that is all.'

'Where were you born, Vijay?'

'I am born in Maligawatta, Miss. We are coming there just in jiffy.'

The taxi turned north into Dematagoda; poverty was beginning to break through the surface of the city like rust. As Clara stared at the dogs picking over the piles of refuse on the street, Vijay pointed to a boarded-up building in front of which a youth of about sixteen was casually bouncing a tennis ball on the uneven pavement.

'Where you are seeing bouncing ball, Miss, there you can be getting drug. Those days only pot. Nowadays heroin is also there.

'Don't the police also know what it means?'

'Miss, most of these fellows having more control over policeman than ball.'

Clara smiled and turned her head to keep in view two men who were pushing a hand cart up the slight gradient. The younger of the two was doing most of the pushing, and she saw that he was retarded, staring wide-eyed at the strange, familiar world around him and gibbering constantly to himself.

'That is just coolie, Miss' said Vijay, looking round for something else to attract her interest.

As Clara watched, the wiry older man took the cart from his companion and set it down on its shafts. Lifting one of the buckets hanging from its sides, he took a stiff brush under his arm and unlatched a rusting, corrugated iron door. In a second he had disappeared into a narrow alleyway between a small tea shop and a decaying tenement building.

'What does he do, the coolie?' Clara asked.

'He is Tamil cleaner, that is all.'

'What is he cleaning?'

'He is cleaning out all bucket-houses, that is all'.

The taxi was still stuck at the lights when Clara saw the old man emerge from the alleyway carrying the bucket which was obviously now full. He was glistening with a faint sweat and flies were hovering around his arms and settling on his neck and open khaki shirt. For a second, he stood in the shade drinking something from a tin mug.

'So there is no sanitation, no pipes or anything?'

'Some houses are having sanitation. Rich people are having sanitation. Some people are having pit latrine type *sulabh shauchalaya*. Some still having just bucket only'.

'Does the coolie call every day?'

'Must, Miss. Otherwise buckets starting to sing.'.

'Who pays him?' asked Clara fascinated.

'Town Hall is paying him small salary. But he is also having *santhosam*.'

'*Santhosam*?'

'It is very small tip. One, two rupees only. Each house is giving.'

'And sometimes they also give him tea?'

'Sometimes also he will be taking tea.'

They watched as the coolie turned to hang the tin cup on a nail.

'Cup is there only for coolie, Miss Clara, no-one else in family is using this cup.'

The taxi pulled away, leaving the coolie and his assistant pushing the cart to the next house. Soon they were entering Maligawatta.

'Over there is illegal drinking place, Miss. Inside they are putting wooden barrel in ground. Then everything is being put. Mainly it is rotten fruit. Apple, pineapple, mango. Even potato is there. Afterward whole thing being dammed up for months on end. Bricks are going on top, also sand, so no one is knowing. One fine day they are opening. Now, very strong drink is there. Then they are having ladle to be putting into glasses, but they are having also small net to be getting centipedes, beetles, caterpillars, cockroaches, everything. Very cheap way of getting drunk for poor, Miss Clara. You can be breaking down wall when you are drinking. You are in heaven. Only afterwards you are dying.'

Clara smiled again and the smile remained as they passed

a long line of white-uniformed children, the girls proceeding demurely, immaculate in their clean white dresses, shining black hair held back by coloured plastic slides, while the boys sprawled along behind, noisily showing off, walking in that uneconomical way in which boys everywhere walk from school. The taxi stopped again at the lights. The first children were now passing what looked like the entrance to an alleyway from which a drain flowed into a grate on the street. She watched as one or two of them disappeared into the gap, stepping over piles of rubbish, rotten vegetable leaves, empty tins, sodden paper bags, food wrappings, fish bones, coconut husks, which lay on the pavement by the drain.

Clara wondered whether she could ask to see where Vijay himself lived but decided against it and sat up higher to try to see whether the bridge was carrying them over river or railway line. Just down the embankment, twenty or thirty women in saris queued with water pots at their feet.

'Do most people get their water from the street, Vijay?'

'Poor people yes, Miss. Water is no problem. Everybody is having water within two minutes of walking. Problem is not water, Miss. Problem is queuing. Usually there is only very small pressure. Sometimes tap is being stolen. We are queuing ten minutes for water, ten minutes for toilet, ten minutes for washing. Queuing. Queuing. Queuing, Clara.' No sooner had he succeeded in pronouncing her name than he was overwhelmed by how inappropriate it had been, said at the wrong time, at the wrong point, with the wrong intonation. For the next minute the deafening blunder echoed through the dungeons. He would not attempt it again. The taxi lurched into Mihindu Mawa.

Everywhere Clara looked, thousands of lives were flowing around her as the taxi weaved its way back through the Pettah, people of whom she knew nothing and to whom she meant nothing. How many of them, she wondered, carried some great secret which isolated them in these crowds, or were weighed down with the knowledge of a mortal illness, or were inwardly supporting some twisting agony of mind? How many had in prospect some act of unselfish love, or contemplated some desperate crime, or had suffered some great triumph or humiliation in the course of that long day? The crowds converged on the Pettah bus station and began to divide themselves up among the railings and the pedestrian islands, mingling with the throbbing engines and the cries of vendors, and from her great distance she surmised that all outside the window of her cab would be able to point to a more direct and intimate connection between what they were doing on that Friday evening and the need to put food into their stomachs, clothes on their backs, a roof over their heads, to take care of a family or to fulfil the demands of some strongly held belief. And what of herself? What was the connection between her presence in this scene and any of these necessary things? As they crossed back onto Slave Island, her thoughts seemed to exaggerate the distance between the world inside the taxi and the world outside. No matter what she did or did not decide during these two weeks, she would never have to worry about the things that occupied almost all of the people who were passing by her window. And as she looked she felt a new and different dimension of her removal, knowing that since the beginning human kind had been preoccupied with food, shelter, fuel, and the web of reciprocal relationships, obligations, beliefs, which had protected and insured such needs. But now a minuscule percentage had been released, and were blessed or cursed with being the first to cross the narrow, difficult mountain trail from which they had descended onto the vast and trackless plain where they now stood looking at one another and wondering which way to go and why, and whether to travel together or alone. Fort had been left behind. They were within sight of Galle Face Green, and she saw how disorienting was the removal of old imperatives, the props of old axioms of being, the established criteria giving way to this ever-widening expanse of new terrain for which she and all who strove with her, the well-educated, the sophisticated, were so profoundly ill-prepared. The little release of a tension that had become habitual, the small relaxation which seemed so simple but had proved so elusive, came to her bit by bit as through the window of the speeding cab she saw for the first time a past which had led her to this afternoon, a present in which she might be forgiven, and a future in which, if she were brave enough, she might find her way.

As they turned along the coast road, she breathed deeply and felt as though she were letting herself go out to the preoccupations of the people heading in all directions across the Green, content that her existence mattered not one jot to the man with the worried frown coming down the steps with a newspaper parcel under one arm and wearing a piece of string for a belt. She sensed that she could exist here without being gullivered by threads of expectation. She enjoyed being nobody in this city, and she glimpsed again a fragment of the unconscious truth which had driven her here, knowing that she was exhausted by the effort of filling all the space in her universe by her own efforts, weary of the burden of significance which she had attached to her days.

Vijay too was preoccupied as the taxi crossed the narrow isthmus between the lake and the open sea. He had planned to get out at the lights and walk the length of Galle Face Green to the hotel. But for the moment he sank back on the worn leather, limp with the effort he had made. In the end, he told himself, he had come through, scraped together a little solidity, a quantum of assurance. But now, as the taxi approached the lights at the beginning of the Galle Road, he was once more divided: one part of him despaired at the thought of the evening shift on the verandah; the other thought with relief of regaining the tiled room under the hotel and wrapping on his white sarong.

Clara smiled understandingly when he said he would walk the rest of the way.

'Thank you, Vijay,' she said. 'It's been the most enjoyable afternoon I've spent in a long time. I wouldn't have understood anything without you. You've been a wonderful guide.' She was suddenly aware that something inside her wanted to reach out to Vijay and, on an impulse, she stretched out her hand to touch him on the sleeve of his white shirt. Through his smile she saw again the fright deep in his eyes and took away her hand as the cab rolled to a stop on the edge of Galle Face Green.

Vijay watched her rejoin the traffic on the Galle Road. Dusk was just beginning and the first red tail lights glowed through the dust and fumes. He crossed to the seaward side and looked the full length of Galle Face Green toward the distant façade of the hotel, gleaming white through the brown haze. He began to walk, suddenly alone and wondering which world was real, struggling for a grip on the afternoon, trying to reattach it to the rest of his life. As he neared the hotel, he thought for the first time of the Food and Beverage Manager; but his disorientation persisted and he was unable to decide whether his act of defiance had been trivial or momentous. In any case, he told himself, no one need know. He thought of what Lal would say and resolved to reply, if anyone at the hotel were nosy enough to ask, that it was his own time and he had spent it chatting with the Queen of England.

More than once he was nodded to or greeted by acquaintance or friend as he crossed the Green, sometimes stopping to exchange a word and enquire after family and job, and supposing that he might have been more careful. He had set out intending to take Clara only to those parts of the city where he would be unlikely to be seen by anyone he knew, but in the end vanity had bundled wisdom out of the window; he had taken her the full length of Sea Beach Road where the men from the Maligawatta slum gardens were in the habit of standing and waiting for casual work; he had directed the driver to proceed slowly past his old school building, over the St Sebastian Bridge, and into Mihindu Mawa; he had stopped outside K. J. Muhammad's tea shop which was only a stone's throw from the New Bazaar Bridge. Now, he approached the front entrance of his own hotel, turning inland at the last moment to head for the staff entrance on the Galle Road. He had seen no one he knew, and on the whole he decided that the afternoon's outing was unlikely to attract any attention.

But Vijay, who had told Clara so much about his city, could, unblinded, have pointed out to her the impossibility of one of its sons driving its streets for a whole afternoon with a European woman without being noticed by any of his accumulated acquaintance. Vijay Jayasinghe and Clara Lane were seen in Maligawatta by Adeline Pancras, who was taking her four-year-old to the ear, nose and throat clinic in Hultsdorf and who was the sister-in-law of the woman who lived next door to Sithie Zanoobie whose husband had deserted her and who would forever be grateful to her friend Chandra for helping her in her hour of need. They were seen by Donatus Perera, who was forced to give way to the taxi at the Borella roundabout and who was the surly assistant to the van driver who regularly delivered the day's vegetables to all the hotels on the Galle Road. They were seen by two unemployed Tamils who happened to be leaning on the parapet of the New Bazaar Bridge, waiting for the betting shop to open, and who had only the previous week had occasion to visit Godfrey Jayasinghe for a decision on the old question of whether a run was higher than a flush. They were seen passing the cricket ground by the tri-shaw driver who was struggling to ferry an overweight lady to the Maradana Mosque but whose regular patch was the quiet lane between Galle Face Green and the dignified white hotel which provided most of his customers. And they were seen in Grandpass by a Mrs Priyanganie, proprietor of the Sinhabahu Hotel which, although having only six bare rooms without bath or WC, nonetheless admitted her to the Association of Hoteliers where she liked nothing better than to discuss the trials of the profession, as one hotelier to another, with the likes of Miles Perera.

As the shadows lengthened on Galle Face Green and Vijay ended his walk, almost everybody in the city who would have had any interest in his spending the afternoon in the company of a fair-haired, well-dressed, European lady had already been informed of the fact.

23

Most of the residents of the garden had turned up out of respect for the priest, and two hundred people were now gathered beside the latrine blocks, the only area large enough for any assembly. The men and some of the older women occupied most of the strung plastic seats that had been brought out from the verandahs. The younger women crowded in at the back by the washrooms. Just in front of Chandra, on the last row of seats, Godfrey was keeping her informed of his impatience by a series of elaborate grunts and sighs. At the front the priest, his robe glowing an unearthly colour in the early dusk, was intoning his sermon. One plump, glossy arm held a delicate pointed-leaf fan motionless across his chest as he stood stiffly behind the little table which Mrs C. J. Periera had covered with a pristine white cloth, the marks of its careful ironing still visible in spite of the humidity. Behind him, a rolled black umbrella leaned against the garden wall, decked with white flags. He hurried on with his sermon, looking as though he could not wait to tick off garden No. 178 in the little accounts book in which he recorded which of his half-dozen slum-sermons he had preached in which garden and what the total amount collected had been.

Chandra stood on tip-toe to see if she could catch sight of Susil who had insisted on sitting with the older boys at the front where boredom was being alleviated by furtive fights and unravellings of the rush mats.

'The Lord Buddha taught us that the first step to overcoming our difficulties is to correctly identify them,' intoned the priest, his shaven head slowly turning as he spoke, like a directional fan, gleaming in the electric light of the latrine wall. The only object on the table-cloth was an old chromium alarm clock at which Godfrey was staring as if mesmerised by the possibility of the alarm going off and bringing the sermon to an abrupt end.

'Many cases which turn up at the police station or at the hospital begin as arguments at the water tap or the latrine,' the priest went on. He paused to hitch the glowing robe more firmly onto his left shoulder and began to wave the fan at the flies and midges which had been drawn to the saffron glow in the gathering dusk. One of the mothers moved to the front to extradite the ring leader of the fighting going on below the level of the table.

Only five metres from the priest stood the concrete cubicles, and for the first time in many nights there was no smell. Those of the women who had considered the job beneath their status had at first fallen into a sullen silence as Mrs C. J. Periera and Chandra Jayasinghe had cleaned the latrines together; but while Chandra had organised the younger women to do the job for the next two mornings, Mrs Periera had had a quiet word with some of the more prominent among the original defaulters all of whom had agreed to re-establish the rota system, commenting that it was fine so long as everyone took their turn, as they personally had always been willing to do.

The priest's fan was waving a little more energetically now and, as if keeping time, his delivery had also speeded up. 'There are always those people who will try to get a grip on the Garden Council for their own ends,' he warned. 'Beware of such people. Make sure that it is you that your representatives are serving and not themselves.'

Chandra's mind began to wander. The warden had talked about something similar at the health class that afternoon, only he had made it more interesting. He had begun with felt cut-outs of various animals, sticking them up on a piece of material draped over the blackboard. At first he had only asked the women to describe the characters of the animals in traditional stories and they had begun calling out, laughing at being asked to play a children's game, giving him the slyness of the fox and the greediness of the rat. Suddenly he had put up felt cut-outs of a man and a woman. Amid much behind-hands laughter, he had begun asking them to think about the specific characters they all knew in the slum gardens. The women, shy at first, had gradually been drawn in and had eventually given him the pitiless, never-satisfied mother-in-law; the inconsiderate neighbour; the violent, alcoholic husband; the lazy, do-nothing brother; the leering husband of a best friend; the stone-faced moneylender. In each case, he had pretended to set such people in front of the meeting, imagining that he was holding them up by the hair, prompting all the women to join in with their thoughts, and what had started as a childish game had rapidly become emotional as the women of the slums vented long-subdued or never-before spoken feelings and saw that many of the other women were also having to contend with anxieties similar to their own so that the trickle of release had quickly become a flood of shared emotions. After all the characters had been exposed, the health officer had asked them 'And how do we cope with such people?' and the discussion had become serious. He had several times addressed his question to Chandra, and seemed always to look at her while he was speaking so that she was forced to lower her eyes to the floor where the ants were still filing in perfect order in the grooves between the tiles.

In front of her, Godfrey seemed to have despaired of the priest's alarm clock and was looking around him as if to see if there might be any way of escaping without being noticed. Any minute now, Chandra thought, he was likely to begin raising bets on which of the two flies on the priest's robe would fly off first.

'The Lord Buddha also formed a Community Council,' the priest intoned. 'The Lord Buddha also said' - he paused the fan for a moment as if to emphasise the point – 'that it is the particular duty of all organisations to help those who are in trouble, those who are exploited, those who are vulnerable.'

At the priest's words, the face of Vinitha presented itself with terrible clarity again in Chandra's mind. The women had still been chattering excitedly about the afternoon's discussion as they had crossed the dusty compound outside the clinic. Chandra had stopped for a moment, not quite able to place the woman who stood alone on the steps, a child wrapped in her arms. After a second, it had come to her that this was Vinitha, whom she had sometimes sat with at the ante-natal classes. Vinitha, she remembered, had also had a son, born about a week before Susil. She had greeted her warmly and enquired about the child. But the flow of conventional words had stopped as she turned to look at the little boy in Vinitha's arms. He was little more than half the size of Susil, his face the shape of an old man's, pinched and drawn, the hair sparse and grey. Only the enormous clear brown eyes, sunk deep into gaunt sockets, were still the eyes of a child. As she looked, the filthy cloth he was wrapped had fallen away to reveal a shrivelled grey leg, wider at the knee than at the thigh. Chandra had turned to look at Vinitha not knowing what to say. But there were no pretences left to be kept up; the woman's face was racked by her pain and humiliation, and Chandra had instinctively reached out to touch her arm. Vinitha could hardly speak.

'I have no food,' she had said simply.

'Your husband has no work?'

'Nothing for six months.'

'They will look after him at the clinic, Vinitha.'

Vinitha had nodded. After a moment to recover herself, she had explained that she had had to borrow a blouse even to come to the clinic. Slowly, she had told her story. Her husband had been sacked after a failed cart drivers' strike. Evicted, they had put up a shack on the only place they could find, in a small shanty on a waterlogged marsh near the Kandy Road. But the rains had come early and their home was now ankle-deep in muddy water. They had put the bed-boards up on stones, but there were leeches on her legs when she woke up in the mornings. She had taken work carrying bricks and cement on her head at a building site in the Pettah, working from six in the morning until six at night for ten rupees. Her back and neck gave her constant pain. She had had to ask her older child, a bright girl of ten whom Chandra had met once at the health centre, to leave the school in Grandpass and find work. Chandra came near to tears as the voice of the priest droned on over the garden and she remembered how Vinitha, holding her malnourished child, had finally broken down on the steps of the clinic. The ten-year-old girl had succeeded in finding work as a domestic servant to a house in Cinnamon Gardens, thirteen hours a day, seven days a week for eight rupees a day. Late on the previous Friday she had come home without pay for her week's work. Two plates had slipped from her fingers as she had carried them from the table, and by the time she arrived back at the waterlogged shack there had been ugly bruises rising on both sides of her face and her ribs had hurt so much that she could not lie down. As she had told Chandra the story, Vinitha's shoulders had come forward in her borrowed blue blouse until finally she had bit hard into her lip and let her head fall over the frail child. Chandra, resting her hand on the defeated woman's arm, had felt the sobs that racked the body but could not be shown to the world.

The flies were buzzing all around the saffron robe now and some had even had the audacity to alight on the polished olive skin. Working the fan, the priest was bringing his sermon to a hurried close. 'If you want to improve your lives here in the slum garden,' he concluded, closing the little pocket book on the white table-cloth, 'then you must follow the example of the Lord Buddha. Do not drink alcohol. Do not commit adultery. Do not gamble. Support your Garden Council. Be careful to choose only good and reliable friends.'

There was an outbreak of shuffling and stirring as the inhabitants of the garden prepared themselves for the next speaker, an official from the Town Hall, who had been waiting with commendable patience to hear himself speak.

'I hope we have all noted what the *bhikku* has been saying about helping ourselves,' the official began, his skin as sheltered and pale as that of the priest. 'Because I am here tonight to tell you that the city council will help you, but only if you help yourselves.'

Godfrey turned in his chair and gave Chandra his bored, cynical, here-we-go-again look which made her lower her head in silent laughter. The official droned on. She really couldn't ask Vijay to help Vinitha as well. He was already supporting her mother and helping Sithie Zanoobie with a little money now and then. She thought of Sithie sewing up dusty cement bags in the near darkness on the other side of the canal. They had to help Sithie. She and Chandra had grown up together in the shanty; they were practically sisters. For two years, Sithie had worked in the Middle East; in all that time she had spent nothing on herself, sending all of her earnings back to her husband who was supposed to be looking after their young son and saving the money so that, when she returned, they could go through the wall, like Vijay and Chandra. But Eustace had found other uses for the money. Through Godfrey, Chandra knew that he drank and gambled heavily at one of the arrack houses near the Railway Works. He had also begun buying presents, perfumes and jewellery, for a vain beauty who lived in a nearby shanty. When Sithie had returned, after two years in Kuwait, he had not been at Katunayake airport to meet her. Wondering what could be wrong, she had made her own way back to the shack on the banks of the St Sebastian canal where she had found her home collapsed, her husband and son gone. Numbed, Sithie had sought out her mother's hut where she had been presented with a son who no longer knew her. There she had learnt that her husband had gone to live with a young girl in Bloemendhal, taking with him anything that might have been left of her earnings from the Middle East. She had not cried. With Chandra's help, she had woven new cadjan and repaired the sagging roof of the shack as best she could. Then she had set about finding work. She had applied for tea-sifting, coir-making, stone-breaking, even brick-carrying, but there had been nothing except a wretched job re-sewing used cement bags which were dumped and collected at the entrance to the shanty each morning and for which she was paid eight rupees for the ten bags she had contracted to sew each day. With this income, plus a ration card and food stamps for five measures of rice and one tin of milk powder, she was still not able to feed herself and her son. When the roof had collapsed for the second time, Vijay had bought a sheaf of poles and two sheets of corrugated iron to replace the rotting cadjan.

'The most important thing in a garden like this is to have a strong community council,' said the official from the Town Hall, speaking in Sinhala, his fist pounding gently on Mrs Periera's table-cloth. 'Unless you organise to help yourselves, we cannot help you.' A note of anticipatory exasperation had crept into his voice.

Chandra was telling herself to be sensible and devote her energies only to the arrangement with the Sweet Tooth until they were completely confident with the new stove and knew what was involved in baking eight trays a week. Only when they were sure they could cope would she try for another similar arrangement in Grandpass or New Bazaar. If it succeeded, no matter what Premawathie said, she would invite Sithie to share in the little business. Until then, all she could do was to help out with a little money and sit with her sometimes to share the lonely task of resewing the dust-laden bags on the floor of the shanty. Without daring to articulate it even to herself, she also knew that if things went well then one day she would ask Vinitha to do some of the delivering.

'We have found,' the official was saying with great gravity, 'that the key to improving life in the slums is people's participation.' He beamed at the assembled inhabitants of the garden as if he had announced that they were all to receive double food stamps. 'That is why,' he continued, 'we are here to consult with you this evening about the question of the new latrines.'

Chandra began to concentrate.

'That is why we are sharing with you all the details so that we can decide together what is best.'

With that, the official passed around a few sheets of paper which gave details of the extra latrines that the Town Hall was prepared to install.

Godfrey turned around again to Chandra.

'New latrines are not even built and already they are handing out paper,' he said loudly. There was a stir of laughter which caused the official to glance in their direction disapprovingly.

'As you will see,' said the official from the Town Hall, 'if each household pays ten rupees per month for two years this will be enough to pay for the new installations.'

Godfrey turned to Chandra: 'Why does he always say participation when he means we have to pay ten bucks?' he said in a loud whisper followed by more suppressed laughter. Chandra refused to look at him but instead studied one of the sheets of densely printed paper which had just reached her.

'The first thing for each garden to decide together,' said the official 'is where the new facilities should be sited.' His audience remained silent. The only possible place to build anything was in the open space next to the existing latrines.

'Next,' said the official after this matter had been duly decided, 'we have to decide on the responsibilities for the maintenance of the new latrines.' Slowly he explained what the inhabitants of the garden already knew; the planned new latrines would work on the same two-pit system as the existing ones: when one pit was full, a metal plate must be pulled out from the main pipe and reinserted at a different angle to divert the effluent into the second chamber; when that too was full, the first chamber could be opened and its contents, by now theoretically dry and odourless, could be emptied and sold as fuel or fertiliser. It was soon agreed that the Tamil scavenger who performed these duties in the existing latrines would be invited to look after the new latrines as well for a suitable increase in his remuneration which would be added to the monthly levy on each house in the garden.

'The next question,' said the official, 'concerns how many new latrines there should be. I now throw this open for discussion.'

The secretary of the Garden Council immediately asked how many latrines the Town Hall was prepared to install. The official replied that this had been determined on a per capita basis for the entire population of the gardens in the wards of East and West Maligawatta, in relation to the overall capital budget for the current financial year of the budget sub-committee of the Common Amenities Board, and that for a garden the size of No. 178 the number of latrines available was 2.38. He then took several more sentences to explain why it was not possible to build 0.38 of a latrine and was finally interrupted by the secretary who demanded to know if the answer to the question was two.

'I may say,' said the official, 'that for all practical purposes and for the foreseeable future, we are prepared to consider two latrines in garden No. 178. Are there any more questions?' The priest had already gone and the official too was now anxious to be away to his own home. But at that point, Mrs C. J. Periera, who had also been reading the densely printed handout raised her hand at the back of the meeting.

'Why can't the new latrines be built by our husbands instead of the contractors employed by the Common Amenities Board?' she asked.

A buzz spread through the assembly, and Mrs Periera had to raise her voice to continue.

'We have plenty of men who can do that kind of work. And

with the money you have down here for the contractors we could build more than two latrines. We could put another standpipe in, and a new washroom as well.'

The audience was paying attention now and several of the men voiced their agreement. The official looked exasperated.

'We can also buy materials cheaper than you have put down here,' joined in K. K. Mundi, the casual labourer who lived next door but one to the Jayasinghes. 'We can get bricks cheaper, cement cheaper, sand cheaper. All we need from CAB is the squatting plate.' Another murmur of assent arose from the assembled population of the garden.

'I am afraid that cannot be agreed to,' said the official, rising to his feet to quell the mutiny with the lash of bureaucracy. 'It's a question of quality control, and building to certain specifications to comply with the requirements of the Health and Safety Act of nineteen hundred and forty-eight. That is why we can only use licensed builders. The Board has experienced contractors for all such jobs.'

At this point, Godfrey struggled to his feet and bellowed loudly: 'Also Board is getting kickback from contractors.'

As the crowd roared in agreement, the Vice-President of the garden also rose to his feet. 'That is also true,' he said angrily, 'Common Amenities Board is getting bribes from contractors. Then contractors are making money on shortcuts and not doing job.'

Before the official could reply, another voice had called out. 'Go yourself, sir. Look at the plates in the latrines. Both are cracked. It's because they used sand and cement five to one instead of three to one. Then they went off somewhere and sold the cement that was left. They also sold the bricks. They built the latrines with the old bricks from the bucket-houses you paid them to pull down.' Another roar of approval rose from the garden, forcing the official to his feet.

'Such mistakes might have been made under the previous Council, but steps have now been taken to make sure that things like this don't happen. Now, are there any final questions?' The official began stacking his papers ready to put them into the leather satchel which he had already lifted from the dusty floor onto the white table-cloth.

'Yes, please, one question,' said Chandra from where the women were standing at the back of the meeting.

'Yes, young lady,' said the official, relaxing a little as he saw a questioner unlikely to give trouble. To Chandra, an unnatural silence seemed to have fallen.

'On this paper, it says that each latrine is six thousand rupees. But just the roof alone is almost three thousand rupees.'

'That is correct. The walls of course are very straightforward. The roof is more difficult,' the official explained in the tone of one who is called upon to teach the obvious to the benighted. 'The roof has to be pitched like so.' He raised his hands into a patient steeple. 'And then there has to be a metal chimney to get rid of the smells. And the chimney has to be fixed into the slope of the roof with tarmac boards to stop water getting in. Then the roof has to be bonded to the walls.' The official smiled and continued fastening the buckles of his satchel. One or two people began to drift away.

'But why do we need a roof at all?' said Chandra above a renewed murmur. 'If there was no roof then there would be no need for the chimney. There would be no smells. Also, it would be light inside the latrine instead of pitch black.'

The official clicked his tongue and smiled.

'Everybody in this city will be laughing up their sleeves if we build latrines without roofs,' he said dismissively and picked up his satchel from the table-cloth.

'They may be laughing up sleeves, but we are shitting in daylight,' said Godfrey, standing up. The laughter bounced off the latrine walls and even the women giggled into their hands, all except Premawathie who was giving Godfrey a look which would have turned him to concrete had he met her gaze. The official waited for the laughter to subside and then opened his mouth, drawing in a deep breath.

'And what happens when it rains?' he said patiently.

'When it rains,' said Chandra, 'we get wet walking up the garden anyway, and the rainwater will all go down the latrines. The health warden is always telling us how important it is to put water down the latrines.'

The crowd had grown interested again, and there was silence as the official looked down at his satchel with pursed lips.

'Also,' continued Chandra, 'if there were no roofs the cost would be half, and we could have four more washrooms with taps instead of two.'

The crowd knew when to be silent.

The official was desperately looking for a back door now.

'It's a very interesting suggestion,' he finally said, recovering his confidence, 'and it's just this kind of little thing that we've arranged these consultations for, so we at the Town Hall can hear what you, the people, have to say. I'll be making a full report of everything said here this evening at the next meeting of the Common Amenities Board on which I have the honour to serve. Thank you all. Good night.'

The President of the garden moved quickly to take the official's place behind the little table and held up both hands, calling out that the meeting was not over just because the visitor from the Town Hall was leaving. The garden's own business remained to be transacted, he said to an audience which was rapidly thinning as the women went to settle their children for the night. By the wall, groups of men were loosely gathered, waiting their turn to step through the gap on their way to the arrack parlours and meeting houses around the bridge. Chandra looked to see if Godfrey had gone, but he was motioning her to come and sit on one of the empty seats beside him.

The President of the Garden Council was calling the meeting to order and looking cross at facing less than half his original audience.

'First item. Three members of the garden council have not attended any of the last three meetings,' the President was saying. 'Their places are now forfeit. I call for three more nominations to the Garden Council.'

Two friends of committee members had been put forward when Mrs C. J. Periera spoke up again. 'Town Hall says there must be two women on every Garden Council. I propose Chandra Jayasinghe.'

'I am seconding,' Godfrey called out to more laughter. Chandra looked down at the beaten earth as the President asked for other nominations to contest the three places. There were none, and the meeting moved on.

Later that night, Chandra lay on her bed-board. From somewhere down the garden came the sound of a radio, and she could hear the lowered voices of a card game on the Mundis' verandah. In the darkness beside her an insect scratched its way across the floor. Susil breathed evenly at her side. She was staying awake, waiting for Vijay to get back from the late shift, eager to tell him about the calculations she and Godfrey had done that afternoon, about her election to the Garden Council, and about the silly story about his being seen that afternoon, in a taxi, with a famous American film-star.

24 ∫

Vijay changed in the locker room under the hotel while Lalith, already in uniform, sat on the bench quizzing him about his afternoon with Clara but succeeding only in prying loose monosyllables. Lalith lit the half cigarette he had saved from lunchtime.

'Come on, Vijay, you are taking somewhere more interesting than Wanathamulla!'

Vijay tightened the sarong and poked one bare foot under the bench to retrieve a *chapal*.

'I am telling you already, Clara is wanting to see just ordinary life of city.'

'Oh, it is Clara now is it?' said Lalith, drawing some satisfaction from the conversation at last. He leapt to his feet and grabbed the wooden coat stand from which Vijay had just lifted his tunic top.

'Clara, Clara, Clara,' he cried passionately to the coat stand, hugging it close to him and guiding it round the locker room as if dancing in the old ballroom. Vijay's other *chapal* narrowly missed him as he waltzed round the far side of the lockers. He picked up Lalith's cigarette which was burning into the wooden bench and helped himself to a drag, grinning despite himself.

'Lal, seriously I am asking, what is union hearing?' He tried to keep his voice casual. Lalith danced the coat stand back to its position, bowed courteously to it, and held out his hand for the cigarette.

'Rumour only. Minister is leaning on Miles Perera to be finding jobs for two unemployable cousins.'

'Gamini says we are having to have two sackings to be making places. He is hearing that word is in from bosses – no more hirings until troubles going away.'

Lalith came and put his hands on Vijay's shoulders.

'Not worrying, Vijay,' he said, looking good-humouredly into his friend's face. 'They are not sacking Vijay Jayasinghe for having mad passionate affair with Clara.' He pronounced the name breathily, as if with the last gasp of emotion in some epic film. 'They are firing some room-boy who is not staying awake, not star waiter with catering college diploma who only cannot be keeping hands off lady guests.'

'They are still needing excuse. They are not just firing,' said Vijay, trying to get a purchase on his world.

Lalith saw his friend's concern. 'Vijay, Vijay,' he said impatiently 'they cannot be sacking for taking taxi ride in own time. I am telling you they are having Hotel Workers' Union down neck before you are saying Bob is uncle if they are trying anything of this nature when father of chapel is Lalith Surasena.'

Vijay was less reassured by this than Lal might have hoped as the two of them made their way up the stone steps to emerge, at precisely half past six, into the evening sunlight.

Clara dived cleanly into the cool green waters of the pool, gliding a delicious half length, hair streaming behind her, the cold rushing refreshingly through her mind, washing off the dust and the traffic fumes, the beggars and the street hawkers, the sweating bucket-men and the shouting vegetable traders, the belching trucks and the lumbering bullock carts. The city rose to the surface of the pool in Clara's wake and evaporated with a shimmer under the still warm sun.

Three of the pool waiters watched, hypnotised, as she swam length after length in a steady crawl. Ten minutes later she lay on the wooden lounger, pulled out from under the shade, glistening with a light sun cream.

The pool-attendant arrived with lemon tea. Sitting up on the lounger, she looked out over the rim of her cup to the vast sunlit ocean which was beginning once more to turn the colour of steel. Her pores absorbed the steady, indulgent warmth of the six-o'clock sun as she began to allow the day's experiences to sink in, letting the pieces drift back to earth, seeing how the patterns reformed, fitting new with the old. The heat radiated back from the hot sand and vibrated in the balmy air. She half dozed, the tea barely touched.

The insistent bitt-bitting sound awoke her and she let her head fall sideways to see the middle-aged woman, seated about fifty metres away, knitting a shapeless garment and occasionally smiling at her daughter who sat staring out to sea.

The sun was disappearing now in a dull red glow over the ocean, losing its ardour, and she lay back in the arms of its less intense affections, closing her eyes. Minutes passed. A defeated man was sitting on the corner of the street holding one end of a ball of wool that was unravelling her as she walked away from him down the Galle Road. She awoke before she was entirely undone. The woman and her daughter were still there, consulting the pattern together. Her tea had gone cold. The warmth closed her eyes again and her own mother's face, smiling and fond, swam towards her. She began to wander, remembering her last visit home, how awful it had been, how the family and friends she had met had been just voices murmuring outside the room with no doors. And when she had tried to speak she had felt as though she were at a far remove, talking through glass walls, going through the motions from thousands of miles away inside her own mind, every sentence thrown across a vast space. With her sister's little girl, she had tried to imitate what she had observed others saying and doing. She had seen her mother and sister attending to an elderly aunt at the dinner table, or making childish conversation with the little girl, or chatting inanely with neighbours whom they seemed genuinely glad to see, but only by the greatest of efforts could Clara maintain even the pretence of being part of it all. Her whole visit had passed in this way, a prisoner watching a film of a world which she might never be allowed into again, the deceased watching her own ghost.

She shivered on the sea front. Night was falling faster than she had ever known and already one or two lights were appearing out to sea. She stared, wondering whether they were the lights of ships or the first faint stars appearing where sky and sea were merging into a common deep.

❄

Vijay watched Clara leave the seafront and cross the lawns. He turned away, hoping she would take her place at dinner before the scene was desecrated by others. For the moment, both restaurant and seafront were deserted apart from himself and Lalith, standing expectantly in the no man's land of the pre-dinner period, neither their own men nor anybody else's, the timeless statuary of the verandah.

Above them, Gamini stood in the semi-darkness of a first-floor window. At night, he often left his post on the landing for several minutes on end. Usually he paused for a while at the point where the gallery looked down on one side to the old ballroom and, on the seaward side, to the dim verandah below. It was dark, but he knew his way like a bat through the maze of the broken furniture and it suited his mood to stand in the gloom looking down on the lamp-lit tables. How fragile, how vulnerable, they looked in the foot margin of his page, against the enormity of the night. He half sat on the window-sill and looked with a sharper sadness at the two slim figures standing alone by the little desk, their tunics and sarongs lit yellow by the lamps, waiting for the first guests. Already he had heard from three separate sources that Vijay had spent the afternoon touring the city in a taxi with the English lady staying in room 107. He sighed softly through his teeth and wished he could send down the wisdom of his years to calm what he knew to be the agitated soul of Vijay Jayasinghe. Vijay, Vijay, he murmured to himself, the sigh mingling with an ill-defined nostalgia for a half-imagined past. Lalith he had given up on long ago, Lalith who wanted instant utopia by turning the world upside down like a child knocking over a patiently constructed tower of wooden bricks so that all would be scattered across the floor, rolling everywhere, equal and free at last, never mind the disorder and derangement which would mean that no one would ever find his place again and each would be an insignificant, insufficient whole, equal in purposelessness, free in running any way they liked in ever-tumbling aspiration and never-ending restlessness until they rolled to a stop, nowhere, alone, lost without place or purpose. But Vijay, he had hoped, would subdue his discontents, maintain his dignity, find his place.

Gamini leaned back against the balcony wall and looked up into the night sky as if unable to maintain the struggle: order was gone, gone in the name of the foolish notion of equality which served only to open the flood gates to a ceaseless surge of unfulfillable ambitions, pride, greed, all of it pouring and rushing into rivers of disillusionment and demoralisation that finally stagnated into pools of indignity. He had seen so many bravely flying their kites, their foreign cigarettes bulging in their shirt pockets, pretending that some day soon they were going to be a man. But the years passed and they did not become men. Their pretences wore thin like the soles of their imported shoes, and with each passing year it became more and more evident that as things were, so they were going to be. And so slowly they subsided to become the toothless, stubbled old men in vests and sarongs with comfortable *chapals* on their feet. Some of them, those whose ambition had not flown too high, descended gently to earth in later years of resignation and disappointed contentment; but many who had let themselves soar out of control had so far to fall that in the end they could only live with their disillusionment by inhabiting the toddy houses, the arrack dens, and now the heroin parlours which had sprung up all over the city. Only there were they able to preserve the illusion of still being aloft, of being a man, even as they were dragged along in the dust, respected by no one, not even their wives. They had aspired too much; they had been allowed to entertain the romance of the unattainable against which all reality was disappointment. The possible had been beneath them: they had known no sense of their place, and so they had never known the peace of that knowledge, never known the dignity which can come from behaving according to what is expected.

On the verandah, Vijay was struggling with the idea that Clara would not be dining in the hotel, that she must have gone instead to the grill room at the Oberoi or the Capricorn. The thought churned in the pit of his stomach as he was called into action by the arrival of a large party of tourists who were streaming in from the bar, brushing past the chairs and hungrily casting around for a table for twelve with a view of the sea.

When Clara finally came onto the verandah at a quarter past eight his heart lifted dangerously and in hurrying to get rid of the tray he was carrying he moved too quickly for the sarong and almost fell full length, earning a long sarcastic look from the captain who stepped forward to lead Clara to her table. Vijay stood back. The captain exchanged a few polished words, raising one hand regally behind him without turning around. Vijay stepped in with the menu which the captain placed open before her with a glossy beam and a small bow.

'I can specially recommend the lobster tails this evening M'moiselle,' he said unctuously, even glancing over his shoulder to suggest that no one else that night would be privy to this information. Vijay, standing to one side, waited patiently.

The captain took Clara's order with a little brass-knobbed pen and handed the chitty to Vijay while he lingered to converse with a favoured guest. Having been close enough to hear Clara's words, Vijay was able to transfer the indecipherable scribble to his own pad. After a few minutes the captain motioned the wine waiter in and, taking a little beaming step backwards, left Clara to her meal. As soon as he had gone, Clara's eyes travelled to seek out Vijay. She smiled good evening to him and rolled her eyes in commentary on the captain's clumsy solicitousness. Vijay smiled at her steadily, relishing to the depths of himself the bond of intimacy which had been thrown to him like a lifeline down the length of his verandah. Clara turned to look through the white arches across the lawns to the dark sea.

The Australian was leaning over the back of his chair impatiently. It was one of Lalith's tables and Vijay motioned him in with a perfect imitation of the captain's imperious manner. Lalith stuck two fingers up behind his back as he moved in to present the bill. Vijay approached Clara's table as soon as she had finished the small serving of chairman's curry.

'I thought I'd be brave and eat local,' smiled Clara.

'Chairman's curry is good,' said Vijay, instantly distressed at the banality of his words.

'Why don't they make you captain, Vijay? You'd do a better job than old smoothy.'

Vijay did not quite understand the term but smiled at what he knew was a light-hearted compliment.

'Have you ordered main course, Miss?'

'Yes, he recommended the lobster tails.'

'Twelve are being ordered on Fridays. They are being specially recommended until all are gone.'

Clara smiled, and Vijay grinned back sheepishly.

'I keep thinking of all the thousands of people we saw today, Vijay, and wondering what they are all doing out there, right now, in the darkness.'

'Most are also eating at this time, Miss. All city is having lobster tails about now.'

Clara gave him a look of mock reproof, amusement sparkling in her eyes, and he gloried again in the intimacy.

'Seriously, Vijay . . .'

There was a discreet cough and Vijay withdrew to make way for the captain who began to make meticulous enquiries about how Clara had found the chairman's curry.

The captain was still talking with Clara when Vijay returned a few minutes later with the lobster tails, turning to take the dish from the tray in order to present it to Clara personally. Vijay returned to his station. When the captain had withdrawn, Clara's eyes once again sought him out and gave him a long-suffering look. Vijay smiled back and scanned his other tables, noticing that a new guest, a young American wearing an elegant dinner jacket, was being shown to the table just across the aisle from Clara.

A few minutes later, as he walked back down the verandah after taking coffee to table twelve, Clara lifted her head to beckon him over.

'Vijay, I was just thinking, I really ought to try at least one of the other restaurants in the city while I'm here. Can you recommend one?'

'Capricorn is there. Also Intercontinental. Also Meridian. Also Oberoi itself is there.'

'Are there any that are just restaurants, not hotels?'

Before Vijay could think of a reply her attention had been distracted by the captain cruising in to ask if everything was progressing satisfactorily. Vijay retreated, waved away by the subtlest motion of a plump hand.

He took up a position next to Lalith by the little antique desk, the two of them standing side-by-side, their hands behind their backs, facing down the verandah. Lalith began to speak out of the side of his mouth.

'Lady getting drunk at nine. Big tip coming at seventeen. Fourteen eating fish with fruit knife. Little bit of chairman's curry falling in cleavage of Indian lady at twenty-two. Flies not being done up at twelve.'

'Betting two roops tip at eight bigger,' said Vijay, just stopping himself from also speaking out of the corner of his mouth.

'Listen Lal,' he continued 'Clara is asking what other restaurants are there. I am telling her Intercon, Cap, Meridian, but she is wanting restaurant and not wanting hotel at all.'

'Then there is Seaspray, of course,' said Lalith.

'Of course, why I am not thinking of this.'

'When you are thinking of taking Clara to Seaspray?'

'When I am getting tip of one year's salary from table eight.'

He moved off to present a bill for signature, stopping again by Clara's table on his way back down the verandah.

'Miss, there is Seaspray. It is having fresh fish and they are saying it is top restaurant.'

The captain loomed.

'Yes, Seaspray is very good, very good, very good, Miss Lane. They are serving fresh fish every day, sea fish, lobster, shark steak is there, also chicken tikka, chicken curry . . .'

Vijay shuffled slowly back to the desk. A movement in the reception area caught his eye and a sudden coldness spread over him as the Food and Beverage Manager walked to the end of the verandah entrance and stared down at the scene, lifting his chin to indicate that he was busy counting the diners for some official purpose. His eyes took in each of the waiters in turn and lingered unnecessarily long on Vijay.

Disconcerted, Vijay set off again in response to an imaginary summons and was saved from the possibility of being seen heading purposefully to nowhere by Clara stopping his progress down the aisle.

'I've just been thinking, Vijay,' she said, looking at him directly. 'To say thank you for this afternoon, I would really like to invite you to this Seaspray place – if you have an evening when you're not working.'

Seeing the instantly startled scare deep in Vijay's eyes, she added, smilingly, 'Just to say thank you, before I go back to London.'

'Of course, I would like to be sitting at Seaspray,' he said, not knowing how to finish, and was again saved by Clara asking him about his evening and morning shifts. Glad to have questions he could answer, Vijay gave her an extraordinarily detailed account of his duty roster, which she took to be an acceptance of the invitation.

'So it's Saturday or Monday then?' she asked.

Vijay's mind raced. Saturday was tomorrow. No time to think about the undefined problems which swarmed all over the idea of going to dine at the Seaspray with Clara Lane. Also, something told him, he must not be rushing around making himself available at any time.

'Saturday in evening I am unfortunately engaged in some business.'

'Fine. Monday evening then? Let's make it eight o'clock, there at the Seaspray.'

Clara smiled and Vijay retreated, the fanfares on the parapets drowning out the screams from below. Back at his post, he tried to resume the quiet stance and subdued look appropriate to the evening time on the verandah, but his face was unable to mask the panic in his mind. Before he had had the chance to calm himself, he was summoned by a small gesture to speak with the captain.

'F and B is wanting you in office, Vijay,' said the captain, in his 'you wouldn't be told' voice. Vijay remained where he was for a few seconds. Lalith was nowhere to be seen. The American at table eight was looking at Clara Lane. The captain was strolling between the tables, hands linked behind his back. The breeze from the ocean had turned cold, and the lights of the verandah seemed to have retreated into the distance as Vijay remained in his place, knowing that he must compose himself. After a few seconds, he turned and walked numbly through the double doors into the lobby of the hotel. An acre of polished tiles faced him. Out through the wide arches to his left he could just see the dim oil lamps of the drinks-carts and the peanut vendors on Galle Face Green. The eyes of the two receptionists followed him as he set off across the sea of tiles, heading for the small office under the main stairs.

He knocked quietly and went inside. The Food and Beverage Manager was sitting at his desk and made a show of finishing whatever it was he was writing before looking up.

'Jayasinghe, I am hearing that you are defying warning given this day only. All over town you are going with guest of hotel. All and sundry telling this.'

'Before warning,' said Vijay, his throat dry. 'Such arrangement I am making before warning.'

The Food and Beverage Manager looked at him as if this were irrelevant, but said nothing.

'Also,' continued Vijay, 'it is my own time I am taking just to show Miss Lane city.'

'This is not of any account in matter. Hotel rule is hotel rule and you are defying. Also defying after warning.'

'This is rule when there is Raj, that is all. It cannot be meaning anything in here and now.'

'Do not be giving me Lalith Surasena nonsense,' said the Food and Beverage Manager sternly. 'Having nothing at all to do with Raj. Rule is rule, Jayasinghe. What is Tour Guides Union saying when they are knowing that waiters in certain hotel are also doing moonlighting? Having money and all for being guide?' He held up his hand to forestall Vijay's protest. 'I am telling you what they are doing. They are having hotel put on blacklist so tour companies cannot be recommending and booking rooms and all. That is what they are doing, Vijay Jayasinghe. And that is why rule is there.'

'I am not having any money from Miss Lane,' said Vijay, sensing a subterranean sympathy and urgently pressing on his case. 'She is not wanting to be seeing any of tourist places. She is wanting to be seeing only ordinary places and all, everyday life I am showing. What is harm? What is wrong in this I am wanting to know?'

'You are not telling what is wrong. I am not telling what is wrong. Staff rule is telling what is wrong. I am telling you Vijay, even silly bitch from Sinhabahu Hotel is running to GM this very evening, not one half-hour ago, telling staff are running all over town with guests and all waiters doing moonlighting for guides so that everybody is gossiping and laughing and hotel is getting bad name. We are not Capricorn, Mr Perera is saying, we are not Intercon. Dignity of this hotel is what we are having.'

Vijay said nothing, distressed at the General Manager's involvement and realising how naïve he had been.

'So I am not knowing what GM is doing, Vijay, but here and now I am giving second warning.' He paused. 'And I am hoping sincerely I am not hearing any more foolishness, Vijay Jayasinghe.'

There was a softness in the older man's voice, as if appealing to Vijay, who remained silent, still standing just inside the door. The Food and Beverage Manager nodded, not unkindly, and Vijay bit his lip and turned to go.

The captain was watching him as he came through the double doors. Vijay avoided his eye, refusing him the satisfaction of a significant look. Immediately he was summoned to table eight, but his way was blocked by the elegant American in the dinner jacket who was crossing to Clara's table. Vijay waited while table eight made up its mind about dessert, but he had ears only for the conversation behind him.

'Excuse me,' the American was saying in an attractive, steady voice, 'we both dined alone tonight, I thought perhaps . . . you might like to join me for coffee?'

Vijay pretended to be writing as the woman in the low cut dress and heavy necklace changed her mind several times between the Ice Cream Adam's Peak and Pear Belle Hélène. But all he could see was Clara and the American sitting at the little table together, united in the intimate pool of lamplight, leaning towards each other as they talked, like an advertisement in a magazine. Then he heard Clara's clean, clear voice behind him, relaxed, in control.

'I'm sorry, you'll think me very antisocial, but I came here just to be on my own for a week. I do hope you don't mind.'

'Have you got that?' said the woman in the necklace.

Vijay looked at his pad and took a wild guess at summarising the dessert order.

'Why do they employ people who can't speak English?' he heard her saying as he headed back down the verandah after sorting out the mess.

When he returned, carrying the tray of four desserts, Clara had gone. Her table stood empty, its lamp still on.

Back at the desk, Lalith caught up with him and raised his eyebrows. The two of them looked slightly away from each other so that each appeared to be surveying his own sector as Vijay gave him the gist of the interview with the Food and Beverage Manager.

'Better watch out now, Vijay,' said Lalith, without changing the blank expression on his face. 'Word is getting out. Two of Minister's cousins are getting waiters' jobs. One is having very bad twitch.' Lal held his hand up with splayed fingers as if carrying a tray of food and began to jerk head and hand violently. 'He is just standing here and food is going all over verandah. We are not needing waiters. Better to be putting food on ceiling fan I am thinking. Other cousin is cretin.'

'I am thinking this is only rumour,' said Vijay. 'Minister can be getting them government job, desk job, where no one is noticing.'

'Even if cousins not coming, I am thinking lay-offs are there. I am seeing all figures. There is circular from HWU. Bookings all down, even January, even beach hotel. All hotels same thing. Over-manning, bosses are saying. Any excuse now they are giving sack.'

Lalith glanced at Vijay. His friend looked worried.

'They are not firing only man with CCC diploma, Vijay,' he said, confidently. 'Also, Vijay Jayasinghe and Lalith Surasena only ones speaking half-decent English. Hotel cannot be firing fifty per cent of English-speaking staff at fell stroke.'

Vijay smiled uneasily as Lalith moved off. There were only two guests left now, both in Lalith's sector, and he turned his back on the restaurant to look out between the arches. A movement caught his eye. Clara had not gone upstairs; she was standing on the moonlit lawn by the edge of the chessboard, gazing out to sea. Behind her the rigid squares of black and white formed a matrix for the subtle, flowing lines of her black sleeveless dress and pale moonlit limbs, and an indescribable tenderness flooded through

Vijay as he watched her vulnerable beauty at the edge of night and ocean. Suddenly, he was seized by the apparent certainty that this was what he wanted, yearned out into the night for, the source of all restlessness, something unalloyed, devoid of dross, something which called out to him, something ennobling, something fine. It was as if all his dissatisfactions, his gnawing anxieties and his permanent sense of despair with himself, had fallen away; he had become as one with the monochrome beauty of the night, and the moonlit square, and of Clara, who was pushing her hair back from her face in a gesture that struck him with an almost physical pain.

Old Gamini, too, looked down on the tableau of the verandah and the lawn. He too was moved by the monochrome romance of the sea with the waiters in their white sarongs looking out from the little oasis of lamp-lit civilisation across the dark lawns to where the palely lit Clara stood alone on the edge of the chessboard against the vastness of the night. Memories too deep for words stirred within him, troubling him as he had not been troubled for long years, asking him questions which he knew had been asked before, long ago, and which he had never answered. In Gamini too, a memory of something deeper than all his memories stole out across the lawns to Clara. Too late, he tried to call it back, but it was out of his grasp, and he stared out into the darkness with a sudden and unaccountable sadness which he had thought to have left behind so long ago. His eye fell on Vijay, slim in his tight sarong, gazing out through the white arches. Vijay, Vijay, he was about to say to himself, cautioning the boy against disorientation. But instead he looked, and felt, and despite his long marriage to contentment his heart went out to Vijay on the verandah below.

25

With the whole weekend stretching emptily before her, Clara did what she had vowed not to do, and within an hour of enquiring at the desk in the lobby she was heading out of the city in a tourist board car complete with a driver-cum-guide and a reservation for one night at a small hotel a hundred and fifty miles to the north.

Gradually, the film in the small screen of her window became more rural; but without Vijay to explain, the images came and went and were as quickly lost to her. All the windows were wound down to catch the rush of air, and the noise in the back of the little Wolseley was too much for all but monosyllabic exchanges with the driver. She had wondered about sitting in the front, but had sensed that this would not be expected. Slipping on her sunglasses, she let her head fall back onto the vinyl bench-seat and watched the slow drama of the countryside roll by, undisturbed by her questioning.

After a few more minutes, she tore open a sachet and wiped her face with a tissue soaked in eau de cologne. Even from inside the car, the fertility of the island was threatening; fronds of lurching palm trees grabbed wildly at the narrow strip of sky over the road while below the vegetation ate hungrily at the broken edges of the tarmac, trying to reclaim it for its own. Here and there, through the swaying curtains of the palms, she glimpsed slow, muddy rivers or the clear, calm acres of a lagoon shimmering in the morning sun. The car lurched on. She became drowsy in the heat and humidity, though it was not yet eleven o'clock. Consciousness flickered like a faulty electrical current, her doze broken intermittently by the blare of the car horn as the driver grew impatient with the carts pulled by leathery buffalo that refused to be hurried by whatever century it happened to be.

With the slight feeling of sickness brought on by the constant braking, Clara's mood began to change. It seemed pointless now, this journey to nowhere; a running away, a giving up on the daunting and untrodden paths offered by a day relaxing by the ocean, a settling for the easy, well-worn trail to places unknown. Beside her on the seat lay the guidebooks which had been thoughtfully sent up with the compliments of Miles Perera. She looked out of the front window to ward off her sickness, her eyes drawn to the thatched huts standing back from the road where children were spinning long lengths of coir on iron wheels. Another broad, slow river came and went. The roadside now was lined with women who were crouched on their haunches breaking piles of stones into smaller stones, swinging hand-hammers with nothing to shield their eyes and only their saris to protect them against the midday sun. Soon they were gone, their places taken by fragments of fishing villages glimpsed through palm trees. These were scenes different from any she had known, yet after a few seconds her interest faltered and died. All that was left, she reflected with a renewed onset of anxiety, was an obligation to be interested, a husk left over from a time long ago when interest would have welled up from some clear spring that was now as dust. The heat was intense in the back of the little car, but the idea arose within her as from an ice-cold subterranean sea that she might be losing entirely that little temporary purchase on the world, that minuscule engagement, that genuine, unforced involvement in the life around her. The pretence would then be all that there was, requiring a constant effort, drawing on an unrenewable energy. The car horn blared for long seconds as both the Wolseley and an oncoming lorry held the middle of the road, neither willing to fall away into the ragged margins until, at the last, both swerved and passed within a hand's-width of each other, blasting compressed air through the windows. Can it happen to a person, she wondered: could one contract limitlessly into some dense black hole of the self from which no light could ever escape and into which no light of others could ever reach?

'Village of pineapple, Miss,' said the driver, slowing to a crawl through a straggle of stalls. On either side of the road, tables made from poles and plaited palm fronds stood in the rich earth, laden with the heavy fruit.

'Can we stop?' said Clara, reaching for her bag.

The car pulled into the dust by one of the trestle tables that stretched through the village. Before the handbrake had been applied, the tiny woman standing behind the stall had begun wielding a machete that flashed wetly in the sunlight, skinning and slicing great shards of pineapple from the still-crowned core which stood for an instant, naked and bleeding before being thrown into the rotting pile on the roadside. Clara reached through the window for the fruit which was being handed to her on a fleshy green leaf.

'Five rupees is OK,' said the driver.

Clara gave the woman a ten-rupee note and waived away the change with a smile. The woman's face, quick and sharp as her machete, continued to stare as the car pulled away.

'Would you like some?' she asked the driver, who had taken note of this encouraging excess.

'Miss, I am eating only tinned pineapple.' He smiled in the mirror.

Clara concentrated on manoeuvring the heavy boats of fruit into her mouth without drenching herself in the juice of a fruit which seemed to have lent taste-buds to her whole body.

Soon they were in open country again, heading towards a range of low hills. Through the little screen she saw what she assumed to be paddy fields, rectangular lakes of unapologetic green, framed by bunds of mud on which dark-legged men in knotted white sarongs walked unhurriedly between air and water. As she watched, some stirring of interest moved her, seeming to say to her that all was not eagerness and ravishment, that there was some purpose in this warm and unambitious light, some beauty in these low, gentle hills which bathed their feet where pure white herons stepped through wet fields and muddy buffalo struggled through another year.

In this slowly oscillating state Clara travelled northwards until, as evening approached, they reached the far off town where she had a reservation for a single room at the only hotel.

'Where will you stay?' she said to the driver as they turned into a driveway of damp red earth lined by lascivious, flowering shrubs.

'Miss, drivers' quarters are there.'

Thinking that he had driven all day on difficult roads, Clara offered to pay for a room in the hotel. He politely refused, saying that he would prefer to stay where he always stayed.

Her own room was a small cell, immaculately clean, with dark, heavily varnished woodwork and sunny yellow curtains hanging against a roughly plastered wall. In a determined moment before dinner, she had stopped at the hotel desk and bought a guide to the ruined town, a leaflet about the famous *dagoba*, and a small booklet entitled 'Buddhism in One Hour'. All through the meal she swayed between a determined interest in the sights she would see on the morrow, and a resigned admission that they would hold nothing for her. She sipped the last of her coffee and her patience with herself snapped: I must be dead, she told herself brutally, not to have any enthusiasm for such a day as tomorrow promises to be.

She was in bed by nine o'clock, browsing through the books and leaflets, but she could retain nothing, and by half past she had resolved that the best preparation was a long night's sleep. She took one of her three remaining pills and floated into oblivion with 'Buddhism in One Hour' lying open on the old-fashioned candlewick bedspread.

She awoke just in time to see the dawn as it cracked the mould of night across the back of the low hills. For several minutes she gazed at its unasking wonder, and then let her eyes fall to the bed where the books and leaflets still lay from the night before. She swept them onto the linoleum floor and strode to the bathroom; there would be none of this distracting business of names and dates which would be forgotten within hours; she would instead give herself up unconditionally to whatever the day presented, letting any mystery or meaning it might hold come to her without straining or searching, absorbing herself in her surroundings rather than her surroundings in herself;

for a whole day she would keep her thoughts turned outwards, remaining in the sunlight, bravely being normal, resisting the retreat into herself. From such little determinations did Clara weave herself a whip to correct her indulgences, and by seven thirty she was drinking gritty black coffee under the jacaranda trees in the hotel garden, looking forward to whatever the day would bring.

On the map it had looked like an important town, but in fact only the one municipal building stood more than a single storey high, and there appeared to be just two surfaced roads intersecting at a set of redundant traffic lights. The rest of the streets were dusty tracks where starved dogs rummaged and peed around the rotting refuse and makeshift shacks of woven palm and naked concrete blocks. The cities that Clara knew were dominating places where it was possible to go for years without seeing raw earth, except perhaps through a peep-hole cut into the boards of a building site, or in a tired park where nature was given permission to remain by authority of the surrounding concrete. But the town she drove through now was perched only precariously on the earth's crust, a thin skein of human activity drawn between earth and heaven, an intrusion into the scheme of things that a stern wind might soon remove all trace of. The last of the ramshackle buildings disappeared, and the car headed out into acres of mouldering walls and broken arches that were all that was left of the ancient capital of the island.

As they approached the *dagoba*, Clara asked the driver to stop. With a wave of his arm, he pointed out where he would be waiting in the shade of a few withered trees and began reversing the car into the dust.

Clara was left alone in the morning heat, knowing only that what lay all around her was the remains of a long gone civilisation. Without a guide, she set off into the silent centuries of stone.

So bright was the sky that she kept her eyes lowered to the pattern of the foundations embedded in the parched grass, and did not at first see the famous *dagoba* rising above her. Only when she came to the iron railing at its base did she begin to follow the shape upwards, but even then its dazzling whiteness could hardly be seen against the brightness of the sky. She circled the rail, stepping between broken walls, until the sun disappeared behind the *dagoba* and she could make out its huge, gentle shape. She sat on a wall in its shade, the great dome rising above her, more perfectly whole than any building she had ever seen. After gazing at it for several minutes she opened her diary and began trying to draw its shape as it rested against the morning; but even when she had achieved something of the unforced symmetry in its outline, she found that what she had drawn conveyed nothing of the proportions or the beauty of the *dagoba*, surmounted by its golden cupola. She tried again until she had covered all the remaining pages of the month of March, but its subtle perfection still eluded her and eventually she gave up, putting away her diary and dropping her hands in her lap. For long minutes she sat below the temple, marvelling at what manner of people, what concepts of their own and others' lives, had lifted its perfection to the sky, attending to what it had to say of men and gods and little lives like hers. At length, it teased her out of thought. Its immortal calm, its endless and respected silence, stole upon her until all time seemed one and all meaning encompassed by its steady presence. Little by little, the sun neared the edge of its curving mass, darkening its shape. Trying to overcome her blindness, she looked down at the intense nearness of the ancient wall at her feet. She stood up, newly aware of earth and stone, and approached the compound in front of the *dagoba*. Beggars sat patiently in the shade. She gave, unanxiously, without any demand being made, and passed through to where shaven pilgrims in saffron and white were slowly circling an ancient tree, its tired arms resting on iron props. To her right, by the temple wall, one or two visitors were lighting wax candles. She watched as they carried them to the spikes of what appeared to be a wrought-iron replica of the sacred tree. The driver was suddenly by her side.

'Miss, day is going.'

'I'm just coming,' said Clara. 'Can you tell me what the candles are for?'

'Miss, anyone who is on a journey is lighting candle. It is usually some prayer just for safety of those leaving behind.'

The driver retreated again. From somewhere nearby came a slow fluting music, hoarse and wooden. After a moment's hesitation Clara placed a few rupees in the round tobacco tin and stepped forward to light a candle from one that was already burning on the iron tree. She tried to think of those whom she had left behind, and stepped forward to set the candle on a vacant spike. Doing as she had seen others do she stepped back, bowing her head and bringing her hands together for a moment before the Sacred Bo Tree. But to her disappointment she could feel only her own embarrassment, and a strange vertiginous feeling of having betrayed herself, as if she had given in to some cowardly impulse to relinquish the struggle, she who was not a believer in anything, a maker of gestures of faith, a surrenderer of self, a hander-over of responsibility. She watched the flame of her candle as it steadied and merged into the pattern of a hundred others, burning quietly on the iron stand.

The road to the East was virtually empty and the landscape was harsher now, dry and glaring. Clara sat back and watched the passing bunds, sinking within herself, aware that the great *dagoba* had affected her in the way that it was designed to, thousands of years ago, moving her to a fleeting reordering, insisting on the timeless over the temporary, the significant over the immediate, the inconceivable whole over the fragments that can be grasped, offering her some vague promise of release, some small allowance of faith in another self. The driver was pointing at something but his words were drowned in the rushing air. Ahead of them, the great rock of Mihintale rose without preliminaries from the plain.

A few minutes later they were pulling into the deserted car park. The driver backed the car deep into the shade and wandered around forlornly, eventually finding a notice nailed to a tree: all tours of the rock had been suspended until further notice. Full of apologies, he explained that this kind of thing had happened often since the troubles began, and that perhaps the best thing to do would be to drive south to Sigiriya. Clara looked around the little clearing. They were quite alone apart from a tethered deer which grazed contentedly in the shade of the rock. The guidebook had been among those swept to the floor and she knew of Mihintale only as the holy of holies, the place where monks from India had first preached the message of the Buddha, sounding the bell which had rung down through the centuries.

Without offering to climb with her, the driver warned her about the steepness of the climb, the dangers of the heat on the rock, the smoothness of the steps, the untrustworthiness of the handrail. But he had long ago concluded that Clara was not the type to be dissuaded from going her own way, and his eyes followed her for only a few seconds before he stretched himself out on the front seat, his bare feet protruding from the passenger window.

Clara stood captivated by the tethered fawn. In mid-graze, it raised its elegant head and stared back at her with large-eyed calm, the low sun caressing its gentle brown flanks and casting a long-legged shadow across the grass. Clara strained to look up at Mihintale, towering above her.

The path started gently, but gradually the backs of her sandals began to cut into her ankles and she found herself breathing hard. The heat smote her from the side but she could see that the track would soon disappear under the shade of a deep overhang. It was obviously intended as the first resting place, and she was just about to stop when she became aware of a presence in the shade: the figure, scarcely distinguishable from the rock itself, was huddled under the deepest part of the overhang, dark rags pulled all around itself so that not even the face was visible. Only the cupped palm held out in supplication made the figure human, fingers stiffly spread like the branches of an ancient olive tree. Clara pushed a note between the outstretched fingers and climbed on.

The path was steeper than it had looked from below, and at the next widening she leaned against the cliff face, unable to see anything but the glory of the slowly sinking sun. She closed her eyes and it occurred to her that this long day was the first on which she had not thought of the thousand prospects, anxieties, decisions, plans, speculations, which filled most of her conscious moments. A small shame for a life of such preoccupations bubbled to the surface of the pool and burst into the dazzling sunlight. Clara looked for a moment into its depths, perceiving only the trivial urges, the lust for sensation, for the constant novelty, for the ways of topping up the drug of stimulation, of warding off the vastness of boredom, of trying to fulfil the great vain mass of expectation. The path beckoned upwards, curving away out of sight. Perhaps such preoccupations were just a desperate attempt to reach some kind of climax, a fulfilment which would consummate the victory over need; or perhaps they were just an increasingly desperate attempt to find something to put in its place, to fill the void left by necessity's long occupation. She did not know. The great rock still rose above her as she bent to remove the sandals, leaving them by the path and setting off barefoot on steps smoothed by centuries of pilgrims.

The sun was left behind again as the path worked its way across the eastern face. The iron handrail quivered to her touch, and for a moment she caught sight of the drop to her right. She wondered whether to go on. But the sun beckoned, and soon she was emerging onto a wider shelf where a worn stone seat looked safely down over a sunlit land.

Clara sat and surveyed several hundred square miles of the island's dry zone. At first it appeared that the landscape was barren, unpopulated, but soon the low sun began to search out minute white figures, walking along dusty tracks, crossing dried up fields, gathering in little groups and dispersing again across the plain. She leaned back against the cliff face. Thousands had rushed past her window during her drive; thousands more were gathered below her now, unaware of her existence, sufficient unto themselves, people who were neither players with whom she must engage nor audiences before whom she must distinguish herself, people to whom she brought none of her conditioned responses, none of the wary guarding against potential relationships, the mutual awareness of all the infinite nuances of unspoken communications whose function was to define place. For a few moments, she called to mind the people of that other landscape, those whom she did know, those with whose lives she was engaged, those who were her fellow-players and her audiences, and she sickened to the knowledge that they were as far removed from her as any of the figures on the plain below. She resumed her climb, the tendons at the back of her ankles giving rhythmic protests of pain.

A few minutes later she emerged from between the iron railings that had been driven in to succour the weary over the last steps. She could feel the cooling wind now, rushing over the summit of the great rock. There was no path any more, only a surface of stone rising towards the ridge. She was quite alone, and for seconds on end she saw clearly that it was this lust for the consummation of her own significance, constant and cramping and mean, that was causing the faltering within, that had sentenced her to the prison of the self, the loss of all joys, the inability to live in the present, the loss of reciprocal joys and obligations, the deprivation of all that was genuine, the separation from all source of renewal, condemning her to the long, melancholy withdrawal. And did it all come, she wondered, from accepting the vile imposition that one's own individual life was somehow more precious, driving the urge for consummation, sought through the recognition of others, through constant acknowledgement? So occurred the absurd striving for the separateness of the self and its corollary, the relentless relegation of the rest of the world, the steady, wilful progress towards a meaningless aloneness, the petty point proved. So had the momentous mutual withdrawal occurred; so had she proceeded to her desiccated state.

Clara walked against the wind towards the little promontory on the western edge of the rock, a natural pulpit giving out over the plain below. But now the wind was becoming a gale, roaring in from across the vast plain as if outraged by the existence of the great rock which rose to obstruct its passage, pushing rudely past her face, forcing her to screw up her eyes, pressing her damp cotton dress cold to her body, seeming to fill her with its violence, threatening to sweep her like a grain of sand from the rock. She braced herself and pushed forward to the very edge. There was more sky than she had ever known; the whole earth was below her; she was intensely alone in the middle of a vast universe which was suddenly intent on showing her all its congregated might; and at Mihintale, with the mighty weight of air streaming into her from the plain, her hair flying behind and her hands hanging in limp surrender at her sides, Clara Lane cried her tears of opening and relief, dried by the roar of a careless, rushing wind.

26

'I am telling, Vijay. I am telling Mrs Seeliwathie and nosy woman who is always with her,' said Premawathie, sitting on the verandah with her hands gripping her knees. 'I am telling it is also job to be looking after foreign visitors. It is because Vijay is speaking better English than manager of hotel even with St Thomas' education. Obvious, I am saying, that someone who is speaking Queen's English is having this work. But what is hurting is, I am hearing it from Mrs Seeliwathie, Vijay, with putting up of hands to mouth and half finishing what she is saying and giving knowing look and all. If I am already knowing then I am telling before they are mentioning and then they are not being interested. In this garden, interest only there if thinking they are having scandal. Why you yourself not telling, Vijay?'

Vijay lit his third cigarette of the day and put his feet up on the wall, tipping back in his chair and letting the smoke trickle upwards from his lips as if the question was too tedious to bother with.

'Also why you are taking to low-class areas, Wanathamulla, Dematagoda, of all fine places? Foreign lady, from home too I am hearing.'

Vijay drew on his cigarette. After a few moments' thought he decided to accommodate her.

'Amma, sometimes tourist is wanting to see not only just pile of stones at Polonnaruwa. English lady is wanting to see what tourist is not seeing. She is wanting . . . just to be seeing all ordinary things, how everything is, how people are getting along, all such things. She is not wanting decorated elephant and Kandy dancer and all such things being there just for tourist only.'

There was a pause while Premawathie digested this. Vijay, sensing her retreat, took the chance. 'And I am telling you now I am taking again on night of Monday next.'

'What is to be doing in evening?' said Premawathie, suspicious of her pride.

'Amma,' he said impatiently, 'she is wanting to know what is going on in city any time.'

'That is all good and well,' said Premawathie, 'but why I am hearing from Mrs Seeliwathie and stall-wallah on Bodhiraja? Why I am not hearing from you, Vijay?'

'Because, Amma,' said Vijay, giving the impression he was nearing the end of his extraordinary patience, 'I am thinking big tip from English lady. But not like other fellows always boasting about what they are having. I am waiting until tip is sitting in pocket before telling.'

'I am knowing this, Vijay,' said Premawathie, mollified now and anxious to place herself once more in solidarity with her son. 'It is also what I am always telling.' She waved her hand dismissively down the garden. 'I am telling all this. It is part of job to be taking foreigners here, there, this place, that place. He is not mentioning because only telling if it is big person he is taking.'

From next door but one, the sound of the child being beaten again seemed to create its own space of silence as the garden waited fearfully to hear the boy's solitary pain. Only the insensitive dogs and the suddenly louder music from the radios kept up the din as the tortured cries, fragmented by attempts to breathe, caused anxious looks to be exchanged from verandah to verandah. But soon the din arose again around Vijay, coming at him from all sides, uncontrollable, without order or meaning, assaulting him with impunity. His cigarette hissed into the drain.

His mother followed his eyes to where her husband was negotiating himself, sideways and not without difficulty, through the gap in the garden wall. Unaware of his wife's disapproving glare, Godfrey stopped for a moment by the light of the latrines, refastening the sarong pulled loose by the edges of the brickwork, and began to wander slowly down the garden, hands behind his back, looking from side to side in the manner of one who would not at all mind being interrupted for a little afternoon conversation. Passing No. 36, he was persuaded to step up onto the verandah to join in a last few hands of cards. Premawathie's expression relaxed and, a few moments later, she disappeared back into the house.

Vijay looked the other way down the garden. Near the entrance, where Premadasa had run in a wire to his house from the street lights on the main road, the electric blue of a television flickered inconstantly through a rattan screen. At No. 18 the haloes of candles could just be seen in the inner room where old Weerakone was laid out. He turned his head again as a burst of raucous shouts and a cry of 'Lucky blighter, Jayasinghe' floated down from the verandah of No. 36 where the thick white smoke of cigarettes ghosted out from under the eaves. Outside, a few dogs had found something worth fighting over in the drain.

In a moment, Premawathie reappeared carrying a tray. Glancing up the garden, she placed the two-tiered chromium cake stand before her son and stooped to pour him a cup of thick, orange tea, noticing as she did so that a button was coming loose on his sleeve.

For several minutes Premawathie sat on the bench greedily watching her son eat. He had seemed distant of late, preoccupied, and to digest him eating her cakes seemed somehow to return him to her. Vijay, eating to satisfy his mother's appetite, finished the second of the pink-iced buns, their sweetness soured by the stale taste of his mother's sacrifice. A few crumbs were left on the plate and a jackdaw landed heavily on the gutter of the roof opposite, clawing for balance before thrusting its head forward and taking stock, greedily, warily, in preparation for a bout of aggressive cawing. Premawathie clapped her hands, but the jackdaw of the slums is not easily scared and it sidled along the gutter screeching its defiance, until the broom was fetched. Vijay closed his eyes. His mother, watchful of his every expression, reached forward to scoop up the crumbs, offering them to her son in her closed fist. But the noise seemed to have started off the woman opposite who had begun yelling at her daughter, and this in turn had set off a new round of barking and crying, causing No. 27 to turn up the radio. Vijay clenched his teeth and a small air-pocket of temper bubbled up from the depths of his dissatisfaction.

'Amma, who is putting up batik instead of calendar?'

Vijay's sudden change of tack alarmed Premawathie.

'Calendar is old,' she said, trying not to provoke him further. 'Batik is from Mrs Goonatilleka. She is giving because of cakes I am making. She is giving tea for Adeline.'

'I am not liking batik, and we are not having in house,' said Vijay, getting to his feet, ashamed even before the words were out. He jumped the two steps from the verandah and headed for the breach in the garden wall.

Once through the wall his pace slowed. He thought about crossing the canal to Sithie's where he knew Chandra would be, but he could not bear the thought of an hour spent in the shanty. He had given Chandra twenty rupees for Sithie only that morning. He decided to walk the first leg of the journey to work, and soon he was climbing the steps of the embankment just opposite the Cheltenham Corner.

An hour later, he crossed the road towards the permanent taxi rank at the front of the hotel.

'We are making regular thing?' asked the taxi driver. Vijay clicked his tongue as the man counted out the notes into his hand.

'Maybe once in while, if no one is knowing,' said Vijay.

The cab driver gave him a satisfied nod and he recrossed the road towards the hotel.

The verandah was dead and his shift was endless, blunt, lacking all bite, like the non-alcoholic lager which he and Lal had tried when the hotel has begun ordering it in response to the new demand. He knew that Clara had left for the north, and wondered who was acting as her guide. The fifty rupees made a small packet in the top pocket of his tunic, and as the evening wore on he began to feel it more and more as a badge of shame. He told himself that it was only what anyone would have done, that fifty rupees was fifty rupees, that Clara would never know about it, and wouldn't care if she did. But he could not banish the notion that it was an unworthy act, an act of betrayal, of Clara, of the afternoon they had spent together, of himself, of what and how he wanted to be.

Throughout the endless evening on the verandah, the feeling of cheapness deepened into desperation, and the conviction grew that he must somehow redeem the act, do something that would show he was not just a waiter grubbing for tips, something that would reflect a different relationship, a different self, something that would be the act of a friend, an equal, something honourable and unselfinterested, something that redefined things as he wanted them to be.

His shift ended at last and he changed in the old boot room, so subdued that Lalith eventually stopped provoking him, eliciting no response. On the corner of Galle Face Green the taxi was still there; the driver, bored elbow protruding from the window, raised his hand at the wrist in desultory acknowledgement. Vijay thought for a moment about giving him back the fifty rupees, but he felt the absurdity of it. In any case, his evening of absorption in the problem had yielded a larger hope of redemption.

It was while he was waiting for the first of the bus rides which would bring him to Maligawatta that his amorphous hopes of a transformation, of some deeply redefining act, first crystallised. A memory arose of Clara lingering over the glass display cases as they had left the cool lobby of the Oberoi, gazing long at the island's gemstones, garnet and topaz, cat's eye and amethyst, under the brilliant lights. She had glanced at one or two of the smaller emeralds, and dwelt on several of the milky moonstones, but had looked longest at a tiny ruby, like a drop of spilt blood on its cotton wool bed. She has even asked the price; it had been nine hundred and fifty rupees plus tax. In Sea Street it would cost only half of such a sum. No sooner had the thought been born than it became full-blown: standing amid the late crowds in the bus station he imagined himself presenting the gem to Clara at the Seaspray, watching her as she lifted the lid of the box. His whole being exulted. This would not be the act of an underling seedily arranging kickbacks. She would look into the deep, red gemstone, cut, polished, perfect, a gift worthy of her, of himself, of all that he wished to be. In one act it would redefine the world as he wanted it, put everything onto a different basis, say all that he felt; and in that one instant of conviction he saw that nothing else would do.

He returned to the hotel, showing his pass again and making his way to the lobby. A late-departing guest was checking out, and he waited by one of the pillars. The clerk looked up at him suspiciously; he was not supposed to show his face in the reception area without good reason. When the guest had departed, he asked to see the cashier and was allowed to go through into the inner office. There, without offering any explanation, he produced his thrift card and asked to withdraw five hundred rupees. The cashier gave him a disapproving look and, after finding his wire spectacles, began consulting a ledger. Eventually he assembled the five sheets of carbon paper and typed ponderously for a few minutes. When Vijay had signed in several places, he closed the book with a dusty thud and unlocked the cash drawer, taking his time to select the notes that were grubby, worn thin, torn.

Vijay had passed the end of the narrow little street in Hetti Veediya a thousand times. It was variously known as Sea Street, Gem Street, Jew Street, or even Chitty Street after the chitties which were given to those who came with their gems and bangles of gold and left with only the sad little pieces of paper. But never before had he run the gauntlet of the brightly lit gem houses from whose open doorways soothing music enticed and an occasional proprietor smiled invitingly when business was slack. After he had walked twice up and down the length of the street, ignoring the calls of the snake charmers and the tarot card readers, the sellers of charms and curses, he decided, for no particular reason, on the Gem Emporium. As casually as he could manage, he stepped up into its narrow gloom.

After a glance in his direction, the two assistants carried on polishing the glass counters. There was a smell of methylated spirits in the silence as Vijay waited to be asked to sit down on one of the black plastic chairs bolted to the floor in front of the long line of display cases. When nothing happened for several more seconds, Vijay straightened his shoulders. I am a buyer not a beggar, he told himself, and walked out the Gem Emporium. But the same thing happened at the Moonstone Palace, even though he had adjusted his frame of mind and entered the establishment looking not lost and ill at ease but brisk and confident, even a little bored. Discouraged, he walked once more between the flashy, cheaply built façades of Sea Street, eventually stopping outside the True-Cut Ruby Mine. In the doorway stood a kindly looking older man who politely asked him his business.

'I am maybe wanting to buy ruby,' said Vijay. 'Small one only. Well cut. It is present for English friend.'

The man whom he judged to be the proprietor motioned him inside, graciously inviting him to sit on one of the chairs in front of the glass cases. Circling to the far side of the counter, his host clicked on a powerful lamp and unfurled a black velvet cloth onto the surface of the glass. Loosening the cord of a small pouch, he poured out a dozen rubies, spreading them carelessly in a small profusion onto the blackness where they winked pricelessly under the light. At Vijay's side a cup of hot, sweet tea had suddenly appeared.

Vijay sat forward and saw for the first time why such a fuss was made about the island's gemstones. Each of the rubies had a depth and concentration of colour which seemed impossible in something so small. They glowed on the blackness of the velvet, intensely perfect, intensely precious, intensely steady, and he saw in that same instant that they were not just stones but a capturing of something elusive, a making permanent of a sad beauty, of a quiet grace, of a completed perfection; and from the depths of him Vijay felt the rightness of his idea.

After a few moments he returned to the world of Sea Street and realised that he did not know what to do next. Taking a sip of the tea by his side, he made a show of peering at some of the gems more closely than others as the proprietor manoeuvred the arm of the lamp to search out the perfections of his children. He remained quiet as Vijay looked at a smaller than average stone which had the colour of the deepest wine. He asked the price. It was a fine choice. A discriminating choice. These were not ordinary rubies. They came only from Ratnapura. They were cut only by the finest stone cutters, not by these

Johnny-come-latelies whose fathers had been butchers. There were no finer on the island. The price was eight hundred and fifty rupees.

Vijay felt the sudden drop of disappointment. Eventually, he asked the price of one or two of the smaller stones and lingered over one at six hundred. He knew he should not pay anywhere near the asking price, but had no idea at what level to pitch an offer. The owner of the True-Cut Ruby Mine remained silent, waiting. Vijay continued to stare into the galaxy of red scattered on the velvet night. After another indecisive sip of tea, he was rescued by his father's voice seeming to tell him that there were plenty of other shops and plenty of other stones. 'Offering five hundred then going,' he heard Godfrey saying confidently in his ear.

'I will give five hundred rupees,' said Vijay, still looking at the rubies spread before him. 'But not for the small one. For this one.' He pointed to the perfect stone that his eyes had first lit upon.

The owner smiled condescendingly and, without a word, began pouring the rubies back into the velvet bag. Vijay stood up, refusing to be intimidated, and walked out of the True-Cut Ruby Mine.

'I am letting you have for seven fifty only.'

Vijay stopped but did not go back into the shop. He turned and spoke, his head still ducked under the low doorway.

'Five hundred is maximum and I think I am finding ruby.' Without glancing back he left the little shop and strode over towards the Emerald Isle on the other side of the street. He had walked past another two shops when he felt a small tug at his sleeve. It was the owner of the True-Cut Ruby Mine.

'Robbing is what I am calling, but I am not selling one stone all this long day. This is only reason I am taking five hundred.'

Vijay allowed himself to be steered back across the street and back into the gloom of the True-Cut Ruby Mine. The stone he had chosen was now sitting alone in the centre of the black velvet cloth, watched over by a smiling younger man.

'Gift box must also be there,' said Vijay in a resentful voice.

'Red leather box we are giving.'

He counted out the money from his shirt pocket and held it in his hand while the owner picked up the stone in a small square of black velvet and began looking at the shelves of boxes behind him. Vijay looked around at the faded photographs of gem workings on the walls. Overhead, the caged ceiling fans raged. The small box was placed before him, the ruby glowing intensely on its soft black bed, exactly like the one at the Oberoi which had been priced at nine hundred and fifty rupees. Vijay counted out the notes, refusing an offer of more tea.

'She is visiting that woman,' said Premawathie stiffly when Vijay asked about Chandra. He lit another cigarette and rested his feet on the verandah wall.

'I also am going,' he said, as much to provoke Premawathie as to announce an intention. There was no response. In the drain lay a dead rat, split open but not eaten by one of the garden dogs. Here and there the faces of his neighbours were dramatised by the yellow light of oil lamps; shadows came and went as children were settled for the night and the women emerged onto the verandahs to sit for the last few minutes of the day. At the top of the garden he saw Godfrey squeeze sideways through the wall. As his father approached the verandah, Vijay could see that he had had another win.

'What are odds,' he smiled, making room for Godfrey on the verandah.

'Four to one only,' said Godfrey, 'but I am laying fifty bucks.'

Vijay raised an eyebrow; it must be at least the third win that week, though it had always been easier to glean information about his father's winnings than his losings.

The old man began to cajole the radio. At Vijay's feet, two more cockroaches were taking a risk. From the roof opposite, a jackdaw dropped into the alley and began picking warily at the carcass of the rat. Over the drain the midges were beginning to gather and the fresh smell came and went in waves. In the shadow lands beyond the latrines more dark figures could be seen negotiating the wall. Vijay eventually stood up to go and Godfrey looked up questioningly from the crackling radio.

'Chandra is with Sithie?' he asked Godfrey, by way of an explanation for his leaving. Godfrey made a face to say he did not know and returned his concentration to the radio. Vijay headed for the wall. Passing No. 18, he took a glance inside the doorway to see the old man laid out on the table surrounded by garlands of white flowers, dignified and peaceful, hands across his chest, his grandchildren playing on the floor beneath him.

The electric lamp on the latrine block wall came on as he approached, and was immediately surrounded by moths of all sizes, greedy for the light. Skirting the smouldering pile of refuse, he stepped through the wall and made his way along the embankment at the back of the shanty. Here and there he exchanged a word with those he had known since boyhood. Some of them, he sensed, resented him; others may have felt a vicarious pride. He glanced down one of the alleyways to his left. His old home had changed hands again and was now occupied by a family from Polonnaruwa with six children, kinsfolk of the people next door. Every day the space in the shanty seemed less. It could not be long, he thought, before it was entirely covered over, acres of poles and plantain and corrugated iron stretching unbroken to the bridge, the inside becoming a continuous warren where homes and lives flowed together in a communal darkness. Climbing the stone steps, he looked down on the precarious latrines built out on stilts over the water where groups of men were bathing and cooling themselves, children splashing, women washing clothes.

Once over the bridge he dropped down again into the shanty, making his way through a maze in which the evening wood-smoke did little to mask a smell which appeared to be worse on this side of the canal. His mother objected to Chandra's constant visits to Sithie's shack, and especially to her involving herself in the degrading work of sewing cement-bags. He, too, wondered why Chandra found it necessary to involve herself so intimately; he helped Sithie with cash when things were desperate, and a few extra bags sewn would not amount to much. Now, as he twisted left and right towards Sithie's shack, he realised with a faint sense of disturbance that it was prob-ably just an act of simple friendship, of solidarity, of a little solace in hard times, to sit sewing with Sithie for a few hours on the floor of her hut. Some of the women smiled at him respectfully as he picked his way down through the shanty, wishing that someone like him would come for one of their own daughters.

Reaching Sithie's hut he saw that her bed-board was propped against the wall outside, along with the pots and pans and her few possessions. He ducked under the low doorway. In the light of the feeble oil lamp on the floor he could just make out the two figures sitting between the piles of sacks. They were old women, slim and delicately boned but with grey hair pulled tightly back from thin grey faces as they sat straight-backed on the floor of the hut. As his eyes grew accustomed to the dark he saw that everything around him was covered in the same fine grey dust of age; only Chandra's lovely eyes were still liquid and clear, shining like jewels as he stood framed in the doorway. She was dressed in her oldest clothes, and when she smiled he saw the fine film of cement dust breaking up on her face and falling in little trickles of powder to the floor.

27

Not since her childhood had Clara felt the sadness of a holiday coming to an end. It was Monday morning. There were two more days left.

The remains of coffee and a slightly sandy sandwich lay on the table beside her. Outside her ellipse of shade, the sun beat down from an empty sky. The sounds of the ocean soothed, and she looked forward to thinking calmly about the unarticulated hopes that her weekend had brought, turning the little beginnings of relief over in her mind, consolidating the promise that all might not be lost. In this mood she had swum and showered and applied her sun cream; and by ten thirty she was once more stretched out on the edge of the ocean. Yet when the moment had come, she had found herself postponing the contemplation of her weekend and deciding to relax for another hour.

Her thoughts turned to the evening at the Seaspray Restaurant. If it were dark she would take a taxi. She would also, she decided, try to get to know Vijay a little better, loosen his tenseness with her, lower the barrier that he obviously thought should exist between them. She shifted her position and pulled her feet in under the shade. It would help, she thought, if he could lose some of his obvious admiration for her. It rendered her uncomfortable, made her feel a fraud; yet she subtly played to it. Lessening people's admiration was not something she had had a great deal of practice at, and in any case she had the sense that it would in some way be letting him down. The poolside waiter approached and she raised her hand and shook her head to keep him at bay. Lying back again, she thought of Vijay on the verandah behind her and wondered if he might be watching.

What must it be like, she wondered without any great energy, to be poor and to pass one's life watching the rich spending vast sums of money idling away their time. She wanted him to know that she admired him too, his gritty involvement in the life he led, his diligence in a job which, she guessed, demanded only a small proportion of his abilities. Lazily, she rubbed more cream into the hollows of her shoulders. She had intended to give him a large tip at the end of her stay, although the thought now occurred to her that his sensitive soul might be hurt by it. She decided that she should give him something more personal. But anything she could buy in the gift shops would not be very appropriate; something from England would have been much better. She was emptying more cream onto the palm of her hand when the idea came to her. It was rather extravagant, but she had just the thing in her room. She had bought the gold cigarette lighter in the duty-free shop, a birthday present for the only one of her friends who still smoked. It was elegant and expensive. It would mean so much more to Vijay. She would give it to him at the Seaspray. And with this pleasing thought she relaxed all of her muscles and tilted her head back to expose her still-white throat to the sun.

Towards noon, she went for a second swim, just for the pleasure of it, feeling the clean water rushing past her as she dived deep and long, not counting the lengths or checking her time against the clock. She pushed off from the side and stretched her limbs out in a luxurious glide, turning to float on her back in the middle of the pool under a midday sun that seemed to have come down from the sky to watch. Almost silhouetted on the roof of the building next door, which she had gathered was the Indian embassy, a uniformed soldier stood at ease, hands resting on his automatic rifle, looking down with interest at Clara floating on her back in the pool. She imagined him hot and bored in the tight black beret and khaki uniform and, on impulse, she gave him a wave and a sympathetic smile. He immediately straightened and gave her a fierce salute, followed by a flashing white grin. Smiling back, she allowed herself to sink under the water, hoping she had made his day.

Later she lay down again under the open sun, allowing its caress. Five more minutes, she thought to herself, and then she would begin gathering up the fragmented perceptions of her weekend. For she knew that at Mihintale she had sensed the prospect of life returning, felt the sap pushing through restricted capillaries, confronting what was dead with life, and she had told herself that whatever the consequences might be she must find a way to close with whatever it was that she had gained. The sun burned down, pinning her in place, and in a sudden fit of determination she stripped herself of false armour and stood her ground for thought, knowing that only some form of accounting to herself could render permanent the truths which were now in the air around her but not yet within her grasp. And as she gave in again to the sun's warmth, her mind stopped and steadied on the one great challenge, aching with the loneliness of it, with the not knowing how to move against it, with the realisation that it could not be met by the deploying of her abilities, that she was disabled under the sun's majestic brightness, that she did not know how to approach these gentle hills as she would have known how to meet mountains.

She felt herself burning and struggled to pull the lounger back under the thatched shade. Her muscles relaxed of their own accord, and it seemed as if she were conscious for several minutes of the great luxury of sinking into sleep. But as she drifted away, she experienced a floating of a different kind; she was swimming in a vast open sea at night; there was no land in sight but the sea was warm, and there was a full moon thinly veiled by a skein of cloud; she did not feel afraid as she swam, easily, rising and falling with the swell of the gigantic, gentle waves that were slowly coming towards her like low, dark hills. The pleasant sensation lasted for unmeasured moments until, lifted by the enormous swell, she seemed to notice that the horizon was strangely uneven and, as she sank gently into the next warm valley, she thought she could sense a far away murmuring sound in her ears. When she rose again in the great sea the vague noise was louder, the sky seemed to have changed colour, and she felt a sudden rush of colder air on her face. And then she saw the wave: it was the size of a mountain range, the moon glinting coldly, wickedly, on its sheer face, as it advanced towards her. Her limbs went suddenly cold as she descended into the next deep valley. She seemed to be in its depths for an eternity, praying she had not seen what she had seen, that it had been a trick of the light, but when she finally rode to the top of the next swell she saw the silent black mass of the Himalayas advancing towards her at the speed of darkness. And then the nothingness happened. The mountainous wave lifted her tenderly thousands of feet into the night and the enormous body of water passed powerfully under her leaving her to descend steeply but gently into the calm sea. She was warm and unafraid again in the undulating foothills of the ocean. A minute later, far in the darkness behind her, she heard the horizon tremble to the thunder of the wave on a distant shore.

28

Since twelve o'clock, Vijay had been waiting for Clara to return to the verandah for lunch. From time to time, he caught a glimpse of her across the lawns. Twice he had stopped, hands full of balanced plates, while she had walked the length of the hotel front to the swimming pool and back. Only Lal had noticed.

'It is OK, Vijay,' he said in a small martyr's voice, 'I am not minding doing your tables while you are taking dip with Clara.'

Vijay tried feebly to keep up the repartee with Lal. It was obvious that Clara would miss lunch altogether now. His mind went forever forward to the evening at the Seaspray, and he brought to it in equal parts an exquisite anticipation and a churning dread. The ruby was in his locker, along with his white shirt and slacks, a new pair of diamond-pattern socks, his resoled leather shoes, a bottle of coconut oil, and a half-full bottle of an expensive aftershave which had been left behind by a Swedish tourist and later auctioned in the old boot room.

Two hours later, when his shift had ended, Vijay lingered on in the locker room, leafing through a copy of a magazine. Gamini came in to change and began giving him looks, each one of which was a complete and well-rounded sermon. Not wishing to talk, Vijay started to change into his normal clothes. At three thirty he checked the contents of his locker and left the hotel.

Over the seafront a dozen kites were flying high, yearning against their lines, stretching out over the ocean. He resolved to make his decision before he reached the end of the sea wall. On his left, the shimmering ocean stretched smoothly out across the world, its fathomless power playing gently on the soft sand at its edge. To his right lay the defeated grass of Galle Face Green. For a while he walked with his mind in neutral, his thoughts floating numbly over the spikes of his anxieties. But eventually he could no longer stay aloft. He had two courses of action, both of which were unthinkable, and any train of thought quickly became a well-worn track which he struck out on only to retrace his steps as soon as he arrived at his predictable conclusion. Over and over he heard the voice asking him what he was doing buying gems for wealthy tourists when he was supposed to be saving every rupee for the rent, when the floor of his home needed a new concrete skin, when they did not even have a place to put their clothes, when his wife was sitting on the floor of Sithie's hut sewing old cement bags. He passed by a group of listless men who had probably been squatting all day on the patch of bare earth and the same voice asked him what he was doing risking his job, putting in jeopardy all those who were dependent on him, squandering his savings, jettisoning all his priorities and obligations into a formless ocean. And for what? Clara would be gone in two days, and he entertained no thoughts of her which extended beyond the evening at the Seaspray. Yet whenever he neared the obvious decision it repelled him like the opposite pole of a magnet, not letting him make contact, veering him away to one side or the other so that he eventually began to listen instead to the voice that sounded from deeper, less accessible chambers. To break the engagement at the Seaspray, said the voice, would also be a betrayal. It would be a betrayal of his belief in himself, of his quest for a moment of dignity that would prove to him that he could be something else, someone else. He looked out to sea and told himself that he would be standing on his verandah for forty years, keeping to his place as old Gamini had done, and that finding a way to stand equal to it, be at one with his surroundings, was all that could sustain him. The memory of being admitted, accepted, would succour him through all that was to come, help him find a self that could not be ruffled by every bitter wind that would blow through the verandah in all the years ahead. Without it, his verandah would be a place of mortification, of perpetual rebuke, of ceaseless agitations. If he turned away now, then the disappointed ghost of the evening at the Seaspray would mock him always, saying to him over the years 'And what happened, Vijay Jayasinghe, on the one occasion when this pathetic illusion threatened to come true, even for an hour?'

Vijay turned at the end of the sea wall and stood for a moment, stranded in indecision. He still had most of the afternoon before he must decide. The afternoon heat beat down on Galle Face Green, and it seemed to him that all his life, the entire complex structure of its concerns and emotions, was on the march, leaving all settled places, setting up temporary camps in the forefront of his brain. He struggled for some control, but the ramshackle march would not be turned back; too powerful for any discipline, it trampled its way over all of the certainties he put up to direct its route. He was walking quickly now, though he walked to nowhere. He thought of Clara lying on the sunlounger only a few hundred metres along this same sea wall. And in the heat and dust and squalor, he longed for the cool, ordered elegance of the hotel. In an instant, the idea came to him: he would go to Kelaniya, to the cool temple of his boyhood, the temple of his mother's family, where white lilies floated in the pond beside the gentle *dagoba*, where there would be temple flowers and running water, where the air would be cool inside stone walls, where the ancient tiles would be cold under his feet. He thought how perfect it would be. There, if anywhere, he would still the armies that marched and return all things to their proper place. With a formless hope inside him, he cut across the heat-seared earth towards the cluster of high-rise buildings which marked the downtown area of the city. It was less than forty minutes by bus from Pettah.

There was a twenty-minute wait for the bus to Kelaniya. Opposite him, not far from the spot where a bomb had killed more than fifty men who had been waiting to go home to their families at the end of the day, he noticed a small crowd gathered around the flickering window of an electrical shop. He crossed the road. Over silhouetted heads he saw a bank of a dozen televisions screening the same video of an all girl rock-group silently miming their way through a pop-song. They looked Swedish, young and thin and blonde, wearing black high-heeled boots and the briefest of shiny black panties which sliced up from the crutch to the waist, emphasising the hard mound. At first he thought that they were naked from the waist up, but now he could see that they were wearing flesh-coloured bands of fine muslin, flattening their breasts, showing the nipples. And as they gyrated noiselessly against a background of swirling electronic colours, he also saw that they were flailing whips, writhing and leering to the music, thrusting their white pelvises out rhythmically from the twelve television screens into the crowd of working men waiting at the bus station in Pettah. No sound came from the televisions, and the ordinary noises of the afternoon – the throb of idling engines, the hiss of releasing air brakes, the bored cries of the lottery vendor, the meandering sounds of music from a dozen radios – seemed far away, as in another country. Minutes passed. From inside the shop the rhythmic thrustings and silently revolving colours seemed to exert a dreadful fascination on the men gathered on the corner. Vijay too was transfixed. But when, in response to a small sound, he glanced to his left he saw that the old man next to him was crying silently. He looked more frankly at the man, wondering if he should speak, but before he had made up his mind the man had turned his stubbled face to look at him.

'I think,' he said, his face overwhelmed by some deep trouble, 'I think it is end of world they are showing us.' Vijay put his hand for a moment on the old man's shoulder, and then crossed the road to the bus-stand.

The shop window and the long wait, amid the diesel fumes and the throbbing engines, had only increased his longing for the temple. He thought of the old priest, long since dead, listing the senses which were touched by the temple's rituals, the eyes resting on the calm beauty of the *dagoba* and the purple flowers, the taste of spices given to him as he knelt, the dry texture of the ashes on his hands, the scent of incense and burning oil, blooms in the garden, and the timeless, patient music. These thoughts grew on him like a thirst as he boarded the vibrating bus and hung on to the handrail in its packed insides, clamour all around him and the stale smell of sweat in the air.

The bus had been twenty minutes late setting off and had also been delayed by the closing of St Joseph's Street, forcing a detour through the rubble of a half-built industrial estate where buses and trucks wedged themselves across tight corners and

passengers descended to yell advice at harassed drivers. By the
time they had reached the Victoria Bridge, beyond which was the
open road, Vijay was already beginning to wonder if he still had
time to get to the temple and back. They had stopped again, and
after some minutes one or two of the passengers began calling
abuse. Eventually a khaki-uniformed policeman sauntered up
to the cab and said something to the driver who leaned down
and switched the engine off. As the noise and vibration died, the
voices of protest inside the bus grew louder. Vijay looked again
at his watch.

'It is President,' said a fat passenger who had struggled to the
front to have words with the driver and who had now turned
himself into a public address system. 'Presidential motorcade
coming,' he shouted self-importantly down the bus. 'Presidential motorcade coming.' The passengers began disembarking
to escape the intense heat and to watch the motorcade as it
passed. Vijay followed. It was a quarter past five. Hundreds of
cars and carts, buses and trucks, had been stopped and a crowd
had gathered where the great bridge touched down on the city
side. Another ten minutes passed. Out over the estuary, the sun
had begun to dip towards the tops of the palm fronds.

A buzz spread through the crowd as someone saw the first
outriders nearing the crown of the bridge. Advancing steadily,
all power in reserve, the half-dozen riders stared straight ahead
through cruel sunglasses, proceeding slowly down the ramp of
the Victoria Bridge. Behind them followed the limousine, an
immaculate maroon Daimler in which the President, all in white
and still wearing his garland of flowers, sat back waving to the
crowd through the closed windows with a tired, sad little smile
designed to impress upon one and all the responsibilities of office.
Vijay stared over the heads of the crowd as the Daimler passed
by, imagining what it must be like inside the air-conditioned
coolness, sinking into the quiet cream hide seats, the delicate
perfume of the garland, one arm lying along the beautiful
polished wood of the door cappings, gliding calmly, silently,
through the great disorder of the city.

The passengers began climbing back into the bus, many of
them already arguing politics. Vijay looked at his watch and
stood rooted to the kerb as the bus pulled away without him.

✱

It was a quarter past six when he arrived back at the hotel. A little furtively, for he was not on duty, he showed his pass at the staff entrance and crossed the vestibule to the boot room. To his relief it was empty, and he quickly stripped off to wash in the stone sink. With a little coconut oil he combed the day's dust out of his hair. Hesitatingly, he sprayed the straw-coloured aftershave on his chest, unsure how much he should use. He took out his clothes, neatly folded in the locker, knowing that the creases would soon drop out in the damp warmth of the evening. Last of all, he reached inside and took out the small red box.

It was when he went to check himself in the full-length mirror at the foot of the stairs that he was seen by the day captain.

'Vijay is on?'

'No, I am just coming for changing.'

'That is good because F and B is wanting you in office.' Vijay did not like the look in the captain's eyes. He looked at his watch anxiously. Six forty. Whatever it was it would do no harm for him to see the Food and Beverage manager in his own time, out of uniform, and looking smart. He climbed the stairs and made his way along the verandah where none of the guests recognised him. He tapped on the wooden door under the stairs and went in. There was a little start in the eyes of the Food and Beverage Manager, but it was perhaps only the surprise of seeing him on an off-duty night, and in his best street clothes.

'Ah, Vijay,' he said recovering himself.

'You are wanting?'

The Food and Beverage Manager stared at him for a second and then pursed his lips before opening the top right-hand drawer of his desk and drawing out a dog-eared batch of papers held together by an elastic band.

He placed the little bundle of papers in front of him and pushed them forward, eyes cast down. Vijay recognised the insurance papers, the provident fund booklet, the chitty fund card, the union membership booklet, and an unopened pay packet. He looked up, but the face of the Food and Beverage Manager was staring at the wall.

'One week's pay is there,' he said finally, pointing to the brown envelope, 'but finishing now.'

Vijay stood silently in front of the desk, thinking that he should reach out and pick up the bundle of papers. But he did not move.

'I am not deciding. GM is deciding,' said the manager, impatient for the interview to be over. Vijay realised that the man was suffering, that he had had no part in the decision and could do nothing to rescind it. But he had not seen Clara since the last time he had been warned. He looked into the eyes of the man who had hired him more than five years ago.

'I am not having final warning?'

The manager looked at him, all-knowing.

'Looking very smart tonight, Vijay.'

Vijay looked down from the manager's eyes.

'No reference,' said Vijay quietly.

'Cannot,' said the manager.

Vijay reached out for the bundle of cards. In the silence the man broke through the manager's mask.

'I am giving you personal letter if it is helping, Vijay.'

Vijay picked up the bundle. He looked into the manager's eyes to see if there was any last hope there. There was none.

'I am sorry, Vijay. You are knowing position. There is nothing I can be doing.'

Vijay picked up the bundle of papers in one hand, the little red box still held tight in the other, and turned to leave the office under the stairs.

29

Clara arrived early at the Seaspray and asked for a table out on the terrace. The last indigo of the day was fading, and the sky and sea were renewing their deep union over the ocean. In the garden below, the crickets had started up the electric current of the night.

The waiter appeared, black tie gleaming on a stiff white collar. Clara smiled at him and ordered a drink. The evening was still warm and she was somewhere near contentment as she looked out over the palms to the darkening sea. After her day of contemplation she was subdued, a little humbled by her own thoughts, but with her expectations wound down, ceasing to require some new fulfilment from her every moment. She was conscious of looking forward to the evening, genuinely, not pretending that she was looking forward to it, not thinking she ought to be looking forward to it. And this evening she was going to find out more about Vijay himself, to learn a little of his own concerns and hopes, to cross over and see another's world through another's eyes, and try and bring him into her universe. She had been lucky to make friends with someone who knew the city intimately from its meanest tea shops to its international hotels, and when he relaxed his conversation fascinated her. She would write once in a while; maybe one day she would visit again. In her handbag, ready to give to him, was the slim gold cigarette lighter in its soft, dove-grey suede pouch.

When, by half past eight, Vijay still had not arrived, Clara began to wonder if anything had happened to prevent him coming.

'Second cocktail, Miss?'

'No thank you.'

'Miss, dining?'

'I don't know yet, I'll wait for a while.'

'No problem, Miss.'

A fresh bowl of spiced seeds appeared on the little glass table. The wind was strengthening off the sea and beginning to tug at the ragged edges of the palm fronds. Clara pulled a fine woollen cardigan over her golden shoulders and wondered whether to go inside. Something told her that Vijay would have moved heaven and earth to be there, and a faint worry arose as she paid her drinks bill and left.

The taxi set her down outside the softly lit façade of the hotel and she decided to have a light supper on the verandah. As she took her seat at table ten the first warm drops of rain had started to fall and the wind was bullying the candle flames in their glass bowls. There was no one among the verandah staff whom she felt she could ask about Vijay.

An hour later she wandered up the wide staircase to the first landing. There, like a fixture, was the elderly room-boy in his white coat and sarong. He straightened and blinked, preparing to give his small bow, as always, as she crossed the landing.

'Good evening, Miss, rain coming.'

On impulse, Clara stopped in front of him as he spoke to her. She paused for a second, feeling a need to explain, and then decided there was no need for subterfuge. The old man had come wide awake, sensing that he was about to be addressed.

'I was wondering if you could help me with something. I arranged to meet Vijay Jayasinghe tonight. The young man who works on the verandah? He has been kind enough to show me something of the city while I've been here and I invited him to dinner tonight as a way of saying thank you. But he did not turn up. You don't happen to know if he's ill or anything?'

The old man's face stiffened, his eyes shifted to the far side of the landing.

'Vijay Jayasinghe is getting sack, Miss.'

Clara's smile vanished.

'Tonight?'

'Yes, Miss, tonight only.'

There was a silence on the landing. Somewhere a floorboard creaked.

'Do you know why he's been sacked?'

The old man's face remained stern, almost bitter. He gave a small, sad, shake of the head.

Acting on instinct Clara asked: 'It's nothing to do with me, is it?'

The old man continued to stare into the distance, lips sealed, and then, as if the words were being wrung from him, he answered her.

'Fraternising with guests outside of hotel not allowed, Miss.'

Clara felt very cold. Somewhere down the disused corridor the wind had freed one of the shutters and was banging it mindlessly against the wall. The sound echoed down the empty gallery.

'He can't have been sacked for meeting me.'

'Someone having to be getting sack, Miss. Actually two people are needing sack.'

Clara looked at him and read something of the life that had been written in those furrowed lines.

'We'll see about this in the morning,' she said as calmly as she could. 'Thank you for telling me. Good night now.'

'Good night, Miss.'

Clara lay awake listening to the wind tearing angrily at helpless palm fronds and violently banging the shutter somewhere in the disused part of the hotel. She was suddenly grateful for the Clara who could get things done, the Clara who would put things right in the morning. She lay awake for half an hour taking the inventory of her weapons.

For much longer, old Gamini stayed on his feet on the first-floor landing. The heavy layers accrued over all the years were telling him he had always known that this was how it would end. He blamed them all, Vijay, Lal, the English woman, agents and victims all of a universal disorder. She had seemed a cut above most of the tourists he saw these days, he had thought so all along, but even she had been seduced by disorder, neglecting the fundamental for the fashionable, the whimsical, the indulgent, living on a graph whose lines have lost their axes. She should have known better. He could have told her, as he had tried to tell Vijay. But underneath the weight of years, Gamini felt the pushing of a tiny shoot, the faint cry of a hopeless voice: Vijay had tried and failed. But I never once tried. He stilled the voice, it was wrong, it was the voice of disorder. He crossed the landing and looked out of the window to the storm-lashed lawns. And his mind gave way to thoughts more important than these, to his full measure of sorrow, a sorrow amounting to love, for a man who was somewhere out there, a man who had gained and lost so much in so short a life. Why could it not have been Lal, he asked himself, why could it not have been me?

30

Vijay had walked for an hour, at first without direction, and then towards the Maligakanda crossroads beyond the park where he eventually found the grubby tenement block. He called up the stairs, suspecting that his friend would be out at some meeting. Lal's head appeared round the door and then withdrew. A moment later he came slapping down the stairs in his *chapals*, tying his sarong and looking as if he had been asleep.

'Getting sack, Lal,' Vijay said simply, showing his bundle of papers and trying to keep his voice normal.

Lal looked up at him with shock in his eyes, but said nothing.

'You are letting?' said Vijay, unable to stop his hoarseness.

'What to do?' said Lal, his eyes large with sadness but without fight.

'What about defending interests of proletariat, protecting rights of working man, all such things.'

'Vijay, Vijay,' said Lal, sitting down on his parents' steps. 'Cannot be calling out hotel.' He looked up at his friend, his face suggesting that anyone could see the reasonableness of his position. He pulled Vijay down beside him.

'Look Vijay, time is not right. No tourists are there. Laying off all over place. Union itself is having only half membership since troubles beginning. If we are having strikes and all, bosses are laughing up sleeve, Vijay. Scabs will be running here, there, everywhere. Bosses happy if not paying wages. We are needing big, big reason, Vijay, then we can be appealing to all workers in city, having protest marches, solidarity, getting dialectic going. Cannot be doing all that, Vijay, because friend is being sacked.'

Vijay nodded. He had known as much but had no other stone to turn. He felt Lal's arm through his.

'Listen, Vijay, I am telling what is happening. When we are calling strike, and after some time getting down to brass tacks with bosses, putting down bargaining chips and all that, I am saying quietly on one side "also Vijay Jayasinghe is getting job". It will be small chip and they are saying OK.'

There was a silence.

'I am doing level best Vijay.'

The suggestion was to save Lal's face, and Vijay allowed it to pass.

For another hour he walked. The wind had begun to swirl the dust on the streets so that it clung to his freshly oiled hair and turned red the narrow bottoms of his new white slacks. He headed eventually for Sea Street, for the only thing he knew for certain he must do.

He was kept waiting for a quarter of an hour in the True-Cut Ruby Mine, picking nervously at the foam cushion of the seat where the black plastic had peeled away. From time to time, he had the feeling that he was being watched. He looked around the dingy room. How many thousands had sat here waiting to sell or pawn, he wondered, all with their own desperations. He went again over the ground; the ruby had been priced at eight hundred and fifty; he had bought it for five hundred. They would surely give him four hundred for it. Surely it would not be less than three.

Eventually the young assistant came to stand behind an empty display case. He looked up at Vijay in a bored fashion. Vijay placed the box on the display cabinet between them.

'I am wanting to be selling back. It is ruby.' He lifted the top of the box to reveal the stone lying on its bed of velvet.

'We are not buying,' said the young man. He did not even look down at the ruby.

'I am wanting to see proprietor.'

'Not available.' He made no attempt to be convincing.

'I am selling for less than I am paying.'

'I am already telling. Not buying.'

The young man reached for the bottle of cleaning fluid and began pouring it onto a cloth. Vijay took the box and walked out of the shop, replacing the lid as he went. It was after nine o'clock but every gem store in Sea Street was lit up. Music wailed from open doorways. Strip lights beckoned everywhere.

'Cards are telling you, cards are telling you,' an old woman shrieked at Vijay from the pavement, reading the look on his face and pointing to an elderly green parrot which obligingly turned over a card and cocked one wrinkled eye at Vijay. With dread he entered another gem store, not even noting its name.

'Pawning?' he was asked when he produced the box.

'I am selling,' he said miserably.

'Here, only pawning.'

It was the same story at the next three gem arcades. No one wanted to buy when they could pay far less against a six- or twelve-month pawn, with a high chance of it never being redeemed.

Eventually, Vijay gave in. 'How much you are giving if I am pawning?' he said to the young man, younger than himself, in the brightly lit shop lined with faded batiks. The assistant picked up the ruby unceremoniously and screwed a black eye-glass in before holding it on his flat palm under the lamp. He let the jewel drop onto the display case between them.

'Glass only,' he said simply.

Vijay felt his heart go cold as he stopped the ruby from rolling to the floor. He put the stone back in the box and jammed on the lid. He looked up desperately into the man's face.

'Anyone is telling same,' said the young man, and he turned to go up the three little stairs at the back of the shop.

Vijay did not waste any more time in Sea Street. Knowing that most jewellery business was transacted in the evenings, he hurried the few blocks to the Fort. After queuing for half an hour at the State Gem Corporation, he was ushered into a little booth where a clerk in collar and tie sat behind a wire grill toying with a pair of balance scales. Vijay sat down under the harsh lights and pushed the little box under the wire mesh.

'I am needing certificate for ruby,' he said, his voice unsteady.

'Testing ten rupees, certificate also ten rupees. Both you are needing?'

'First testing,' said Vijay.

The clerk opened the box. Unimpressed, he took the eye glass hanging from a cord around his neck and twisted it quickly into one eye. In an exaggerated way, he opened both eyes wide, letting the eye glass drop on its cord. He smiled at Vijay and pulled a heavy metal device towards him. The device had a lever, like the machine used for embossing the hotel's letters. Slowly the clerk held up his ruby between thumb and forefinger and squinted over it through the metal grill at Vijay.

'This is a little piece of glass we are having here,' he said jauntily, as though the discovery had made his day. 'I am showing you proof positive?'

Vijay stared at the little point of red cushioned between the fleshy tips of the man's fingers. Receiving no reply, the clerk placed the ruby on a tiny metal plate attached to the machine and took hold of the lever. Still smiling, he pressed a matching plate down on top of the stone. A sick, empty feeling gripped Vijay's stomach as he heard the first little grinding sound of the glass beginning to disintegrate. The clerk stopped and raised the lever again, a torturer relenting. On the lower plate, the top of the ruby had turned to a whitish powder.

The official smiled. Only about twice a week did he get to deliver his favourite line.

'Elephant on this end of lever is not crushing ruby.'

With cruel ceremony, the piece of glass with its fresh white bruise was placed in the exact centre of the velvet and the box was pushed back under the grill. Vijay covered it with the lid and turned to go.

'Testing is ten rupees.'

He paid from the wad of notes in his shirt pocket and walked back through the cream painted corridor out into the street.

He walked to Maligawatta, the wind getting up, his steps taking him home but his mind unable to contemplate returning to the garden with his news. Blow by blow, the awful truth struck home to him as he turned into the Pettah: he had lost his savings and his job; without a job, he would be unable to secure the loan for the advance rent; without the year's rent, they would be evicted. There would only be the shanty to go to. He stopped under a street lamp halfway across a bridge, the wind tugging at his clothes and the first rain beginning to fall. Apart from an occasional lonely oil lamp, the shanties were in darkness. How can a man go home to tell this, he asked himself as he looked down at the dark trickle of water flowing slowly between the muddy banks. He took the box from his pocket and picked out the bruised ruby. He held it for a few seconds between thumb and finger, and then let it drop through the night. He could feel the cold of the river in the air and the rain was becoming more insistent. By the light of the street lamp he could just see it still, the tiny bead in its bed of mud. He stared at it until the little gleam of red began to stretch like a lance across his vision.

31

Clara had to use all her businesswoman's sang-froid to take breakfast as usual on the verandah. She was sure that the rest of the waiters would all know that Vijay had been sacked, and that they would also all know why. She felt it essential that she should pretend it was just a normal morning, ordering her fruit and toast, smiling good morning to the day captain, reading her newspaper, gazing out across the lawns to the ocean and the dazzling sun.

She was not pleased by the outcome of the interview she had just had with Miles Perera. She had asked to see him at the start of the day's business, even before breakfast, to stress the immediacy of her reaction. He had at first pretended not to know anything about Vijay Jayasinghe, and had telephoned to the Food and Beverage Manager to ascertain the facts of the case. But Clara had recognised the call as merely a managerial ploy, exclusively for her benefit. When he had replaced the old-fashioned phone on its cradle he had smiled reassuringly across the leather-topped desk.

'This matter is nothing to do with meeting you or anything of that nature,' he had said, spreading his hands, a priest giving absolution. She did not believe a word.

'That is not what I have heard, Miles,' she said, smiling back. He leaned back to deliver another bland waiver in her direction but she forestalled him before he could say anything which would make it more difficult for him to agree to her request.

'Whatever the reason is, Miles, I want to ask you to extend your already great kindness to me and to do me the very great personal favour of reinstating this man.'

Miles Perera's expression had changed. Thoughtfully, as if about to reveal a confidence, he had leaned towards her, arm on the leather desk top, his head below hers.

'We are both business people, Clara. May I call you Clara? The fact is, Clara, I am having to lose two staff. Having to. Having to.' He leaned back again in his chair. 'You may know even better than I why this is,' and he had given her a sly, knowing look. 'This Vijay is coming only recently, his work is not good, so we are letting him go, that is all.'

'And there isn't any way that you can do this for me, even as a personal favour?' said Clara, conscious that she was on weak ground.

'Anything. I would do anything, Clara. But this I cannot do because, as the Americans are always saying, I am in the middle of a rock and very hard place. Only if the order is coming from London, then I am not needing to lose staff.' He smiled, and then instantly changed his look to one of sincere regret.

'And Clara, you should know that there are so many like this fellow Vijay in this city. He is only one of ten thousand, hundred thousand,' he said finally, dismissing the matter. 'Please do me the honour of being my guest for breakfast.'

Clara had declined, saying that she had one or two urgent calls to make. It did not seem to have worried him. She forced herself to linger a few minutes over her coffee as normal. At a quarter to eight she signed the chitty for the day captain and returned to her room. Determined not to worry about herself, or how it would look to others in the company, she made the call to London and briefly explained what she wanted. She was sure the call was also being listened to on the switchboard downstairs.

'I can't explain everything now, Paul,' she said, making an effort to sound her normal, rational self, 'so would you please just take my word for it that it's important?'

'But what are you asking me to do, Clara?' The voice had acquired a faint note of exasperated condescension.

'I am asking you to ring your opposite number at Stateline and fix it for me. All he has to do is make one call to this man Miles Perera. I mean we do own the hotel don't we?'

'Yes, but Clara you must see how absurd this all is.'

Clara's voice did not change.

'I am aware that it's an unusual request, but I wouldn't be calling if it weren't important.' There was silence on the other end of the line. 'Paul,' she said, dropping her voice to a friendlier tone, 'sometimes senior executives doing these little reciprocal favours for each other is the only way to get things done.'

Five thousand miles away the Director of Personnel needed micro-seconds to appreciate the import of 'reciprocal' and to realise how difficult Clara Lane could make things for him from her new office in Strasbourg.

'Clara, you know if it's important to you then that's enough for me. But I've got to tell you, just last week there was an unholy row at Stateline because they said Graham was reneging on non-interference. Can you imagine if I ring Colin up now to talk to him about some waiter in one of his hotels that he's never even heard of? It would go all the way to the top, Clara. They'd beat us with it every time we sat down over there. Clara, believe me, anything else I would do . . .'

Clara had persisted only a minute or two longer before realising she was beaten. Paul was right. She would explain it all to him when she got back. Now she had only one card left, and moving more quickly than she had since she arrived on the island she changed into her most stunning black silk blouse and matching skirt and sprayed a touch of perfume to either side of her bare and sun-tanned neck.

32

Vijay lay on his bed-board watching the star through the little gap in the tiles. It had been after midnight when he had finally come home and the house had been in darkness. Out on the verandah he had smoked two cigarettes, the gardens strangely quiet all around him. Now he wanted desperately to go to sleep, to find relief in unconsciousness, to wake up with the shaft of pure sunlight falling into the room telling him it was all just a dream.

'Are you still awake, Vijay?' Chandra whispered beside him.

'Awake,' he said quietly.

She reached out her hand to touch him. 'It is late.'

Vijay blinked at the star.

'Chandra, I am losing job.'

He felt her hand go tense and cold in his. There was no sound. Chandra seemed to have stopped breathing.

He heard his wife turn onto her side, towards him, her hand still in his.

'Why, Vijay?' she whispered, squeezing his hand.

'Two nephews of Minister needing jobs. He is brother of Mr Miles Perera. So two are needing sack.' There was a long silence as Vijay struggled for more words in the darkness.

'Also . . . I am behaving very badly.'

There was a long silence. Then she reached for him and took him in her arms.

The next morning, Vijay told Premawathie and Godfrey his news, omitting any mention of his own actions. Premawathie had walked slowly through to the back of the house and collapsed, sobbing, against the kitchen wall. Godfrey had put an arm round Vijay's shoulders and steered him out to the verandah. Chandra joined them.

'Not be getting loan,' said Chandra simply. Vijay nodded his head.

'How much you are needing?' asked Godfrey.

'Again, two thousand four hundred.'

'Whole sum?' said Chandra.

'Whole sum,' said Vijay, not looking at her.

For an hour they sat on the verandah, exchanging only a word here and there. There were no options to discuss. Both Vijay and Chandra had been inside to try to comfort Premawathie, but her sobs could still be heard from within. A neighbour stopped by the verandah and was told the news; over the next half-hour, three or four of the other men came to say a few words to Vijay.

Chandra went once more into the kitchen. Through her sobs the old lady had told her that she could not even face going to the water tap. Chandra could think of no words to say, knowing how much more difficult it would be to go through the wall and back into the shanty. Eventually she returned to the verandah and began to prepare vegetables.

They talked intermittently. Godfrey spoke of putting all the money they had on a horse he had a certain feeling about. Chandra wondered aloud about how quickly they might establish the little baking business. But Vijay pointed out the obvious; they would need the loan in less than a month and it could neither be raised nor repaid without a secure income. After half an hour, the silent group on the verandah were startled by the appearance in the doorway of Premawathie, dressed to go out. She looked at each of them in turn. Though she had dried her eyes, her face looked ten years older.

'Only *kodivina* can be doing this,' she hissed. 'I am going now this minute to be seeking *anjamam eliya*.'

Before anyone could reply she had descended to the drain and set off down the garden, staring fiercely ahead as dozens of pairs of eyes followed the progress of the old lady who had so often boasted of her son's position.

'Fat lot of good *anjamam* is doing,' said Godfrey, struggling up out of his chair.

Chandra looked up questioningly.

'I am also having somewhere to go,' said Godfrey, with a note in his voice which had not been heard for half a lifetime and bore a fair resemblance to determination.

33

Clara sat in the roof-top bar of the Intercontinental Hotel. On the glass table were bowls of fish-shaped savouries and a ceramic tray divided into two compartments containing black and green olives. The waiter reverently placed before her a tall glass of crushed ice over which he proceeded to pour a sparkling mineral water. She did not hear him retreat across the deep-pile carpet. The only sound was the soft whisper of the air conditioning.

She sank back into the soft green armchair and looked down at the view. She had declined a seat looking out over the ocean and below her now the city sprawled inland, its dirty red roofs interrupted by scruffy batches of palms, broken roads and slowly winding canals. She imagined the heat, the noise and the dust, for the wind was not yet spent, and her eyes toured each quarter of the city looking for the slums that Vijay had told her about. Most of all, she wondered about Vijay himself, knowing he was somewhere in the obscure mass of humanity spread out below her.

Her interview with the managing director of the Intercontinental, whom she had met at the little luncheon party at the beginning of her stay, had been as unsatisfactory as her talk with Miles Perera. The troubles had decimated the tourist trade and everybody was laying off all the staff they could. He would have liked to have hired this man as a favour to Clara, for whom he had the highest personal regard, but the times were such . . . and in any case, he was sure she realised, there were ten thousand Vijays in a city such as this.

Clara had only one more day, she told herself, sipping her mineral water and planning the next move. She found it difficult to believe that she could not arrange to get Vijay Jayasinghe reinstated or to find him another job in the city. And as she thought about it, it became obvious what she should do next. It was something which did not depend on asking favours of anybody else, something she could do by herself. Vijay had told her that the going rate for bribing one's way into a job was two thousand rupees. She would simply find Vijay and give him the money. In fact she would give him a lot more than that. Enough to start his own business if that was what he wanted. She drained the last of her Perrier. The waiter was there immediately. She ordered a cold beer to celebrate her plan and got down to thinking about the details. How much should she give him? Thinking back over their conversations she remembered that his monthly pay, with his share of the tips, came to about a thousand rupees. She decided she would give him a year's salary, twelve thousand rupees. Then she thought what that much would mean to her and what it might mean to Vijay, and she doubled it. Paying cash for her half-finished drink, she took the elevator down to the American Express office on the mezzanine floor.

Premawathie sat in the gloom of the little parlour in Maligawatta. Opposite her, a tiny woman was shaking her head at the pile of notes on the paper doily. It amounted to one hundred and eighty-five rupees, all of Premawathie's savings. The dark woman across the table from her looked up sharply. They spoke in Sinhala.

'I would like to help you, but I can't do it for anything less than three hundred.'

'That is all I have.'

The tiny woman, she who could read the light and detect the presence of a *kodivina*, shook her head.

'That is . . . all I have,' Premawathie repeated. There was no response. After a few more seconds the old lady stood up to go. She was almost out of the door when the other spoke.

'If anybody were to know that I have sought *anjamam eliya* for this . . .'

Premawathie turned in the doorway.

'I will not tell.'

The woman paused for a moment and then beckoned Premawathie back in. Struggling to her feet, she took the offered pile of rupees and closed both doors of the little partition. With her back to Premawathie, she counted the notes into a dowry box and locked it with a key suspended from her neck by a chain. Without a word the woman disappeared from the room, leaving Premawathie sitting in the darkness, save for a shaft of daylight entering through the dirty skylight above.

After a few minutes, the medium returned holding a large, glossy betel leaf by the stalk. A spirit lamp was quickly lit. From behind a curtain she took down a jar of dark, oily liquid. Slowly she lowered the jar onto its side until a little of the oil had oozed out onto the betel. Setting the jar upright again on the table, she began smearing the oil with a dark finger over the surface of the leaf. Reverently, she presented the leaf to the glass bowl of the lamp, tilting it to and fro, rolling the stalk between finger and thumb. The oily paste on the leaf glistened and shone. Premawathie's eyes widened in the darkness. The cords of the woman's leathery throat were strung tight and her eyes bulged.

'It is all as we thought,' said the woman who could read the light of the gods. 'It is happening because a *kodivina* has been put on the family of Jayasinghe. They will have recited mantras at the temple. Probably they have also put a thread-bracelet where you are living. Buried I should think, somewhere where you are always passing. But the light says it's bad. This is just the beginning.'

'I knew it,' Premawathie said, triumphant in her terror. 'But who is it who has done this to us?'

The medium shook her head in a sly way. There was not much that she did not know about life in Maligawatta. She seemed to strain, passing her hand across her forehead. Her voice grew distant, tired.

'It is not clearly revealed in the light of the Gods. But it is possible that you are married to a man who has greatly angered someone.'

Premawathie's face hardened. She had known as much. Some

low gambling type, some acquaintance of Godfrey's who had
been cheated, or had lost too much, or who had been ruled
against in one of his pathetic judgements.

'How can it be lifted, tell me?'

The little woman shook her head.

'Only exorcism will work in a case like this. But a *thovilaya*
would take maybe two hours.'

'How much does it cost?'

'You must have the dance. Useless without the dance. Not less
than five hundred for a *kodivina* like this.'

'I will find the money,' said Premawathie fiercely, 'I will find
the money and come back.'

'Perform the ceremony before the end of the month, my dear.
It is then that the *kodivina* will most probably strike again.'

Clara looked at the compliment slip from Miles Perera. He had
referred her query to the Food and Beverage Manager and had
received the attached reply. The paper-clipped note simply said
that the only address the hotel had for the young man in question
was the one given at the time of his employment. This former
employee had not bothered to update his details since, and it was
almost certainly out of date, if indeed he had ever lived there.

This last doubt was raised because, as the Food and Beverage
Manager had shrewdly noted, the address given was the same
as that of one Gamini Senanayake, the first floor room-boy.

Clara read the note again on the verandah, her coffee untouched.
She guessed that by now the entire hotel staff knew what was
happening. She was uncomfortably conscious, too, that the
details of her phone call would be all over the building and
probably several other buildings in the city of London before
five o'clock. She heard Paul's voice and imagined him crossing
his elegant legs in the executive coffee lounge: 'You'll never
guess, our Clara's got herself involved with some waiter over
there. Yes, a waiter. There was this extraordinary phone call at
some god-awful hour this morning . . .'

Clara forced herself to stop imagining what was being said
behind her back, whether six metres away or six thousand

kilometres. It did not matter. She drank most of her coffee in order to prevent another significant detail being fed to the monster rumour.

Upstairs, she crossed the creaking landing to where she could see the white sarong of the old man who was still standing in the dim light before the doors of the Governor's suite. She saw him straighten as she neared.

'Your name is Gamini Senanayake isn't it?' she asked.

Startled out of his routines, Gamini stopped halfway into his almost involuntary little bow and looked up at Clara, shocked to have emerged from anonymity after so many years.

'Yes, Miss, I am Gamini.'

'Then I hope you can help me. I want to find Vijay Jayasinghe. I want to help him. Help him financially.'

Gamini looked at her warily, and then his eyes fell to the floorboards. Clara continued.

'I am told downstairs that the hotel does not have an address for him. The only one they have is an old one, and they say it is the same as yours.'

'Vijay Jayasinghe is giving Gamini's address when he is first coming, Miss.'

'Why did he not give his own address?' asked Clara more gently.

'He is not wanting anyone to be knowing where he is truly living, Miss.'

'Why not, Gamini?'

'Because it is very bad place, Miss. It is having very bad reputation. Hotel is not wanting anyone from that place.'

'He was from the slums?' said Clara.

'Miss, now he is in slums.'

Clara entirely misunderstood the emphasis. She was aware of a vague misunderstanding, but pressed on to the main point.

'Do you know his address, Gamini?'

Gamini hesitated. He would not want to deny Vijay any help that might be coming. But neither did he want to be the one to bring further trouble on the boy's head.

'I am not knowing exactly, Miss,' he said, telling himself that this was in fact true.

'But you do know pretty well?' said Clara. She sensed his

hesitation, sensed also that offering him money would be the wrong thing to do.

'I am knowing only roughly, Miss,' said Gamini, still struggling between truth and right. 'He is living pretty close to canal, Miss.'

'Do you know which canal?'

'Miss, it is Saint Sebastian.'

'You don't know any more precisely than that?'

'I am knowing it is Maligawatta, Miss.'

'You can't tell me anything else?'

'No, Miss,' said the old man miserably. It was almost true.

'You are sure, Gamini?' She thought about the money but her instincts still told her no.

'Yes, Miss.'

Clara thanked him and continued on down the landing.

Back in her room, she found a city map in the hotel's 'welcome pack' and began looking for the names the old man had mentioned. First she checked all the meandering waterways until she found the St Sebastian Canal. Then she followed its course to the eastern edge of the city and began tracing it back in again slowly, looking at every name on either side of the thin blue line. She soon found the area marked 'Maligawatta', not far from the centre of the city. The window was so full of bright sunlight that the contrast made the room dark and she switched on the small lamp over the desk. Checking against the scale, she estimated that the area that was both close to the St Sebastian Canal and within Maligawatta was a strip of land measuring no more than six or seven hundred metres long.

She quickly changed into a pale cotton dress and slipped the map into her bag.

The taxi driver was helpful. He peered closely through much-mended glasses at the crossroads on the map which Clara had pointed to.

'That is Sri Sumanatissa Mawatha, Miss,' he said, straightening up triumphantly and showing a mouth full of dark brown teeth.

'Will you take me there?' said Clara, as the driver showed no signs of moving.

'Miss, I am taking, but there is nothing to be seeing.'

'Take me anyway,' she smiled.

The engine churned and wobbled into what life it had left. 'First time, Miss,' he was saying, as he pulled out into the traffic of the Galle Road, 'first time I am taking foreign lady to such a place.'

It had looked easy on the map in her hotel room, but now that Clara was out in the chaos of the streets her confidence wavered. Six or seven hundred metres could mean thousands in a city such as this. She thought of the one other piece of information she had gleaned: Vijay lived in a slum which had a particularly bad reputation.

They proceeded slowly through the Slave Island traffic, picking up speed as they crossed behind the Town Hall and rounded De Soysa Circus. Here the crowds were thicker and Clara noticed one or two settlements which looked like slums, collections of huts made of bamboo and plaited vegetation, their roofs held on by stones or worn-out tyres. The first ones she noticed were just groups of ten or twenty shacks, but as they drove down the Maradana Road she caught a glimpse of what looked like hundreds of such homes gathered around a huge mountain of rotting rubbish.

'That city rubbish dump, Miss,' said the driver, noticing her look. 'All tourists are wanting to see.' He smiled in the mirror and Clara, suddenly back in the world of other people, smiled back.

'Maligawatta is here, Miss. Where you are wanting particular?'

'Anywhere here will do.'

He coasted the taxi into the kerb and turned, one arm over the back of the front bench-seat. She paid him and slipped out into the heat. On all sides, crowds were flowing in an excited murmur past the shops and the street stalls that lined all four roads as they converged on a tiny roundabout where a traffic policeman stood marooned, perspiring despite his open-necked shirt and khaki shorts. Everywhere, street traders sat on pavements in front of their baskets of fruit and vegetables, household goods and cottons, leather *chapals* and flashy sneakers, bundles of firewood and little stands of fried *sambols*. Clara did not know which way to turn. The taxi driver had put the rupee notes into his shirt pocket and was lighting a cigarette as he watched to see what she would do next. Trying to look in control, she went with the crowd across the road and turned down a street which looked vaguely more residential. Once out of sight of the taxi, she took out her map.

At the end of the street, a bridge rose over what she assumed was a canal. Folding the map to show only the little area she was interested in, she began looking around for street names. There did not seem to be any. But she was almost sure that she was already at the point where the canal entered the area marked 'Maligawatta'. Here and there were groups of makeshift shacks standing on patches of waste ground or on sites where buildings had been demolished. But she guessed that these were not what she was looking for. The old man had said that the hotel would not have employed anyone from the place where Vijay lived. That could surely only apply to a sizeable place, a well-known slum with a name, not these little pockets of rickety shacks. She decided to navigate right around the perimeter of the area she had marked, and then to begin crossing it systematically from south to north.

Less than half an hour later, after walking streets lined only with shops and small businesses, she turned back towards the canal and saw at once what she was searching for. Opposite her was the entrance to what was undoubtedly a sizeable slum. She crossed the road and looked down the rutted, sandy track which ran down the embankment and disappeared into a maze of shacks stretching back as far as the eye could see. It was much bigger than she had imagined, and she felt sure that it was the kind of place that would have both name and reputation. The heat and humidity were almost unbearable up on the road and she wondered what it would be like down in the slum from which the noise and the flies and the smell now drifted up to meet her. She hesitated, as most of the citizens of the city would have hesitated, before plunging into that underworld, not knowing what she might meet there or where and how she would start. But as she stood looking out over the sea of shacks in her fine cotton dress and holding a handbag bought in far-off Florence, she told herself that it was Vijay that mattered, that she had already made a fool of herself at the hotel, and back at her office in London, and that if necessary she would do so again here. Trying to stay calm, Clara Lane made her way slowly down the embankment.

34

Godfrey Jayasinghe squeezed through the garden wall and paused for a moment at the other side, looking down through the shanty. He already knew from several sources exactly why Vijay had been sacked, and his heart bled for the boy. He lit a cigarette and let his eyes travel slowly over the makeshift roofs sprawling untidily down to the putrid canal. For a second the old man thought of the aspirations he himself had once had and a lump rose in his throat. It was hard, he thought, for Vijay to be punished so heavily for so small a sin. Slowly, he began to walk through the shanty which had been his home for forty years and would soon be his home again. He would miss having a verandah to sit out on, but he knew that of all of them he would be the least affected. He thought of Chandra and Susil and felt anew the enormity of what had happened. But when he thought of the wife to whom he had been such a life-long disappointment, his thoughts broke down into chaos rather than contemplate the picture of her living once more on the banks of the canal. She would not be able to bear it, and he ran cold inside, being certain that his wife would choose insecticide.

He climbed the steep sandbank to the end of the bridge. There was only one way of saving them all. And slim as the hope might be, only he, good-for-nothing-Godfrey, had any chance of arranging it. It was the solution that had been taken by tens of thousands of families. A position must be found in the Middle East. Only then could they secure the loan and stay in the garden. And it could only be Chandra. No men were being recruited these days, and even the housemaid jobs were drying up. The contracts were for two years, and in that time Vijay would surely find another position. The trouble was the recruitment fee. So many families wanted to send wives or daughters or daughters-in-law that the recruitment agencies, although paid a commission from the Gulf, were also able to demand five, even ten thousand rupees from the families of each recruit. Godfrey's careful winnings at the Cheltenham Corner over the last week had brought him nearly six hundred. But they had also brought him knowledge that could be worth a lot more.

He hesitated outside the bookmakers. The racing would not start until the evening, afternoon time at Lingfield, Cheltenham, or Goodwood, and he could see that the shop was occupied only by the manager standing in a shaft of brilliantly lit chalk dust as he cleaned the blackboards of last night's odds. Godfrey knew the man well, but he knew also that he was a stooge for the brothers Mahmoud, whom he did not want to know at all. The brothers, Farah and Shari, were local businessmen with a stable of dubious concerns in and around Maligawatta, including the three betting shops, a private gambling saloon, and one of the biggest recruitment agencies for the Middle East. He also suspected that they had some stake in the heroin rackets which had brought a new and terrible despair to the shanties. Only once before had Godfrey ever had anything to do with the brothers Mahmoud. He had been approached, after his gambling adjudications had become a feature of life in Maligawatta, with the suggestion that the Mahmoud gambling houses should also bring all of their little disputes to him and that, on balance, and for a monthly retainer of three hundred rupees, he would find himself ruling in favour of the brothers in all but a few well-publicised cases. Godfrey had been tempted by the regular income, but the next day he had told the emissary of the brothers Mahmoud that he was not interested, and he had never heard from them again.

He entered the cloud of chalk dust in the little betting shop and was greeted by the manager in Sinhala.

'Can't wait to start winning again Godfrey?'

'That's what I'm coming to see you about,' said Godfrey unsure what kind of a voice to use, so unaccustomed was he to having anything serious to say. The manager detected that something unusual was afoot and stopped wielding the blackboard duster. Godfrey plunged straight on.

'I know that you're playing the tapes after the race is finished,' he said simply. 'I want to see Mr Mahmoud'.

Slowly the bookie shook his head and leaned away from Godfrey, arms spreading, indicating that he wanted no part of this.

'*Buddu ammo*! You are asking for big trouble this time, Godfrey.'

'I'm not going to cause any trouble,' said Godfrey. 'I want to ask only one small favour. Then I'll forget about it. That's all. Just telephone, Dilip.'

The bookie hesitated.

'I can't telephone Mr Mahmoud with a message like that,' he said, and turned again to the blackboard.

'If I tell what I know in Maligawatta, Dilip, it will be a matter of a few minutes before a large number of very angry men are coming from all directions to begin very politely tearing one Dilip's head off.'

The bookie recognised this as a simple statement of the truth. He turned again and looked at the telephone. Still shaking his head, he began to dial.

'Someone is coming,' he said to Godfrey as he replaced the receiver.

'Tell him I'll be waiting across the road,' said Godfrey, not wanting to face what he knew might be coming in the darkness of the little shop.

The sun shone and Godfrey exchanged pleasantries with a dozen people in the few minutes that he waited at the foot of the bridge, reassured by how normal the world was, until he saw the new Japanese car draw up outside the betting shop.

More minutes passed. Godfrey ran over his strategy. He knew he could not blackmail the Mahmoud brothers for money. They would assume that it was just the first request of many, and he would certainly end up in the canal. But there was one thing they could do for him that would not cost them anything. And this, if he handled things right, they might agree to. The door of the betting shop opened again and the manager came furtively across the road.

'Mr Mahmoud says to join him for a little talk.'

'Tell him I will only talk out here.'

The bookie disappeared, looking worried. Soon afterwards, an

extremely heavy man in tailor-made trousers and red braces
stooped out of the bookmakers and crossed the road towards
him. He was carrying his jacket and his red paisley tie only came
halfway down his bulging white shirt.

'Godfrey,' he said, as if greeting an old friend, 'come inside,
let's talk in the shade.' He took Godfrey's arm and tried again
to head back across the road.

Godfrey refused to move his feet.

'I would rather be talking here, Mr Mahmoud, sir.'

The younger of the two Mahmoud brothers turned towards
him, his fleshy lips reddened by fresh beetle juice.

'You son of a bloody bastard,' he said smiling benignly, still
with his arm through Godfrey's, 'you are not knowing how
much trouble you are in.'

Godfrey knew that this was not a time to play poker. He threw
his hand on the table.

'I am not asking if not desperate,' he began. 'All I am wanting
is small job for daughter in Gulf. Son is losing job. Soon being
evicted. Having no home. That is only reason I am asking favour.
Afterwards forgetting all about it and racing and all. Not ever
telling.'

Mahmoud hesitated. He knew that Godfrey was well known,
even held in some affection, in Maligawatta, and especially
among the punters in the slums and shanties. Word of these
things always got around; it would not be good for business to
have him beaten, or put into the cement at one of the con-
struction sites. There was also his brother's election to consider.
Maligawatta was a big slice of the constituency. He hesitated for
a moment and then decided.

'No more jobs in Gulf, Godfrey,' he said, still smiling as
if merely passing the time of day. 'Last consignment going
tomorrow night. Then no more till we are not knowing when.'

'Always there is girl not turning up,' said Godfrey, his fears
calming slightly at the tack that Mahmoud had taken.

'This girl speaking English?'

'Speaking English like you and me, Mr Mahmoud. I myself
am teaching.'

'Fair or dark?'

'She is quite a lot dark.'

Mahmoud thought for a moment. It was of course true that out of two hundred or so young women there were always at least three who didn't show, whose courage failed them at the last minute, or who were ill, or who ran away back to their parents' homes. A full quota meant more money at the other end; also there were bonuses to be had for girls if they could speak English; and they were always being pestered for the darker-skinned girls, preferably married, who were favoured by Arab women. Another consideration instantly occurred to him: the girl would be a hostage in case the old man tried it on again, or felt inclined to any little looseness of the tongue. And what he was asking would not cost the brothers Mahmoud a cent. He considered again the ugly reaction if word about the Cheltenham Corner got around the shanties. And there were the three other betting shops to consider. He looked at Godfrey, his fleshy mouth still smiling.

'If you are asking one more little favour after this one, Godfrey,' he said, laughing and looking around as though they were chatting about the weather or the latest score in the test match, 'then I am promising you are not knowing what pain is until that precise moment.' He ended his sentence looking straight into Godfrey's eyes.

'You are fixing?' said Godfrey.

'Only if she is taking place of no-show at eight o'clock tomorrow night. Passport must also be there.'

'What about papers, visa, all that?' said Godfrey, his insides torn between relief and a dread weight of misery.

'All that we are arranging. She is needing only passport and birth certificate. Also photos. Two black and white, two colour. Skirt not sari. Also, medical certificate saying hundred per cent fit. You can be getting anywhere for fifty bucks. What is name?'

'Chandra Jayasinghe. I cannot be thanking enough.'

Mahmoud let him continue, committing himself.

'I am also giving you promise, word of old soldier, you are never hearing from me again after this day.'

Godfrey was about to turn and go when Mahmoud again put his hand benignly on his arm. He brought his great, fleshy face near to Godfrey's ear and whispered benignly and obscenely of the unspeakable things that had been known to happen to girls in the Gulf whose fathers talked too much.

They parted with a handshake and Godfrey remained where he was as the heavy man rolled across the street into the back of the waiting car, the bookie watching nervously from the doorway. Mahmoud glided off without a backward glance and Godfrey began to pick his way back down into the shanty. On his way he stopped at the standpipe. Never before had he felt moved to wash his hands in the middle of the day.

35

Clara tried not to think of the thousand pairs of eyes she was sure were on her as she made her way down the embankment, eyes of the people she could see standing in the alleyways, eyes peering through windows and leaning out round doors, eyes looking down from the road behind her, astonished eyes, curious eyes, alarmed eyes, gleeful eyes. Even before she had reached the bottom of the steep slope, rutted and still muddy from the night's rains, the noise of the slums rose to engulf her. She looked up, not knowing where to begin, or which way to walk or look or smile. Children were already running excitedly towards her. Even from here she could see many smaller alleyways infiltrating hundreds, perhaps thousands, of shacks whose low roofs of corrugated iron or sagging cadjan seemed to join in an undulating sea of thatch and rust. The children were arriving, small, dark, all as intense and alive as the little girl on Galle Face Green, their bodies clothed in an assortment of rags and cast-offs, their hair and skin dry and dulled with dust and poor diets, eyes liquid and clear. A man shouted and the children hung back, dancing a retreat before her, their eyes never leaving her, taking in her hair, her face, her clothes, her earrings, her watch, her bag. She smiled down at them and set off a burst of giggling and jabbering behind hands as more children came pouring out of the ginnels between the shacks to join the bubbling stream. She came to the first of the houses, its walls woven from palm leaves, and smiled at the group of women who were chattering excitedly, some of them pulling scraps of sari over their faces as they leaned sideways to talk, giggling and falling over each other in embarrassment.

Several men were also standing about at the entrance to the shanty, staring more frankly at her, the younger ones sharp and desperate in western shirts and flared trousers, the older more at ease in their knotted sarongs and spreading vests. Clara approached the women in the first doorway, conscious of a sickly warm smell all around her.

'Do you speak English?' She addressed the oldest woman in the group, a tiny figure on whose mahogany face a million lines ran everywhere without ever touching.

'English, English, I no English,' said the woman in a voice like two pieces of metal being scraped over each other, displaying a mouth of bright red gums and a few widely spaced teeth. She said something very quickly in her own language and disappeared into the darkness of her home. Clara did not know whether the woman had disappeared for good or gone to fetch someone. Only when she saw the old woman looking at her from the darkness a few feet inside the hut did she turn and carry on down the path. As soon as she moved the children were all around her, attacking her joyfully with their collected scraps of English. 'Miss . . . one . . . two . . . three . . . four . . . five . . . six.' Others were joining in the chant, jumping up and down with excitement in front of her. She focused on the boy nearest to her, a child of about eight years, a child with the most exquisite eyes she had ever seen. But now a larger boy pushed to the front shouting 'one fine day, one fine day' before he in turn was drowned out by a growing chant of the days of the week which broke down at Thursday amid much laughing and argument as a mischievous looking girl popped up in front of her to say 'Miss, please, thank you!' before covering her face with her hands and disappearing back into the crowd. She was surrounded now, unable to move without pushing against children who were still joyously assailing her with cries of 'once upon a time', 'God save Queen', 'Ell-bee-double-you', 'Missis Thatcher'. Clara decided to push her way deeper into the shanty towards a younger woman who was shouting from a doorway at the milling children. As she approached, she saw that the women's teeth had all been broken and this, combined with the effect of the running red juice from the betel-nut she had been chewing, gave her the look of someone who had just been hit very hard in the mouth.

Her eyes wandered madly as she saw that Clara was going to speak to her.

'Do you speak English?' Clara called above the noise. The woman turned and began calling in a harsh stream of syllables to someone in another room. A girl of about eighteen appeared, holding her blouse together at the top where the buttons had gone. 'My daughter, English' said the woman who had been hit in the mouth, making way for the girl. Clara smiled hopefully at the girl who held her blouse tighter and tighter in her terror.

'I'm looking for someone,' said Clara, trying to be as un-alarming as possible. The girl smiled uncomprehendingly. She too showed the red juice on her lips and tongue, but her hair which should have been young and shiny was aged with dust and poor health. 'My name is Meena,' she said in a tiny, terrified voice, wishing to do her mother justice.

'Do you know someone called Vijay Jayasinghe?' said Clara.

'My name is Meena,' said the girl and turned away in confusion to where her mother was smiling proudly in the darkness. Clara smiled back and moved on.

She was carried deeper into the shanty by the press of children and the oppressive smell began to surround her, hot and sweet. For a moment she thought about retreat and glanced up to make sure she could still see the road; but the conviction that Vijay was somewhere in this slum and the thought of the thousands of rupees she had in her bag made her push her way towards a group of men standing where a narrow ginnel crossed the main alleyway. She directed herself to the oldest man in the group who had been standing with his hands behind his back, chin almost on his chest, in the manner in which she had seen men standing on street corners all over the city. He straightened as he realised that he was being approached and gave a quick glance around to check his escape routes.

'I am looking for someone who can speak English,' said Clara, smiling reassuringly. The man shook his head and smiled inanely, feeling inadequate to the occasion. He had no teeth and his lips were the same colour as his skin so that his mouth appeared only as a sudden hole in his leathery face.

'Chandarasekere speaking English,' said a high voice behind

him. Clara saw that the man who had spoken was blind, his eyeballs like opaque crazed marbles.

'Is he here?' she asked, not knowing where to look as she spoke.

There followed a long conversation in dialect, with much pointing and contradicting, among the group of men. As she waited, still surrounded by children, the noise and heat and stench rose around her like a tide. The argument finally subsided and she waited to be told the conclusion, but the men said nothing; it was as though they had been talking all the while about something else.

'Can you find him?' she asked. A small child was boldly pulling at her skirt. Another brief exchange followed, terminated by the blind man suddenly moving off to his right, saying 'Come, come.' This seemed to settle the dispute and she followed the men, single file, up a narrow alleyway, stepping over open drains and slimy channels, into the recesses of the shanty.

Clara fumbled in her bag for a tissue to wipe the sweat from her face. Her shoes were covered, her ankles streaked with mud. Children and dogs squeezed by on either side. As they crossed another little path, a sudden, sickening smell seemed to overwhelm her, taking control of her stomach. She could not hurry on: the men in front had stopped again. 'Miss, Ian Botham, Miss.' Another small child had forced his way to her side, smiling a smile full of impudence and hope. Clara stroked his head on an impulse and he kept pace with her, squeezing along by her side as they set off again up the alley, walking in a permanent crouch between the eaves of the shacks, the edges of the rusting corrugated roofs and sharp bamboo poles dipping dangerously towards her eyes, her clothes sticking to her in the heat and her face aching from too much smiling. Ahead of her the men were stopping again to debate the path, each argument followed by a new twist or turn so that she was soon lost in the maze of bamboo poles and woven palm-leaf walls, brittle and dry despite the rains, while everywhere the smell of heat on human waste came and went and her eyes began to sting from the wood-smoke which drifted through walls and curled up under the eaves. From an alleyway, a new stream of children flowed in to join the throng and she felt two large dogs pushing past her legs. 'Miss, Beatles, Beatles,' smiled the little boy who had struggled to keep his place at her side.

There was shouting ahead of her now and one of the men almost knocked down the wall of a house as he flattened himself against it to let her pass. She squeezed to the front of the procession and was ushered through a doorway into a dark room where she could see nothing at all. A sour smell struck her, and it seemed that somewhere in the room she could hear a faint rasping breath under the clamour from outside. One of the men seemed to be stopping the children from entering, but he was also blocking out the light and it was a moment or two before she realised that someone was by her side inviting her to sit down. She felt the edge of a rickety bamboo chair in her hand and manoeuvred to perch on its edge, unsure whether it would take her weight. The talk had become a low murmur and the children's voices seemed to have fallen away. She sensed that the others were able to see, and as her own eyes grew used to the darkness she gradually made out what appeared to be the figure of a man lying asleep against the wall. Those who had led her here were standing in silence around the edges of the room, as if reluctant to wake the figure on the bed. But suddenly she knew that the frail old man was not sleeping. She sat quite still. He was naked except for a white loincloth, a huddle of skin and bone on the bed-board, his watery eyes looking at her across the room. Unsure what she should do, she examined the faces of her guides. It seemed to be enough just to sit there. Seconds passed. There seemed to be nothing alarming about this imminent death. The old man was patient and peaceful, and those around him were quite calm. But to her amazement, the skin and bones began to struggle to sit up. She rose from her chair to tell him not to make the effort for her, touching her hands on his arms to motion him to lie down again. But he had surprising strength and managed to sit himself upright on the bed, his talon-like fingers gripping its edges. Clara, finding herself on her knees on the beaten earth floor in front of him, looked into the drained eyes. She forgot why she was there, absorbed by the dignity in the man's face, by the emptiness of his gaze, by the sense that nothing mattered any more, and that there were things in this world of which she had never dreamed. He struggled to speak, swallowing several times, screwing up the dark little cords of muscle around his mouth. She smiled, trying to tell him by her look that there was no need to talk. But eventually he spoke in a faint, leaf-rustle voice.

'I am Tommy in British Army, Miss,' he said, as though this explained all. Clara nodded and smiled. 'I am in France, nineteen hundred and forty-five.' He coughed and shuddered and Clara looked round at the men standing in the darkness, fearing that the effort might be too much for the old man.

'I am wanting to say . . .' he coughed again and came forward, Clara supporting him with stiff arms. There was another long pause while he gathered strength. 'It is great honour . . . in dying hours . . . to be having visit from representative of Queen Elizabeth Second.' He smiled.

Clara looked into his eyes, more humbled than she had ever felt in her life. She smiled back at him, telling him how fine she thought he was. He read the message and smiled a smile of pure happiness that seemed to go right through them both. Clara let his arms go as two of the men came forward and helped him to lie down again on the wooden planks.

Outside in the blinding sun, Clara, moved and confused, followed the men up the little path where the sun made stabbing attacks on her eyes. Just as the children were beginning to find her again, the file of men stopped again in the alleyway. The same little boy was at her side. He smiled up at her, obviously hoping that she would recognise him. She smiled back.

'My name is Chitra,' he said, much rehearsed, and shy.

'My name is Clara,' she replied, astonished by the brilliance of the boy's eyes, the refinement of his features, the perfection of his teeth, the delicacy of his bones, the fineness of his skin, the life in his black, curling hair.

Up ahead, the man in the blue sarong was calling into one of the shacks. After a few seconds, a tall young man appeared in the doorway, dark, well-built, and naked apart from the dark red cloth he was tying round his waist. He blinked in the light and had obviously been sleeping, oiled hair flattened at one side. She was motioned into the little hut, followed by the four men who had now become six, and again she was offered the only chair, a more substantial affair of black iron and red plastic strings. Shouting something to the little boy who had attached himself to Clara and who had also slipped inside the dark room, the young man bent low through a doorway and disappeared.

Minutes went by in the darkness. Clara had no idea what was happening. The heat inside the little hut was intense. Flies buzzed in every corner and the sweat stung her eyes as she struggled to wipe her face on the only tissue she had left in her bag. She could see that her dress, snagged in various places, was festooned with thumb-prints and that her calf was scratched with a livid broken line. By the door the group of men, still standing, exchanged an occasional word. The darkness was retreating and she began to look around her. Apart from the unmade bed, there was a battered metal trunk, rusting in its bruises, and a set of two low shelves on which were arranged a set of six tumblers, a jar of what looked as if it might be hair-oil, a new pair of shoe-laces, and a mouldy black and white photograph of an elderly couple in an elaborate frame. Clara could hear the insects scratching in the wall behind her head and discreetly pulled her chair forward a few inches. On the other walls, pins and rusting bulldog clips held a collection of pages torn from magazines which Clara recognised as *Time* and *Newsweek*, *Harper's*, *Vanity Fair*, *Vogue*, *Cosmopolitan*, and one or two others she could not name. The pages were mostly advertisements for clothes, cosmetics, holidays, suntan creams, cam-corders, computers, cars, and almost all of them featured the young, the perfectly formed, the rich, glaring out into the little hut with an extraordinary thrusting, contemptuous confidence which she had not noticed before. She saw too, as she waited in the semi-darkness, that the expressions of the models were uniformly hard and challenging, deliberately cold and cruel as they stared from the pages and confronted the world with their assurance, their intense and aggressive superiority, their provocative unapproachabilty and violent glamour, their apparently unthought-of possessions, and that nowhere in any of the torn-out pictures was there a smile of any softness, a hint of any weakness, a cedilla of any pity. The only other photograph was an elaborate affair in an embossed tin frame which was held onto the wall by twisted wire and showed a local woman, smiling shyly, flanked by two stern-eyed men in Arab headdress, against the background of an airport. Next to it, a broken shard of mirror was wedged behind a bamboo pole.

The young man reappeared, buttoning up a gleaming white shirt over his sarong. His hair was now swept back in deep black grooves. Pulling a cover over the unmade bed, he sat down to face Clara, shoulders forward, resting his hands on the tightly stretched cloth between his knees. He waited for her to begin, betraying no sense of urgency, as if such interviews happened every day. She was about to begin her story again when the small boy reappeared carrying a chrome-plated tray on which stood a single can of ice-cold Pepsi-Cola, shimmering with condensation. Clara hesitated. A cold drink could never have been more welcome, but her mind raced with thoughts of how much it would have cost and of the times she had ordered such drinks without needing or wanting them. She decided that refusal would be the worst course of action and gratefully took the icy cylinder from the tray.

'Thank you, Chitra,' she said, smiling. The boy's face glowed at being remembered. He gave the whole room a huge, beaming smile and sat down on the floor, arms folded on top of the tray. As Clara held the drink, the young man's wife darted forward to the little shelf and wiped one of the stacked tumblers with the end of her sari. Clara smiled her thanks and forced the ring-pull. It made the same hiss as it always did. She poured half of it into the little tumbler and drank deliciously.

She began to explain her mission, confident from the young man's expression that he was following her without effort, even though he had so far spoken no word of English. She waited for the reaction which would mean that he knew of Vijay. But when she had finished he just stared at her, not seeing, his mind running on what she had said. She poured the rest of the Pepsi and extended her bottom lip to blow air up onto her face. Eventually he leaned back, putting his hands behind his head to think, before depositing them again on the sarong stretched tightly over his knees.

'There is one man who is answering this exact description,' he said with a judge-like gravity, the effect of which was diminished by a voice which was much too light for his bulk. He paused, nodding slowly, preparing to deliver himself of his verdict. 'He is waiter. I am not knowing hotel. He is age like me. He is also speaking English.'

'Will you take me to him?' said Clara.

Without replying, the young man exchanged a few words in dialect with the older men in the room. They seemed to be debating the whereabouts of the person in question and there was a great deal of sweeping of arms in different directions. As if at some unseen signal, they all began retying sarongs and preparing to go, waiting for Clara to lead the way out of the little hut. Clara smiled a thank you at the man's wife and, to the young woman's shy delight, indicated that she had noticed the photograph of her on the wall.

Before she could leave, the silhouette of a young woman filled the bright doorway. She was carrying a bundle of rags. Clara smiled and made room for her to pass through, but it was quickly obvious that the bundle had been brought especially to be shown to her. She stepped forward as the young mother tenderly parted the knitted robe to reveal the pink features of a new-born baby. With its soft folds and creases too big for so small a face it could have been any baby anywhere, and Clara wondered again at the lottery which had planted this particular child, its eyes screwed up tight, its tender mouth almost taller than it was wide, in such a place as this. She smiled admiringly at the infant and then at the proud mother.

'Boy or girl?' she asked. The mother was tongue-tied but several voices from behind told her that it was a little girl. From her bag Clara took out her lipstick and offered it to the little girl first, then, miming it round her own lips, she offered it to the astonished mother. 'For when she is older,' she said, smiling. There was a burst of laughter and delight all around as the mother took the present, covered in confusion. A happiness seemed to fill the little room as the others crowded round the mother and child and Clara swallowed the last of her ice-cold drink.

In the sudden brightness, she did not know which way to turn and the men, having stood back to let her go first, now had to squeeze past her again to lead the way. There were about a dozen now in the procession, not counting the children who scurried ahead as they made their way further into the maze. Behind

them Clara was towed along in the heat, guarding her eyes
against the low eaves of tin and cadjan, stepping over fetid drains
and stagnant pools of slimy water, passing through suddenly
strengthening smells, crossing innumerable alleyways, holding
her breath through the lingering wraiths of wood-smoke and
trying to avoid the worst of the mud beneath her feet. Turning
into a slightly wider path, she began to notice the efforts which
people had made to take the edge off such an existence: the dusty
flowers growing in old paint tins or in tyres that had been cut in
half and suspended from jutting roof poles; the ropes of coloured
beads hanging in doorways; the faded ill-fitting curtains at some
of the windows; and here and there a tiny garden, no more than
half a metre wide, in which flowers struggled behind a wall of
jagged tiles set diagonally into the ground. They were entering
an area now where ugly grey breeze blocks were being used to
replace woven walls, corrugated iron displacing sagging thatch.
Nothing was finished. Dust and rubble were everywhere. Dogs,
cats, jackdaws, chickens, scavenged in the interstices of the slum.
Chitra had again attached himself to her side.

At length they stopped outside another hut and she was once
more invited to enter.

'He is coming,' said the young man who had led them there.
Clara waited in the gloom again, hoping that the next person to
appear in the doorway would be Vijay. A hint of colour caught
her eye in the darkness and she looked up to see a red plastic
toothbrush wedged between the corrugated iron roof and the
bamboo pole by which it was supported.

'He is coming,' repeated the young man, and carried on
looking out of the doorway.

Clara suddenly felt unable to believe that Vijay could arrive
each day on the verandah of her hotel from such a place as this.
Noise came from all directions, filtering through the weave of
the walls, radios wailing, children calling, dogs barking, birds
cawing angrily, women shouting, pots scraping. A stream of
what sounded like violent abuse came through the wall and, in
the distance, someone was hammering with an insistent rhythm.
She looked down. Flies were crawling on the paleness of her feet
and ankles and she brushed them away as unobtrusively as possible. At the window, a pink nylon curtain flapped ineffectually,

revealing two or three curious faces in the alleyway outside. The chair was too low and Clara stood to examine the photographs standing on top of the display case, hoping to recognise Vijay; but the pictures were old and all the men looked the same, their individual features submerged into a common discomfiture.

The man at the door stood back to expose the bright oblong of sunlight which was quickly filled again by the silhouette of another. For a second he seemed to hang in the space, his hands on the pole over the doorway, peering into the gloom.

After a moment he stepped inside, glancing nervously from side to side as if to see who else was there to confront him. Clara shook her head and began to apologise for troubling them. The press outside forced the two young men into the room and they were followed by eight or nine others, all of them talking at once. The new arrival spoke to her in English.

'Miss, there are those in shanty speaking English like me, but I am thinking I am only one having hotel job.'

'You're sure?'

'Miss, it is not possible anyone having hotel job in this place and myself not knowing,' he smiled. Clara began to thank him but before she could rise to her feet a young woman appeared with another tray on which stood a cold can of Fanta orange. 'Please,' said the young man, motioning towards it eagerly.

'Easier this way, Miss,' said the young man as she finished the drink. She moved with the crowd and soon they were walking again along the edge of the shanty, skirting rolls of barbed wire which looped extravagantly in front of a broad ditch beyond which weedy fields stretched away towards a six-storey block of flats that was nearing completion. The light was beginning to fall and the wood-smoke was oozing through the walls as they passed. Clara ducked into the next alleyway, stepping over a drain almost blocked by rotting vegetables, holding her breath against a sudden smell of warm excrement, of steaming rice and pungent smoke, of the day's heat accumulating on the day's wastes. From all sides, the wail of radios and the cheerful chatter of neighbours advanced and receded in waves as she made her way through the shanty, occasionally catching the blue flicker of a television. A sudden squawking at her feet made her stumble and she saw that she had almost stepped on a scrawny, featherless chicken which had now resumed pecking at invisible seeds in the rapidly drying mud. Somewhere just ahead she could hear the fluting of a songbird but she concentrated on watching her feet until a voice in front said 'Minding head, Miss,' and she looked up to see a wire bird-cage hanging from a nail and a tiny red-polled bird singing bravely from a twig that had been jammed between the bars. To her left a deafening radio threw out a stream of volume-distorted syllables, interrupted every few seconds by the words 'Anchor butter'. Two more reddish dogs brushed roughly past her legs, their bones almost breaking the stretched skin, their backs covered in sores. The dogs stopped in front of her and she saw that they had begun pawing a dead rat that was beginning to decompose in a pile of refuse at the side of the path. There was still no sign of an exit from the shanty and the radios seemed to be coming at her one after the other, persecuting her with pop-songs which ended with local disc jockeys screaming with false, manic voices, 'I just wanna be your everything, yeah, so just do it, raaaaight.' Clara felt her foot slip part-way into the drain. Sweat ran down her face and neck and into her dress which was now sticking to her as she walked. Flies landed on her at will. Her face stung with the salt of her sweat. Jagged edges swooped at her eyes. In front of her a beaten dog suddenly advanced and growled menacingly, sensing a stranger, baring its diseased yellow teeth and obstructing her path until it was kicked by a bare foot and disappeared down another alleyway, yelping in pain. Clara pressed on, doing her best to smile as she stepped over the feet of a young woman seated in a doorway who was having the lice picked out of her hair.

They reached the main street again as the first huge drops of rain began to fall, warm and soft into the dust. She turned to thank the men who had accompanied her, all of them pointing reassuringly to where the street lights were just beginning to glow on the bridge. She shook several hands and began to walk the fifty metres which would take her out of the shanty, but just at that moment she saw the dim lights of a vehicle turning down from the road. Slowly, it bumped its way down the slope and, as its lights steadied and headed towards her, she heard the tune of 'Pop Goes the Weasel' being played at volume across the slum. The children who had followed Clara all around the shanty danced and scampered excitedly in front of the van as it rolled to a halt, still announcing its joyful presence even though only one or two dark figures approached the brightly lit window, their faces gleaming in the coloured lights. Clara stared up at the familiar, illuminated sign with the words 'Ice Cream' over the rounded top of the cab and then at the high chromium grill of the old Morris, knowing that it was exactly the same kind of van that she herself had run to in the summers of her childhood. Alone now except for Chitra, the lurch of familiarity proved too much and silent tears began to run down her face, hidden by the increasing rain. She stopped on the path that would lead her out of the shanty and, as she looked up at the blurred lights of the van, something which had held firm in her seemed to collapse unbidden. Feelings so hot and intense inside her seemed to melt down all other concerns, sweeping away fixed things, releasing chaos. She hurried past the van and began to climb the steep slope to the road. Traffic was passing by normally as she reached the top, breathless from her exertions and her crying. Chitra was still there at her side, looking alarmed. She knelt down to hug the little boy who had stayed with her for the whole afternoon. He smiled back reassuringly and she gave him several notes from her purse, pointing back down the slope to the other children and to the ice-cream van which had already run out of customers and now stood as if stranded in the gathering gloom.

A blast of car horns passed by on either side as she stood in the middle of the road, blinded by her tears. Misjudging the speed of an oncoming bus, she almost stumbled into the gutter on the far side of the road and was struggling to recover herself when she heard a mild English-sounding voice at her side.

'Can I perhaps be of some help?'

She did not want to look up but had no choice. Bending over her was a handsome, broad-featured face, the large head shaven and shining against the black background of an umbrella. Only concern was written in the face and, glowing through her tears, she recognised the resplendent yellow robes of one of the island's monks.

'No. Thank you. I'll be all right in a moment,' said Clara, aware that everything in her tearful face contradicted this.

'This is my home right here,' he said, pointing across the street, 'I am sure that taking a cup of tea would help.'

Clara smiled and allowed herself to be gently steered across the side road, the monk holding the huge umbrella over her, shielding her from the traffic and the rain.

'Would you mind removing your shoes?' he said mildly, stepping out of his own leather sandals on the threshold. There was more than a hint of humour in the voice. Clara's sandals were in such a mess that she did not at first see that the request had any other significance. Quickly realising, she smiled again and stepped out of the elegant sling-backs with their detritus of mud and drains.

Not a word was said until tea came. Clara occupied herself by looking for more tissues in her bag and pushing her hair back from her face, consumed by embarrassment and trying but failing to find her composure, relight the lamp of her invulnerability. The monk brought her a clean white towel and smiled down at her. After a moment, he moved to the doorway and shook the black umbrella outside. Unhurriedly, he negotiated it back through the doorway and propped it against the wall in one corner of the room. Instead of windows, walls of fretted stonework allowed the small breeze and the rain-freshened air to enter. He took a seat on a wooden bench facing the comfortable cane armchair in which she now sat fumbling with the towel and her tissue, trying to tidy herself up.

Tea was brought by a young man who disappeared again without looking at her. Calmly, the monk poured the thick liquid and added three large spoonfuls of sugar which had caked slightly from the damp.

Still he said nothing, and even his silence seemed to exert no pressure on her, so that she felt it quite natural to finish the first cup before offering him a brief and unsatisfactory explanation of the events that had led to her distressed appearance at the roadside.

He did not reply for some time, but poured her more tea and seemed to be looking through the carved stones to the street outside. Clara had never seen anyone of such an even, unblemished colour, a light olive, as if he were made for the soft and glowing folds of orange which draped his body and swept up gracefully across one shoulder. It was a part of his almost startling calm, this glowing health, this physical beauty, but it was his eyes which warned Clara that the challenges of this day were not yet over. When she remembered those eyes in later years, it was the attractive crease of humour that she thought of, but now it was the steady, open look which startled her, telling her that he was seeing herself and not himself reflected in her, feeling her confusion, jumping to no conclusions, reaching for no tried responses, aware that something uncommon had come before him.

He pushed the sugar bowl towards her. When he spoke, his voice was unexpectedly matter-of-fact.

'Have you thought what would have happened if you had found this man you were looking for?' he said.

'I would have helped him,' Clara said, too quickly.

There was a pause. The monk also took a sip of black tea.

'Perhaps.'

There was another silence, in which Clara was silently invited to examine the reaction of family, wife, parents, neighbours, community, had she succeeded in doing such an extraordinary thing as hunting down a young man in the slums to press a large sum of money upon him. She guessed that the rumours would already be flying about Vijay's dismissal, and she thought of what wild and uncontradicted exaggerations and inventions could by now have surrounded the tale and how much she might have added to them by her escapade of this afternoon. She looked up at the man who had made her think all this with just a word.

'Perhaps not,' she said, feeling another dimension of her defeat. The sound of traffic and car horns through the open stonework seemed far away.

'It was brave of you to go into the shanty,' he said reflectively, without flattery.

'I thought I was sure to find him,' she said, 'but I suppose there are lots of slums like that.'

He smiled at her patiently. 'The place you were in is a shanty,' he said. 'The slums are much more difficult to find.'

Her look showed her confusion, and he explained briefly. 'It would have been a long search anyway,' he concluded. 'There are maybe a quarter of a million people living in slums and shanties.'

'Is this all you have been doing on your holiday?' he asked, the crease of humour appearing again at the eyes. Clara told him a little about her days lying in the sun, getting tired of trying to relax, and her decision to try to see something of the ordinary life of the city. Then found herself struggling for a lightness of tone, and tried to veer away from the edge.

'You speak better English than I do,' she said, giving an impression of recovering herself, returning to normality. 'Where were you educated?'

He looked at her with barely disguised amusement, and in an instant she saw the gulf of the absurd opening under her question. Once more she was taken aback by how much he could make her think by saying nothing at all. She watched the corners of his mouth turn into a smile whose attractiveness slightly alarmed her.

'I studied for some little time in Edinburgh. Also more recently in Toronto. But tell me, what else have you seen?' He was serious again, but the only pressure came from within.

Clara paused for a second, her habitual girding on of armour struggling with some new instinct to discard protection. As lightly as she could, she told him of her weekend trip to the north, but could not help adding that she had also found herself in tears at the top of the great rock at Mihintale.

'And when was the last time you cried before today and the day before yesterday?' he asked, the creases reappearing so that Clara smiled too.

'A long time ago. When I was a child probably.' Her defences rallied briefly at finding herself talking in this way to a priest. 'I should tell you,' she said, provoked by his expectant silence, 'I'm not a religious person. I never could be.' The instant the words were out she felt utterly foolish. The expression on the monk's face changed not an iota.

'Why are you looking like that?' she asked.

'This is the expression I wear when absolutely any reaction would have something profoundly wrong with it,' he said. 'They teach it to you at the seminary. Now why don't you tell me all over again. Take a little longer if you wish.'

She smiled again at his gentle teasing. Her resentment died of its own shallowness. And in the same moment the ties snapped that bound her to the image of herself, and she abandoned the defences that imprisoned her.

It was not an elegant dissertation. She had never presented anything so incoherently in her life, or cared so little for the impression of herself that her words created. It was a clumsy, uncontrolled stumbling from one fragment to another of the unrelated truths she thought she might have come near to in her days on the ocean front and her journey to the north. She related to him as best she could why she had come to the island in the first place, throwing out un-prepackaged sentences to tell him of the faltering enthusiasm, like a disease that could no longer be ignored, of the leaden effort which even supposed pleasures had become, of her suspicion that no genuine passion or motivation was keeping her aloft, only routine and approval, of the frightening sense that something at her core was shrivelling, of her sense of withdrawal to a remote inner cave from which she was forced to watch and listen as she went about her life, of her growing sense that she was cut off from all source of sustenance, of renewal, of the fear that she would be unable to continue. She told him obliquely of the kind of challenges that awaited her on her return, and of her certainty that they were not the real challenges. Finally, going forward knowing that she could not avoid tears, she told him of her realisation that the people she knew, even those whom she was supposed to love and be loved by, had gradually become no more than people to be endured, people to help or hinder her progress, people who were only audiences for her gratification, and of her gradual realisation that even those who were supposed to be close to her now seemed to be retreating, seeing that she was incapable of anything except going through the motions, that they were withdrawing and leaving her behind, she who could not love. Walls that could have withstood a siege came down unbidden. Thoughts and fears were seized unripened, worries that had not been dressed in words were turned out in rags into the world, anxieties and foolishnesses rushed into the sudden breach, seizing their chance to escape, until eventually she stopped, not at any conclusion, but because exposed, spent, not knowing even now whether she was in the middle of something significant or an absurd, embarrassing collapse brought on only by the coincidence of her disorientation in the shanty and the chance meeting with a stranger to whom she had been able to talk as she would never have talked to anyone that she knew.

'Other than that,' she added, trying to return to the Clara that could cope, to lighten the tone, ease her embarrassment, 'I want you to know that you're talking to a very successful woman.'

The monk ignored the remark.

'Family?'

She told him the facts. A mother. A sister. Two nieces. All living more than two hundred miles away. Visits at Christmas, occasionally in between.

'Work?'

She could not face giving him the details. With a smile that tried to be ironic, she gave him one of the small white business cards from her wallet, watching as he raised his eyebrows and slightly sucked in his olive cheeks. 'I've come a long way,' she said, and looked at him with a genuine humility.

He gave it back to her. 'You certainly seem to have come a long way this week.'

Despite herself, Clara fell onto the defensive again. 'Aren't you supposed to say something, now,' she said, 'make sense of it all with religion?' The remark landed with a cheap clatter between them, and she tried to retract it with her eyes. He saw, and did not bother to pick it up.

'And which Clara Lane did you present to our friend Vijay, the one on the card or the one who is sitting here taking tea?'

Clara hesitated.

'You think it was wrong of me to arrange the meetings?'

The monk looked as though the question was not one that would have occurred to him.

'To make friends? To try to learn something? No, what you did was not wrong.' There was the slightest suggestion of an emphasis on the 'did'. Clara leapt on it.

'You mean it's what I am that's wrong?'

'Not you in particular. It's just that it is sometimes difficult for other people to cope with your world. Even just being aware of it from a distance, as it normally is. And if that world is suddenly presented in one person, a person who not only seems to represent all its . . . potency . . . but who also singles you out for . . . personal attention . . . then it might . . . intensify the problem . . . the problem of how you . . . place yourself . . . cope with things that are already difficult to cope with.'

Clara thought. The monk watched. At length, he spoke.

'What knowledge you have acquired, lying in the sun,' he smiled, 'could of course fade with the very beautiful tan.'

Clara smiled back at him but made no reply. She desperately wanted him to go on, torn between a superficial resistance to the idea that a priest would have anything to say to her and a suspicion, even a hope, that this man might have something to offer that she had not encountered before.

'At some time you will have looked into a river and seen a fish, and not wanted to take your eyes from it because when you look again you will not be able to see it, even though it will still be there.' It was not a question. 'When you go back to London,' he looked donnishly down his nose at Clara's card which he still held in his hand, and said with a certain mock distaste, 'or any of these other similar places,' he looked again at Clara, 'it will also be quite difficult for you to see again the things you have just been telling me.'

Clara remained silent. 'Why are all your religions so strong on analogies?' she said, one Clara once more regretting letting the other one speak.

He thought for a while as if genuinely interested in the question. At length he began again. 'Because of course they are vaguely applicable to a wide variety of different situations, and are therefore most useful to those in our profession. Also, they are non-committal, and hard to contradict, and this too is useful.' There was another pause. 'Also, they challenge the listener to find the point, the applicability, so that one realises it for oneself rather then being told by someone else – always pedagogically more powerful I think.' He looked up at the ceiling fan for a few moments. 'And if the meaning is not perceived,' he went on, 'then it can be said that it is the listener's fault, not the speaker's – also quite convenient. And then there is the weight of historical tradition, of speaking in parables, the Lord Buddha, the Lord Jesus, and so on. So it is probably because an analogy does all of these things whilst at the same time giving the impression of deep and incontrovertible wisdom which, of course, a priest must always try to cultivate.' He smiled again and waited for her to speak.

'I read a few verses of the Dhammapada,' she said eventually.

'What about your own Bible?'

'I don't find that much help either.'

'Not even the bit about having to lose yourself to find yourself? Surely that would have been worth five minutes of your time lying in the sun?'

Clara was taken aback. It was her turn to be silent and wait.

'I can see you really do want me to give you the religious answer,' he suggested at length. She looked at him, knowing he was both teasing her and being serious.

'Ready?' he asked, hitching the robe higher on his shoulder.

'Yes, begin,' she said, trying herself to catch the same note of humour and seriousness.

'There was once a very successful businesswoman,' he began, looking at her, the little creases appearing all around his eyes. 'Her universe was very much bigger than most people's.' He placed the little white business card with a small snap on the table between them.

'She was especially good at certain things, and she was at the same time encouraged from all sides to believe that these things that she was especially good at were especially important. Naturally, therefore,' he spread his hands palms upwards over the table, 'she came to believe that her life was especially important because she was especially good at these especially important things.' He smiled again at her, renewing his discourse with a slight frown of concentration.

'Eventually she also came to think, without really knowing that she was thinking it, that her own life was in fact much more significant than most.' He gave her his mock-priestly smile and continued with only a slight pause. 'Now, two things very naturally began to happen. The first was that it became very obvious to her that it was the things she was especially good at which brought her the approval of others, and eventually brought also great rewards. And so it happened that doing these things became . . . her foundation. All of her confidence was built on them. Almost, one might say, she herself was built on them. And so she ceased to pay much regard to those other things about her, those other qualities of human beings which are perhaps . . . more ordinary . . . less rare or special . . . but which are of course not necessarily less important.' He smiled and looked at her for long seconds.

Eventually the priest looked away through the fretted stone-work of his walls, and seemed for a few moments to go off into a world of his own. With another little frown, he turned to her again.

'So the other parts of herself became, shall we say, neglected, starved, as she left her first youth and entered what should have been her maturity all the while confusing her self with her capacities, staying on the ground where she felt strong, where she could always cope, be approved of, attract favourable reviews, so to speak. And so, in time, these abilities of hers became her, rather than just an attribute of her. She had become . . . her own importance. And the building she had erected on these foundations was necessarily a strange affair, though no one seemed to notice this because, of course, there were a great many such buildings all around her.'

The young man who had brought the tea appeared in the inner doorway and made a slight gesture with his hand. The priest nodded once to him. The sounds of the city seemed to have died away as he looked back to Clara for a sign that he should go on. Clara sat back in the wicker chair and waited.

'The second thing that happened to the young lady, because she was especially good at the things which were specially important, was that she came to have what can only be described as an almost infinite secular choice. And having almost infinite choice, and a conviction that her life was very special, she came to have quite an extraordinary level of expectation . . . I might say an altogether *new* level of expectation. And all around her, every second of every day, she was hearing that all of these choices she could make, all of the things she could have and do, would make her life perfect, exciting, fulfilled.'

A truck went by outside and the room which had seemed so

cut off vibrated slightly with its weight. From somewhere in the far distance, Clara could hear the notes of 'Pop Goes the Weasel' above the sounds of the evening rush hour. The monk's face had become a darker olive in the deepening gloom as he placed his palms together and continued with his story.

'At first, things seemed to go well. As long as perfection and fulfilment were in the future, then it was still of course possible to believe in them. But as the future started to become the present, and the fulfilment did not quite come, the first doubts began of course to creep in. Deprived of the consummation she had expected, and knowing of only one means, she strived all the harder in the same direction. Others became only a means . . . and, as you say, an audience by whose applause her progress could be measured. They could not exist in their own right in her world, and, inevitably, they began to retreat from it.'

The young man reappeared and began lighting an oil lamp over the doorway. There was a pause as the flame slowly grew, reflecting softly in the olive skin and lending the saffron robes a quiet glow as the priest continued.

'Meanwhile, with so much of herself retreating almost without her knowing, for only a small part of herself had come to matter to her, she could not of course find any of the fulfilment and perfection she had for so long been expecting. She may have striven even harder, succeeded even more, but of course no amount of more of the same can satisfy a longing for something different.'

He looked at her and Clara, who had never listened so long, knew that her eyes hid very little.

'Go on,' she said, still trying to keep a light tone to her voice. 'I want to know what became of her in the end.'

The monk looked down at the tiled floor and his shaven head gleamed in the light of the lamp. He looked up once more into her eyes.

'What became of her I do not know. In her emptying world no real fulfilment, satisfaction, contentment, was possible. Yet as she grew older, every decision seemed so very important, because it really was time now that her life became as wonderful as she had been led to expect it would be. And so her many choices became anxieties, because she worried that if they were not the right choices then they might not, after all, take her in the direction of this fulfilment that had been promised so long. Her choices and advances and acquisitions turned into worries, doubts, frustrations, because they were not bringing what they were supposed to bring, what all her world around her had always told her they would bring.' He shrugged. 'And so of course her decisions became ever more anxious and her fulfilment ever more distant. Probably, also, there was a growing sense, as the years passed, that the things she was doing were a waste of one's limited time on earth, but she had no way of acting on this because the concept of wasted time implies that time is for doing something, something other, better, than what one is now doing, but of course she did not know what that something was, did not know what time was for.'

There was a long silence.

'But you must tell me,' said the priest eventually, 'what *you* think happened to her in the end?'

Clara had been trying to think about what he had said, but even at this hour she was drawn back into thinking about appearances.

'I expect it all got too much for her and she finally collapsed and got religion,' she said, unable to stop herself from speaking in a way that she despised for its glibness and that completely contradicted her state of mind. It was as if the monk knew. He pulled the little bench a little closer to her. Outside in the street it was almost dark.

'Let us forget about religion,' he said, pulling the robe back up onto the shoulder. 'You are suspicious because you see it as a kind of self-surrender, and you are right to be so suspicious because that is what makes religion so dangerous, so open to such constant abuse by those who believe themselves to be religious.'

She stared up at him in the gloom. She saw now that his concentration was total.

'But you must ask yourself,' he said with a simple intensity, 'what other means are you going to use? How are you going to nourish that which is starved, re-establish contact, raise the possibility of renewal?'

Clara looked as if she might be losing the thread. He leaned forward slightly and looked at her with more intensity than she had ever endured, and despite herself she suddenly felt helpless against the full power of his conviction, his authority, as she looked into the eyes of all that she had been unable to see.

'Clara,' he said slowly, 'Empathy the only God. Ego the only Devil. The road between the only struggle.'

After a long pause, he smiled his serious smile. Outside, the rain had stopped and it was growing cool. Eventually he leaned back further on the bench and continued in more matter-of-fact tones.

'It is of course the hardest road, no matter who you are. Even if you are a priest of the temple. And unfortunately there is no getting to the end of it, no destination, only the journey. The struggle is all there is. And it is such a silent, invisible struggle, so deep inside, that it cannot often be seen even by oneself. That is one reason why people need all these wonderful outside things to help, the bibles and the words of the Buddha, the prophets and saints and miracles, the commandments in stone and the shining eight-fold paths, the sacraments and relics and shrines and pilgrimages, the churches and the *dagobas* and the temples, the hymns, prayers, chants, sermons. Most people need such little regular sustenances along the way. And above all, Clara, they usually feel the need to join with others, others who are sharing, trying, succeeding, failing, resolving to do better, being forgiven.'

He had gradually leaned forward again as he spoke the litany.

'But you, you Clara, you are going to do it all on your own. And in just twelve days. And with only a sunlounger.'

Clara smiled and looked down at the towel in her hands. He waited until she raised her eyes, unsmiling.

'But perhaps that is not challenge enough,' he continued, straightening, 'and so not only will you not enlist any of these other forces that so many millions have found necessary over the centuries, but you will in fact do exactly the opposite. You will make sure that all the other things by which you surround yourself are, if at all possible, pulling you the other way. He picked up the little business card from the table between them and held it up with the fingers and thumb of both hands as if it were an icon. 'All the prophets and bibles of the world you inhabit, all its priests and rituals and sacraments, all the structures of values and beliefs in which you immerse yourself day after day, year after year, all that you really give the power of your mind and your life to, all the standards by which you have agreed that people are to be judged, all the subtle and not-so-subtle criteria by which it is decided that others will be impressed, all of the examples of achievement you have set before you, all of the symbols of success you have behind you, all of these, all of them, will be pulling you the other way.'

He was leaning forward again now, his eyes seeking hers.

'But you, just you, without any help from anybody else, you will change your direction against all of this, you and your twelve days, you and your sunlounger, will you Clara Lane?'

He saw the sadness in her smile and the creases appeared again around his eyes and at the corners of his mouth.

'You will think I am ridiculing you, but that is not the case,' he continued. She looked up at him, surprised at a tone of voice which seemed to suggest a sadness of his own.

'In fact you and your sunlounger may now be the only way.'

She saw that he was not teasing and frowned in puzzlement at the unexpected direction he was taking.

'If there are to be those who will continue the struggle into the future, those who will see that this is the only journey worth the making, and are prepared to set out on it however difficult it may be; if, I would say, there is to be any hope at all, then more and more, I suspect, they will have to be people like you, people who start off on the journey almost alone, against much greater odds than in the past, and with far less help. Compared to this, those who have religion have it easy. The monk, the priest, perhaps has it easiest of all.'

He smiled a lighter, sadder smile and she sensed that the conversation was drawing to an end. He looked out into the street from which she had entered under his protection.

'Only time will tell us if it can be done your way. And I fear for you because it is known how difficult the journey is, even taking the easiest of routes, well-signposted every step of the way, with all possible sustenance. To do it your way would be truly heroic. Truly inspiring. I do not know if you will.'

He looked at her, and in his priest's eyes she saw close up the hills which she had glimpsed in the far distance as she lay in the sun, saw clearly the heroism he had spoken of, saw what it would take to strike out in the direction of her inabilities, her weaknesses. She could not leave with this onus upon her without sending him some signal of her humility.

'You talk as if I am bravely setting off,' she said seriously, 'but I don't even know the direction to go, or even how to put one foot in front of the other.'

'I am a priest of the temple. I could show you my way. But I cannot show you your way.'

Clara stared at the smooth concrete floor. Eventually, she heard the sound of two or three people praying in another room.

'Could I ring for a taxi?' she asked. The monk turned and eventually spoke a few words into the bakelite telephone sitting on his desk. He looked once more at Clara, and she could see that the conversation had in some way saddened him. Standing up abruptly, she pushed herself towards a small cheerfulness for his sake.

'Do they also teach you at the seminary to look at people as though you know what they are thinking even when you don't?'

'Oh, but I do. You are thinking that you can't believe that you've been sitting here talking like this to a priest.' She pretended to frown at him while laughing at his acuity.

'Tell me,' she said, reaching out and almost touching the glowing robe, 'do you really have to weave the cloth by yourself, and pick the saffron?'

'As you're seeking after truth this afternoon,' he answered with a very serious face, 'I must tell you that we import it from Germany exactly as it is.'

Clara and the priest smiled at each other, united for a second in the doorway. Clara bent to put on her mud-caked sandals. Straightening, she turned to thank him, knowing that her words would be inadequate.

'I won't forget this afternoon,' she began, sounding far more formal than she intended. She gave up and simply looked at him. There was a silence, and the strange feeling of something like a uniting happiness passed through her again. The noise drifted across the road from the shanty, where some of the children were still calling after her as she stepped into the street.

'I feel guilty,' she said abruptly, turning towards him at the kerb. 'It's very conceited to think that I can just come here and take up your time. There are people over there who need your help a lot more than I do.'

'That, Clara,' said the monk, smiling, 'is the only really conceited thing you've said this afternoon.'

36

'Thatha, I must know how you have done this.'

Chandra spoke in Sinhala, for on this subject there must be no possibility of misunderstanding; she too had heard what happened to young women who went to the Gulf by the back door.

Godfrey told her about the meeting with the younger Mahmoud, giving her the facts with none of the relish which, for as long as she had known him, had always accompanied his stories of gambles won, disputes settled, deals done.

'So I leave tomorrow,' said Chandra after a few seconds cold thought, a dreadful distance in her voice.

'If not going back into shanty, then I am thinking nothing else for it.'

Chandra looked at him and gave him a light, brave grin. Her mind was already made up. To her consternation, she saw tears threaten in the old man's eyes.

'Chandra,' he said, looking down, 'you know if . . . just for self only . . . I am million times happier living in shanty and not having Chandra in Gulf.' His eyes filled and he looked away as she took his arm.

At that moment Premawathie mounted the two steps onto the verandah and glared first at the back of Godfrey's head with a piercing venom and then questioningly, despairingly, at her daughter-in-law.

'It is tomorrow night, Amma,' said Chandra, trying but failing to make her voice sound light.

Premawathie came and gripped both her arms.

'It is *kodivina*,' she said miserably, with another hate-filled look at her husband. Chandra could not bear to hear it discussed again. Her mind turned swiftly to what had to be done.

'Problem is photo, also medical certificate,' she said matter-of-factly. 'I am having to ask Vijay for two hundred rupees.' Godfrey unbuttoned the top pocket of his shirt and pulled out five folded one hundred rupee notes.

'Where you are getting?' said Chandra in amazement. Premawathie stared at the money in her husband's hand.

'I am winning,' said Godfrey, and sheepishly explained that the Cheltenham Corner had had to keep on accepting some bets on the winners so as not to arouse suspicion. 'As long as bet is small only, they are taking,' he said. 'These days I am having lot of small bets.'

Premawathie almost spat at him in her contempt.

'Money is for *thovilaya*. That is why we are having *kodivina*. Because of betting and living of low life by Godfrey Jayasinghe.' She reached out her hand for the money.

As Godfrey was about to hand her the notes, Chandra moved to his side and quickly took them from him. She turned to face Premawathie.

'Money we are having now, Amma, we are using for best. Better to be burning than spending for *thovilaya*.'

'No good is coming until we are lifting *kodivina*,' said Premawathie fiercely, thrusting out her hand, demanding the money with all her mustered ferocity. Chandra put the folded notes behind her back and faced her mother-in-law.

'These people making me sick, sick, Amma, you are hearing? They are taking money and cheating, cheating people when having troubles. Not one cent from this house is going to that woman. Not one cent, you are hearing?'

So loud and unexpected was the outburst that Premawathie stood for several seconds with her hand out and her mouth open. Godfrey also stared, as if he expected lightning to strike at Chandra through the narrow strip of daylight between the roofs. The noise of the garden suddenly seemed etched against a dreadful silence as Chandra held her mother-in-law's eyes until the old lady slowly broke into sobs. Chandra steered her gently inside. Godfrey hitched his sarong and took the opportunity to make his escape through the wall.

✳

Vijay sat with Chandra out on the verandah. Susil was asleep and Godfrey had not returned. Premawathie could not bear to sit out and remained inside, standing in the darkness with her back to the kitchen wall.

'So having to go,' Chandra concluded, as if she were talking about going to Havelock Town or Mount Lavinia. 'I am thinking it is only way.'

Vijay did not look at her but continued to stare tight-lipped down the garden. At length he spoke, without turning his head.

'You are not going to Gulf,' he said quietly, almost casually, as if thinking about something else. Chandra had remained silent, letting him think it through. After a while he appeared not to be thinking about it at all, and she spoke gently to him again.

'So going back to shanty?'

Vijay did not reply. After a minute he lit another cigarette.

'And what is happening to Susil?' he said, much later, his voice strained.

'I am thinking all time what is happening to Susil,' she replied, no longer trying to make light of the decision. 'Shanty is not any longer same, Vijay. It is not place where Vijay and Chandra are growing. Ten times more of people are there now. Desperate people now, Vijay. No space any more. Half time no water they are telling. River is sewer. Not only disease is there now, Vijay. Now also violence. Drugs. Everything. I am thinking Susil cannot be growing in such a place.'

There was another long pause. Vijay looked down at his hands. The cigarette was crushed at both sides by the tension in his fingers. He seemed to have stopped breathing. At length he blew the smoke out through his nostrils with grim determination, as though he had come to some decision.

'You are not going to Gulf,' he said again, but there was only desperation in his voice as he looked up towards the garden wall.

Chandra let him ponder.

'Thousands of women going to Gulf and returning, Vijay. It is two years only. We are never having opportunity again.'

Vijay's face remained fixed in opposition. He reached into his shirt pocket for his packet of cigarettes and turned it over and over in his hand. Chandra waited for several minutes more before quietly asking him.

'You are also taking Amma back into shanty, Vijay?'

After a few seconds, Vijay stood up and left the garden without a word.

Half an hour later, Chandra also slipped through the wall and caught a bus to the Fort, from where she made her way to the immigration office in Chaitya Road.

37 ∫

As Vijay stepped through the wall the evening wood-smoke rose from a hundred fires so that the huddled roofs of the shanty appeared to be smouldering as they sagged towards the canal. Instead of taking the top path, through what had become almost a tunnel between the shanty and the garden wall, he zigzagged down through the jungle of planks and plaited palms, dipping through the alleyways in the general direction of the bridge. Without stopping he exchanged greetings as here and there a voice called his name. It was almost impossible now to find the house in which he had been born, so overgrown had the shanty become with hastily erected extensions thrown up overnight to accommodate hopeful cousins arriving from some dry-zone village and just needing a place to stay for a few weeks while they established themselves in the city. Eventually he came to the rusting iron winch which had once served some purpose on the canal and which had always been the landmark by which, as a child, he had found his way home. The house no longer stood alone. It was merged into a group of dilapidated shacks, its roof sunk low and in need of repair where the brittle cadjan was breaking on the poles. The open space outside the door where he had played his games or sat listening to his father's stories had long ago been swallowed up. As he stopped to look down the dark, narrow alley, a child of about four, naked except for a pair of khaki shorts, buttons missing down the front and tied at the waist with string, came running out of the doorway. He stopped when he saw Vijay, his large eyes the only life in a dust-dry face, like pools remaining long after the rain. His upper arm was loosely bandaged with a bluish rag stained brown with old blood; scratches and sores interrupted the caked mud on his feet and ankles. Deciding that Vijay was not threatening, the boy sat down with his back to the hut and began throwing small stones at the chickens who were scratching about in the alleyway, lifting their scrawny legs high out of the mud, gleaning the furrows. Flies played on the boy's neck and ankles and a flea-ridden dog muzzled him as he looked up at Vijay. He began throwing the little stones into a puddle outside the door of the next-door shack.

Vijay set off again through the maze of beaten earth and soft mud where the sunlight never reached. Women were queuing down one of the alleyways and, coming to an unrecognised crossroads, he saw that they were waiting for water that drizzled grudgingly into buckets and cans. With a shock he recognized the tap as the one that he had used almost all his life. The open area all around it had gone; dozens of little shacks now crowded around the concrete apron where as a boy he had played cricket so often for his country. Just ahead of him as he dropped towards the canal bank he saw a woman spill the hard-won water from the aluminium pot on her hip as she was knocked into the planked wall by a fierce-looking man coming in the opposite direction; Vijay, following behind, stepped into a doorway to avoid being barged as the young man kept on coming with long unseeing strides, his eyes blazing and his reddened lips pulled back in a snarl as he ploughed through the shanty heedless of anything but the visions raging in his head.

He broke through onto the canal front, still some way short of the bridge. A dozen men were standing almost up to the tops of their sarongs in the slowly flowing waters, lazily rubbing water onto their arms and chests. Further down, at the point where a shallow bay made entry to the canal easier, a group of women were rubbing white soap onto clothes stretched out over the rocks at the water's edge. Others were standing further out in the stream, working in pairs, dunking the soaped shirts and sarongs into the heavy green waters, lifting them out again, twisting them until the water stopped coming and the little bubbles of soap floated away under the bridge.

Vijay reached the end of the shanty, but instead of climbing as usual to the road he ducked low under the first arch of the bridge and disappeared into its shadows. Inside, he found the damp flat-topped stone that he remembered. Hidden in the semi-darkness, staring down into the waters which flowed suddenly faster in an effort to squeeze their volume between the massive stone supports of the bridge, he sat for a while, the dank, mossy stones resting on his back as the underside of the bridge curved out towards the first of the dark pillars.

Slowly, as the water rushed before his eyes in heedless white furrows, he let the facts advance and be recognised. He would not find another job. Thousands of people had been laid off. He needed almost the whole amount of the rent loan. But the news could not be kept from K. W. Matthew or anyone else who might lend him money, even at five per cent a month. And even if he could borrow, he could not repay. There was no way out. He forced himself to confront the practicalities of living in whatever place in the shanty they could find, somewhere at the eastern edge he imagined, close to where the new arrivals were crowding the city rubbish tip and far from the dribbling tap. He saw the five of them trying to arrange their bed-boards on the earth floor of the same room, saw Chandra queuing in the long line down the alleyway, washing in the canal that was downstream from a hundred latrines, being barged into by men driven by the heroin coursing in their veins. And he saw Susil, sitting in the little space outside the hut throwing stones into a puddle and, later, struggling to do his homework amid the crowds and the flies and the noise. He imagined Godfrey, taking it philosophically, missing his verandah. Finally he summoned up the picture of his mother clutching her battered tin trunk as she stepped back through the wall into the shanty that she had not set foot in since they had moved to the slum. The picture could not be sustained. He knew that his mother would not do it, knew also the way out that she would take, the way that others had taken before her, and the certainty of it seemed to bring the weight of the bridge down upon him. He fixed his gaze on the dark waters not an arm's length in front of his face, rushing by in deep, steady furrows, sharp ridges tinged with a dirty white as they streamed through towards the light. He tried telling himself that many families had made sacrifices in order to be able to send a wife or a daughter to the Gulf, that it was astonishing good fortune that Godfrey had been able to arrange it all without having thousands of rupees for the signing-on fee. He looked at the bright arc of light where the water rushed out again into the next stretch of the canal and widened out into the evening sun, and he knew that it was the only way they could stay in the garden. Slowly he lowered his head into his hands. And when the surge of shame and misery had fully claimed him, he looked up into the rushing waters and tried to tell himself that the two years would pass quickly, that tens of thousands of young mothers had gone as housemaids to the Middle East, that tens of thousands of their children were being brought up by aunts and grandmothers all over the slums of the city, and that by the time Chandra returned he would have made good his mistake and found another job. But even as he tried to force himself to stay on the foaming ridges of hope that moved rapidly towards the last of the daylight, the vast volume of his thoughts was flowing in the darkness below, thoughts of his wife being torn away from all that she knew and all that she loved, thoughts of his son not understanding what had happened to the mother who had been there almost every minute of his life, thoughts which ran on and on into ever new manifestations of the calamity he had brought upon them all. He lowered his head again, his little efforts to reduce the proportions of his despair swept away as he stared into the black truth of the evil waters flowing before his eyes.

He shivered in the deep shade and half stood to slither out from under the arch. Heading for nowhere he crossed the bridge, the blade turning inside him, goring his stomach, his chest, his lungs, so that it became insupportable and he plunged this way and that, desperate for any temporary relief.

'*Aday*, Vijay Jayasinghe, why the king so worried, man?' His arms were grabbed and he recognized Kit, a young man of about his own age whom he had known vaguely since childhood and who still lived in the shanty.

'The king has lost his job,' said Vijay.

'*Aiyo* Vijay!' said the young man, his playful grip turning to the light touch of consolation. He had a friend with him whom Vijay did not know.

'No tourists, no waiters,' said Vijay, grateful that he had an explanation that was both brief and convincing.

'Lost my job too,' smiled the other man, speaking in dialect.

'So I'm the only one in luck,' said Kit who as far as Vijay knew had never had a job. He glanced sideways and leaned towards Vijay. 'Fifty bucks at six to one,' he said, patting his shirt pocket. 'We're just going across to have a drink on it.' He turned Vijay by the arm to steer him back over the bridge. Vijay had never much warmed to Kit, but he had no direction himself, and felt desperately in need of a drink.

Soon the three men were climbing the stairs of the little hotel up to a first-floor room which Godfrey would have recognised but which Vijay had never seen before. The walls were of smooth concrete, bare apart from a few assorted calendars from different years. They sat down on plastic chairs around a packing case on which stood a saucer of curried prawns and a Players tobacco-tin lid overflowing with cigarette ends. The floor was the same bare concrete, its meandering cracks filled with dirt.

'Three toddies, chasers,' called Kit to a sunken-cheeked man who had followed them up the stairs. Vijay stared at the floor. Cigarette buts, bottle tops, and bits of food and broken concrete edging had accumulated in the cracks. The drinks came, each tall glass of sweet white toddy accompanied by a smaller, heavier glass of arrack. Another unshaven man wearing a filthy striped sarong had joined them and the three of them had started talking about the bets they had won, leaving Vijay to stare blankly at the wall. Soon the drink had diffused through him with an anaesthetic glow and the knife in his stomach had slowed its turning. He heard Kit shouting down the stairs and, after a few moments, the old man appeared again with a bottle of arrack and another saucer containing two untidy, hand-rolled cigarettes.

Vijay silently held out his glass for the arrack as Kit's friend lit one of the loose cigarettes and took a deep drag.

'Well, fuck the job anyway,' said the friend in a mixture of languages, looking at Vijay who was wondering how the man could speak without losing any of the smoke.

'What job was it?' said Vijay.

'Docks,' replied the other, leaning forward to hand him the cigarette.

Vijay knew he was talking about casual labour, not a job; he had probably only been employed for a week or two. He accepted the cigarette and drew its odd, sweet taste into his lungs. The little room had filled up without him noticing and groups of men were playing cards or talking around the packing cases and metal tables as the smoke drifted up to deepen the blanket that was nestling comfortably against the ceiling.

As he sat back in his chair and let the smoke out slowly, a huge muscular man with a shaven head appeared at the top of the stairs carrying the wreck of an older man in his arms. He dropped his burden on the floor and disappeared. Vijay seemed to hear only the leather *chapals* slapping on the steps and he had the impression that the sound seemed to go on for far longer than the stairs. The man who had been dumped on the floor dragged himself across the concrete towards the first group of card players, the stumps of his dark legs like purses drawn tight with string. He was waving a book of coloured papers in one hand. The tickets, stamped 'national development lottery' were imperfectly perforated, and the old man needed both hands to tear them from the book, trying to balance himself, sitting up without legs so that Vijay involuntarily stiffened and moved his own muscles as if willing the man not to roll over sideways onto the concrete floor. His glass was filled again as he stared at the rough white scratches all over the grey skin on what was left of the man's thighs.

'So what happens now, man?' Kit was saying.

Vijay drew again on the loose cigarette and handed it back. Taking the smoke deep into his lungs he forced himself to say the words. 'My wife has just today got a housemaid job in Gulf.' As he spoke, realisation came to him anew, the words giving the awful truth flesh and blood, letting it out into the real world, its birth sending a powerful surge of pain and misery through his intestines. But his new companions greeted the news with brayings of appreciation and much slapping of hands on thighs, raising glasses which glinted and mocked him in the light of the bare bulb over the table.

'This is the best of all worlds, Vijay,' said Kit loudly. 'You don't have to work. The wife sends you good money every month. And no nagging. And for you, old friend,' he reached forward and put his hand on Vijay's knee, 'the field is free.' There was more laughter and he felt Kit punching him playfully in the hollow of his shoulder. 'You know my sister always fancied you, Vijay.' The other two men made obscene comments and laughed uproariously as Kit leaned back and began refilling all the glasses. Vijay smiled miserably. The old man was dragging himself over the floor. He bought a page of tickets and sat looking at them in the smoke and the noise, not knowing why he did not get up and leave. Tomorrow night, his wife would be gone. What was he doing here in this place with these men? Yet the glasses that kept being refilled and the cigarette that was still being passed from hand to hand seemed to keep something unthinkable at bay, to suspend time, postpone the world, as if whatever it was would not happen so long as he did not leave the cocoon of smoke and voices and the liquid that had at first been fierce but had now grown tame. Yet something overhanging inside his head seemed to tell him he should be going now, and he decided that in two more minutes he would go down the stairs again and out into the street. He stared at the old man who had now dragged himself round all the tables and was waiting patiently at the top of the stairs.

An hour later, he was still with Kit and several more strangers, only now they were sitting in a dark low-ceilinged parlour with fifty or sixty other men. Vijay had not noticed which way they had come through all the back streets but it did not matter; he could not get lost in Maligawatta. The heat must have been building up all day in the windowless room and he could smell the thousand-odoured breath and the stale sweat of the men staring at the video screen which provided the only light. As far as he could make out, a white couple were having sex; but they were being filmed from such a close up position that it was quite difficult to make out exactly what was happening. Suddenly the camera pulled back to reveal the man thrusting faster and faster into the woman, but Vijay had entered the dream world now and he saw only the piston like rhythms of light and dark, moving abstract shapes of light over the heads of men who stared and breathed and murmured like a mass of insects greedily clustered on some rotten fruit. He was becoming disoriented and he looked away, nausea filling his insides. For relief he stared at the flat, cool wall above the bar hatch. At length his eyes focused on the glass of a framed photograph; for several seconds he seemed to be able to see only the glass, but when he eventually broke through he saw that behind it was not a photograph at all but a certificate of long service from the Liptons Tea Company. It seemed to be saying that only the tips would do. Gradually he became aware that the man next to him was explaining that he too had a wife in the Gulf. 'Fantastic, fantastic,' he was saying, waving his cigarette around excitedly as he spoke. The glowing orange end of fine fire and the beautiful transient circles it made in the darkness fascinated Vijay and he followed them until the man, gaining no response, turned his attention again to the screen and Vijay looked away again in the direction of the cool wall. There, in the candle-lit serving hatch, someone was pouring from a huge jar, held in two disembodied hands. The liquid flowed magically into a fine muslin mesh which seemed to absorb it effortlessly; and then Vijay heard the splashing sound, rich and distinct, as if it were much closer, and saw that the liquid was passing though the cloth into a moving line of plastic jugs. He watched entranced as the harvest grew, the net beginning to writhe with centipedes, beetles, flies, caterpillars, the legs of spiders and the fragmented wings of cockroaches. Vijay looked at his drink. It was gone. Someone was tugging at his sleeve and he realised that for some time Kit's friend had been asking him for a cigarette. He fumbled in his shirt pocket. The packet was empty but the fingers took it away.

'One hit, then we're going for last race,' said the man who was not Kit but who now seemed to be leading the group. The words came from underneath the seat on the floor where the man was crouching on his knees, head down between the seats as if praying to the screen where the woman was writhing faster and faster to her climax while sixty men waited silently with parched throats and stinking breath. A match flared near Vijay's feet and exploded behind his retina. When the explosion died away he saw that the man was smoothing out the silver paper from the empty cigarette packet, drawing it between his finger and thumb until it stood out stiffly like the shining blade of a knife. Slowly he turned the knife over while another hand untwisted a screw of paper and gently tapped out a fine white powder onto the dull lining of the foil. The match went out and the little drama at his feet died, devoured by an irresistible blackness. His blood seemed to have run into his head and he looked up to the screen where the thrusting and gasping was becoming slower but louder and a woman's little cries were leaking more and more frequently over the heads of the crowd. A second match flared below and quickly dimmed to a red glow as it passed behind the foil. A dark liquid was running down the silver now, and a sharper smell was added to the dull stew in the room as Kit bent low over the altar, sucking smoke into his nose through the tube of card. After a few seconds he straightened, his eyes still closed as the tableau down below died again until another match exploded and another dark figure bent to pray. At length, after the match had flared and died several times at his feet, Vijay suddenly saw Kit's fist moving towards him, the end of the white tube suddenly growing larger. 'Vijay, just take one toot only,' he heard someone saying to him. 'All troubles are vanishing in here. Come and be a king again.'

The music had risen to a distorted crescendo and Vijay looked up at the screen where the camera was now close on the white woman's face and he saw with exquisite clarity the appalling falseness of her ecstasy. He rose and stumbled his way to the door.

It was dark when he stepped out through the heavy plastic beads of the doorway, dark and blissfully cool. Not knowing where he was, he walked towards the lights. Something in the air, a scent he knew, told him he was not in Maligawatta at all but somewhere downtown. He came out of the alley. He was in a residential street, and the pavements and the low walls and hedges seemed to have a vivid presence as if everything around him were more accessible. He slowed his pace. The pavement was marvellously solid beneath his feet, but the flagstones seemed to undulate softly as if he were walking on a heavy ocean of stone. On his left now was a hedge, each leaf a perfectly formed tongue reaching out to lick him over garden walls. Higher up, the lights of upstairs windows seemed to hang independently in the night, glaring down on him with a friendly flare as if the stars above had closed in to watch him sailing down his sea of stone. In the street, an age away, he saw a young man in gleaming white gliding slowly towards him on a bicycle. He stopped again, entranced by every clean click of every spoke and sprocket as the white shape cycled by. The hedge had somehow turned into a fat cream wall into whose broad inviting top broken pieces of glass had been set at angles, glinting dark and green like little wavelets as he passed. He stretched out his arm, feeling that he could have run his hand over the top of the wall, but instead letting it float and ride a few inches over the waves. As he reached the corner of the street he bumped into someone turning the opposite way and the ungainly confusion and clumsy disentanglement seemed a slow and graceful pirouetting away of two white figures in the gloom. He must keep walking, he told himself, keep walking because the evil that surrounded him was closing in, threatening to trap him where he was, becoming as weighty and solid as the beautiful pavement beneath his feet. And there was something urgent about its closing, something it would have him do tonight. The next corner seemed familiar to him and he crossed the road and began walking towards a distant throb of music and a dull orange glow in the night sky.

Soon only the well-known road separated him from the dark expanse of Galle Face Green and the ocean beyond. He clung to the quarter of a mile of long whitewashed wall on his left. Instead of broken glass, the wall was protected by an arrangement of wrought iron which looked like an elegant design but which, close up, was a phalanx of closely set arrowheads, their tips glinting lethally where the paint had worn away. Here and there along the wall, gates and grilles afforded glimpses of illuminated lawns and lazy fountains, the floodlights creating sudden paddy fields of brilliant green and casting dramatic unnatural shadows in all directions from the trees. At the next gate he stopped and looked through the railings at the discotheque of the Capricorn Hotel, the source of the pulsating lights and the dull, thudding sound which grew louder with each step. Through the iron grille he could see hundreds of people bobbing up and down on the pale wooden dance floor which extended out in a great arc through the vast sliding windows and over the lawns lit by coloured spotlights. Vijay steadied himself to read a notice on the gate: only hotel guests and those in possession of tickets would be allowed into the grounds.

He arrived at the gates of the Capricorn. Under the huge bowls of soft white light, mounted on stone pillars at either side of the entrance, policemen stood chatting with the guards. No one entered on foot, and the pedestrians on the Galle Road were being made to wait for the cars and taxis turning into the hotel. Vijay stood and watched, his world slowly beginning to come back. Most of those arriving were Europeans or Americans, coming from the other main hotels, the Intercontinental, the Meridian, the Taj, the Oberoi; but some were locals, and none of them cast an eye in the direction of Galle Face Green.

The music pulsed through Vijay's blood as he waited for the convoy of winking cars turning in off the road. As they slowed to negotiate the entrance, he took in the faces of the guests; the locals were more eager, the visitors aggressively unimpressed, but for several seconds it seemed to Vijay that he was seeing the same anonymous face passing by time after time, framed for a split second in the window of a car; the face of expectation.

The flow of arrivals ceased and the policeman strolled back to allow those on either side to continue their journeys up or down the Galle Road. Vijay remained where he was, holding on to a piece of the iron grille and still gazing towards the discotheque where all this anticipation was to be fulfilled. The music seemed to be inside his veins as he watched the distant dancers. It was as if each thump of the beat was being produced by some giant drumstick thudding against the underside of the dance floor, sending the bright little figures jumping as if they were coloured gemstones scattered on the surface of the drum. On and on went the music, thumping out into the night sky, constantly agitating the little stones, rearranging them into new patterns with its beat. For some illogical reason, Vijay had decided to wait for the music to stop as his signal to move on. But it did not stop. Instead, some of the little gems seemed to be gradually agitated towards the edge of the drum and then to fall off onto the white tables and chairs which waited for them on the lawns. Whenever this happened, Vijay saw one of the waiters glide across, dignified in a full-length white sarong, and bend towards the stones that had now become still while out on the drum the ceaseless agitation continued on into the night.

One of the policemen was looking suspiciously at him now and he glanced down to see that there was blood on the front of his shirt from a long cut that had suddenly appeared on the palm of his hand. He crossed the road onto Galle Face Green and was confronted by what seemed like total darkness stretching across the grass towards the ocean. A salt-breeze cooled him, and as his eyes readjusted he saw that the Green was not empty at all: crowds of local teenagers were silently dancing on the grass, their pale shirts and saris dimly picking up the flashing lights of the disco as they reflected from the low clouds, changing dull white to dull red, dull red to eerie blue, eerie blue to ghastly yellow, now light, now dark, flickering their fluid movements like an old film as they jumped with silent footsteps to the music from across the road, a drumstick pounding under the ancient earth of Galle Face Green. Even those who might have come to take a quiet stroll in the cool of the evening were being forced to listen to the music, and many of those sitting around on the grass were unconsciously tapping their sandalled feet to its monotonous, insistent rhythm.

He made his way through the pale ghosts of dancers and headed out into the darker areas of the Green. But here too there were crowds that had been invisible from the road, gathering in small groups around the hand-carts where lamps and lanterns glinted among bottles of imported beers. Vijay kept going towards what he knew was the sea wall. Further still out into the darkness, small groups of men were huddling up to the glowing coals that marked the barrow-loads of peanuts and cashews, lighting the faces of those earning their living in this obscurity, weighing out roasted nuts on scales that gleamed in the firelight and handing them in little twists of newspaper to hands that reached for them out of the darkness. Vijay walked through them all into the night, his head beginning to clear, attracting now and then a bold glance from passing dark-eyed beauties as he veered towards the deserted stretches of the Green.

The music had faded to a distant thump, and the lights flickering on the underneath of clouds were as nothing to the vast darkness of night over the ocean. From a distance he had thought that he could be alone in these dark acres, but as he walked he saw that even here the Green was not as empty as he had supposed. Near the sea wall, hundreds of ghostly figures were gathered in quiet groups, smoking and talking in low voices or sitting in silent tableaux on the worn grass.

The pulsing beat could still be heard, like the throbbing of blood in his head, but the lights had given up altogether and with the darkness had come an increasing cold. His shin struck something sharp in the grass and although he felt no pain he looked down to see the slow spread of seeping blood on one leg of his white slacks. There was just enough light to see the sign set at a low angle in the grass and he read the words 'No radios' painted on the metal in two languages. It grew still colder as he reached the sea. It had also become suddenly quieter, as if the small stirring of the ocean were enough to still the puny, impudent sounds of the disco. Even here at the edge, the darkness of the Green was not deserted, though the barrows were dimmer, lit only by candles in glass tubes, dispensing warm beer, sweet white toddy, illegal arrack, and cigarettes waiting to be lit from the smouldering ropes. Here for the unwary were the alcoholics and the drug addicts, the small-time criminals and the pushers of pot and heroin, the inhabitants of the underworld, the legions of the defeated. Vijay looked about him in the darkness. Gone were the clear-eyed young men who still had life at their feet, and in their place came the old, some with hardly more years than Vijay, men on whose faces despair had already spread its blanket, men from whose walk all swagger had gone. They crouched on their haunches or sat on the dark edges of Galle Face Green, occasionally spitting betel juice onto the grass, seeing little, expecting nothing. There was no light, and he could no longer discern the litter, the beer cans, the pools of mud, the excrement, on the untended ground. Out of the darkness a beggar appeared at his feet; the man had no arms and appeared mute, reaching up imploringly with his mouth and making little guttural sounds with his throat. Vijay slipped a note edgeways between the man's lips and walked on into the night until he came to the end of Galle Face Green.

He was facing out to sea. On his left, barely fifty metres away, was the white wall of his hotel and, beyond, his verandah. In his mind he saw the softly lit arches, the warm parchment lamps, the gentle fall of the faded purple table-cloths and the gleam of the brass rail on the antique desk, a tiny ledge of little ceremonious activities perched on the edge of the night. The thought that he would never see the verandah again washed over him with a gentle empty wave, barely troubling the surface of the fullness within him. He turned his back on the ocean to look towards the Galle Road, breathing deeply the sea air that was as pure on this side as it was polluted on the other. His head was almost clear now, and in the distance he could still see the spotlights of the Capricorn pulsing out the muffled beat while here and there the lights of police cars flashed their own sharp blue warning as they patrolled the stretch of road between the discotheque and Galle Face Green.

Vijay climbed the few steps and sat on the cold wall. His shoulders fell forwards, the stained white shirt glowing in the little phosphorescent light of the waves. He watched mesmerised as each wave came in. The ocean, too, grew tired at night, each wave dragging itself wearily up to fall despairingly on the beach, seething to nothingness before being pulled slowly back over the sand into the darkness. For minutes he listened to the waves coming in from the far night, the loneliest, saddest sound in the world, an awful dryness in his mouth, the taste of his emptiness. For a moment he thought he could hear the sounds of the verandah to his left. Lal would be serving his tables. Old Gamini would be looking down from the gloom. His head was clearing fast in the sea air, and he realised to his surprise that he did not long for his verandah, the place where he had set himself the test that had in fact been set by others, where he had tried to define himself by the imprint he could make in that world that had so suddenly been placed before him, a world which had seemed from the beginning to oppress him with his own inadequacy, a world whose illusive, taunting assurance had become the great unspoken challenge of his days, a world in which he had felt always that he was clothed in rags, that he was placed politely but irrevocably beyond some invisible wall, a world whose secret language he had sought to learn and in so trying had unquestioningly absorbed its givens and its gods, a world so attractive to something within him that for its values he had relinquished his own without a struggle. On the ocean front at the edge of Galle Face Green he saw with unquenchable shame the indignity of such a life, and knew with a certainty as irresistible as the sea before him that he had failed because he had tried in the wrong way to be a man.

Below him the little waves seemed strangely detached from the great brooding presence of the ocean. He wondered if Clara knew why he was not waiting on her tonight. And as he thought of her he saw that she too had become a distant memory, and he knew with an unpitying clarity that it was not Clara that he had put before all else; it was himself. In his desperate wish to make an impression on that world that had been set before him, to somehow prove himself against criteria that had grown thick and irresistible like lurid, fertile weeds, twisting his thoughts, strangling his judgement, insinuating themselves into his veins, he had reached with both hands for a meaningless moment while letting fall all that was real, all that was fine, all that was loved. His self-absorption welled up before him and roared in, overwhelming the sea walls as he hung his head on his chest and wrapped his arms around his knees, screaming silently into himself until his stomach contracted and he retched violently again and again as he hung forward over the sea, the spittle falling from his mouth into the waters which seethed and flowed in every direction as wave after wave came in from the ocean.

After several minutes he raised his wet eyes slowly to the sea again, finding the courage to look into the eyes of his wife. Unexpectedly, he saw in those eyes not recrimination but something of her own struggles: the struggle with his mother; the struggle she had waged against her own fears, her shyness, her colour, her lack of any status or acceptance. Her eyes looked at him from out in the ocean, and he registered again the small shock as he saw a woman who had come to be held in respect by his mother and father, by the community in which they lived, by the other young mothers who seemed to look to her in their difficulties. And once he had begun, he saw also the achievements which she had gradually worked towards in the years since they had first passed through the wall, and he knew that they were far greater than his own. He seemed to see her eyes more clearly now than ever he had done when Chandra was before him, and the profoundest shock came when he saw there the assurance which she had gained, the solid ground on which his wife now stood, the integrity which ran through all that she did and said and made it unnecessary for her to be tense, dependent, uncertain of her own lights. He looked into her eyes, way out to sea, and finally saw as if the night were opening its secrets to him that Chandra had won her ground on which to stand not through preoccupation with herself or any process of resolution and torture but through her family, through the people around her, through reaching out, that she was winning through because her aim was not to impress but to identify. He had been lazily proud of her beauty, rejoicing in it as she had walked to the garden wall, missing the inner beauty she had become. Shame rolled in on shame as he thought of the hopes and plans in which he had shown so little interest, of her trivial concerns which had intruded on his preoccupation with a world so much more important than her own, of the plans and hopes that he could have shared, letting her down even as he believed he was supporting her. He looked up into the night and the sea, no longer trying to restrain himself from their enormities. Another wave launched its weight against the wall and he saw Susil growing up without her in the garden, and in the swirling waters of his guilt he saw all the ways in which he had to be a man. He stood up on the sea wall, with scarcely a glance to the lights at the other side of Galle Face Green: he was ready to go home.

38

Gamini straightened as Clara followed the two bell boys down the corridor towards the dim landing. He was used to seeing guests leave for the airport wearing colourful T-shirts, shorts, jeans, and was pleased for once to see a guest properly dressed for travelling in a cotton dress, well-polished sandals, a linen jacket over her arm. But he frowned inwardly nonetheless. This was the woman who had brought disorder because she had not kept her place, not maintained her part in the framework which allowed others to also have their place. And so, as sure as gravity, she had brought chaos. He had said it would happen and it had. Gamini understood the principle and Lal never would. That was why Lal had encouraged Vijay in this foolishness. He would be drawn into no more silly arguments with Lal. None of them knew how to hold things in their proper place any more, not even the elegant English lady-guest who was now coming towards him.

He accepted the tip with a retiring bow, but he could see that she was about to speak to him yet again in too direct a fashion, focusing on him too personally, not allowing him to play his role.

'Gamini, I tried to find Vijay yesterday and I failed,' she said. Gamini flinched. He much preferred to come at things at more of an angle, so that there was the possibility of glancing off, leaving a little room for doubt, a little scope for misunderstanding, a little space for the unresolved. He remained silent, already having heard from a dozen sources about her attempt to find Vijay Jayasinghe in Maligawatta.

'I think if you really tried, Gamini,' she smiled almost slyly at him, much too personally, 'that you could find him, or perhaps there are others who work here who could.' He remained silent but lowered his eyes to the fraying coir strip along the polished wooden floor. He was used to people giving him only passing attention, not trapping him like this so that he had to improvise and could not fall back on any of the stock responses that had served him down the years.

'You see, Gamini,' she persisted, 'I don't believe what I've been told. I believe you. I think I was responsible for Vijay losing his job.'

She remained silent so long that he was eventually forced to look up into her eyes. The woman was incorrigible.

'That's why it's only right that I should help him now,' she said. Having secured Gamini's attention, she handed him her business card with her home address written on the back. Underneath the card was another two hundred rupees. He looked down at the small white card and the folded notes. But she remained silent until he had to raise his eyes again.

'Gamini, in your own way, in your own time, please find him for me. Tell him I want to help. Ask him to write to me.'

She was gone, leaving Gamini with the burden. He struggled with his sarong, folding the notes into the waistband so that they would not be seen in the breast pocket of his tunic. Maybe Vijay would visit him at his home one day; or maybe he would contact Lal. He would give him the card, but it would make no difference. Vijay, he knew, would not write.

All of the first-floor guests had now checked out or left their rooms for the day, and Gamini wandered along, a little earlier than usual, to his resting place out on the old gallery. Wearily he lowered himself onto the edge of the wicker chair and gazed out over the verandah. On the drawerless skeleton of a chest by his side there remained a few dry letters of the word 'William' which he had written in the dust a week ago. He sank back but could not seem to find rest in his accustomed place and, after a few minutes, he wandered along the corridor to the landing. She would have paid her bill and be gone by now, he thought. He looked down at his bare feet and imagined her crossing the great lobby, young Malik toiling behind with the suitcase and the taxi waiting in the drive by the potted palms. He imagined her, at the top of the few white steps looking out onto Galle Face Green, turning grandly to scatter gold sovereigns over the marble floors. My God, what a scramble there would be.

All day, people had been stepping up onto the verandah to say their goodbyes. A dozen young women had come in a group to see her, all of them weeping as they gave her the magnificent red and gold sari which, as they told her, the health warden had contributed very generously to. When they had left and the fuss had died down, Mrs C. J. Periera had come quietly onto the verandah with a box of delicate sweetmeats for her journey and a lined index card with the neatly printed name and address of one of her relatives in Kuwait to whom she had written about Chandra.

As soon as she had returned from the offices of the Mahmoud brothers, where she had queued to hand in her medical certificate and learned that there would be more than two hundred women travelling to the Gulf that night, Chandra had called Susil back from the top of the garden. Sitting on the bed-board with her back to the wall, she had held him close in the gloom and tried to explain what was happening. But it had not been possible to explain to a child who was not yet three that the mother who had tended him all the days of his life and had never left him for more than an hour was tonight going away for two years. Only her strange voice told him of some awful truth, and he connected the awful thing with the constant sobbing of his grandmother in the kitchen and the crying of the other mothers on the verandah, and he too had begun to cry for the world he had known that was now coming to an end.

Eventually she had washed both their faces and got ready to visit her own mother on the other side of the canal. But as she was about to leave she had herself been brought to tears again by Premawathie coming out from the kitchen and offering to go with her to the shanty. Shaking her head, she had kissed the old lady and carried Susil quickly to her mother's shack where she had spent an hour saying her goodbyes. Her mother, not knowing what else to do, had bought cakes for the occasion.

Then she had spent another half-hour with Sithie Zanoobie, who had wept most of all.

Now, as she walked back across the bridge, she forced herself to slow to a normal pace. It was three hours before she would have to be at the agents. She had almost nothing to pack except for the food they had been told they would need for the journey, and Premawathie would already have that prepared. Lifting Susil through the gap in the wall, she watched him run down to the verandah. Hurrying, she continued on up the embankment, to her tree opposite the park. Dappled shadows danced in the little waves as she slipped her feet into the cool waters of the canal.

In the few moments of tranquillity, her heart filled with what had passed between herself and Vijay. It had been late when he had come home and he had been bleeding from cuts on both his hand and leg. Without questioning, she had washed the blood away and seen that the cuts were not deep. In whispers they had talked until long after all other sounds had ceased, sitting on the verandah with the gardens silent all around them. Covered by the darkness, Vijay had unlocked himself to her in fits and starts, telling her as best he could all that had been happening inside him, and struggling often to continue. She had kissed his tears dry and held him in her arms out on the verandah as he had spread his shame before her, telling her things that she would always remember, things she would hold onto always, things she might never have known. At the first slow lightening of the strip of sky between the roofs, they had made their plans. She had told him all of her concerns for Susil, the essential practical things, the areas where his mother's influence must be resisted, the friends who could be relied upon, the particular health warden he should see if he was worried. And she had asked him to promise to sit with Susil for a few minutes every night, to read her letters and talk to him about the mother who still loved him from across the sea and would one day be coming back.

Eventually they had moved from the most painful things and Vijay had told her how he had been stopped by C. K. Munyandi on his way into the garden and tactfully asked if, now that he had more time available, he would accept nomination for the Garden Council. He had accepted, and she would see the difference in the slum when she returned. She had smiled in the first dawn light between the roofs, thinking how happy it could all have made her. Delicately, for she had wanted the suggestion to be his, she had mentioned again the trial run and the long-ago arrangement with Mr Punchihewa at the Sweet Tooth. She had heard from Mrs Periera the previous day that the loan was virtually certain, as there had only been half a dozen applications from the women of the gardens. It would be weeks before it came through, but Vijay had seized on the plan with a harrowing eagerness. His mother would take up the loan and sign the papers, and he and his father would organise the buying and the delivering and the trials with other shops in Grandpass and Maligawatta. Gently, she had told him of how she had intended to make the plan work, of the hopes she had kept to herself. She had quietly fetched the tilly lamp and written down the prices she had negotiated, the quantities and the delivery days, the names of the four other shops she had in mind, and the prices that Godfrey had agreed for the cylinders of gas. At last she told him that if all went well he might need help, and that he should rely first on Sithie Zanoobie. If more help were needed, Sithie would contact Vinitha and her daughter. When all practicalities had been exhausted, a silence had fallen between them; all distraction had been put aside, and they had held on to each other for long minutes out on the quiet verandah. Even after they had gone to bed they had not slept, but lay in each other's arms talking softly until the dawn.

The wind stirred the tall, graceful trees in the park and she knew that it was time to go. But for a moment, on the canal bank, she allowed herself to look into her own darkness, wondering if in some unknown way she too were being punished for her own stirrings of discontent, her ambition to become involved in worlds that were not her own. The thought troubled her but she put it away and began building her resolve, ready to return. She told herself that what lay in front of her had been endured by thousands of other women who had somehow coped, that she would face whatever came knowing that she was making it possible for Susil to grow in safety. She thought of the journey ahead and told herself that it would not be as painful or frightening as giving birth, but she knew the analogy was false and could not bring herself to think of another country. She stood up mechanically, unable to confront or avoid the enormous unreality that she was leaving her husband and her son, leaving her family and her home for another country. Desperate to avoid giving in to tears for herself, she scrambled up the bank of the canal and headed quickly for the gap in the garden wall.

At seven o'clock, Vijay walked silently with her to New Bazaar, carrying the shopping bag of his wife's clothes. When the time had finally come, Premawathie had taken her into the privacy of the kitchen at the back of the house. There, with tears streaming down her face in the darkness, she had poured her blessings on the dark, dowryless girl whom she had come to love, forcing herself through her tears and her sixty-five years of unbending stiffness to tell Chandra that she was all that a mother could ever want for her son and her grandchildren and that, even if it killed her, she would live long enough to see her again.

Godfrey had sat on the verandah on the outside of all the preparations and leave-takings, but the misery had been building up inside him all day. He had convinced himself that he would not see Chandra again, and when the time had come he had not been able to bring himself to speak, squeezing her hand tightly, his eyes brimming with tears, looking away down the garden.

At the last she had said her goodbyes to Susil, who had screamed and clung to her in a last terrible realisation of what might be happening. Leaving him in Premawathie's arms, she had stepped through the wall, as tense and precarious as a china vase, holding herself together, speaking with a strained normality, knowing that she would break when she was gone.

The parting at the agents was as if he were seeing her off for a day's outing to Kandy or Nuwara Eliya. In the milling crowds they smiled and gripped each other's arms, and then she was waving from the window of the old bus, biting her lip, her eyes like jewels. She was gone.

The last British Airways flight had left hours earlier, and the Executive Club was closed. Clara sat in the main departure area, awaiting the last call for flight AL753 to London via Bombay. The air conditioning had broken down and the air smelt of the day's heat and some kind of cleaning fluid. Occasionally the sliding doors drew back and the heat was replenished in gusts, as if driven in by the hot throbbing of the airport bus. All departures were delayed, and boredom sat like heat in the lounge where tourists sat and sweated on the plastic seats, fanning glistening faces with limp boarding cards. From time to time, a stewardess drifted languidly across the tiled hall. All around her, the muted babble of languages echoed slightly against the tiled walls and granite floors. To her left by the Gulf Air gate, two hundred or more women in saris were sitting on the floor amid the plastic cups and the cigarette ends.

She strolled over to the window of the State Gem Corporation to see if she could summon up any excitement over the moonstones, amethysts, emeralds, rubies and lapis lazuli arranged under a single strip-light. She decided she could not, and wandered towards the revolving stools of the coffee bar. A tired sandwich curled under a scratched plastic cover. She would eat on the plane. Instead, she took out the leather portfolio from her shoulder bag and opened out the three slightly damp sheets of paper containing the final draft of a letter which she had been writing until the moment of her departure from the hotel. As she read, the public address system started up with a metallic squawking, echoing unintelligibly down the vast hall. The crowd of women began scrambling to their feet. On the monitor, a light was blinking to tell her that her own flight was also now boarding. Over in the far corner of the departure hall the man in the khaki uniform had begun striding up and down with what looked like a policeman's truncheon, shouting at the women who had begun to move off towards unmarked doors. She noticed that most were pulling one end of their saris across their faces and that some of them appeared to be weeping.

She presented her boarding card and was shown into the first-class lounge overlooking the parking bays. Far away she could see the fringe of palm fronds and knew that beyond them lay the open sea. Below her a bus throbbed. From somewhere to her left came a steady metallic clanging and through the plate-glass window she could see that the women, stretched out in a long line across the tarmac, were filing onto an airbus whose engines had already risen to an untroubled whine. At the foot of the gantry the man in khaki appeared to be banging his truncheon on the handrail as each woman passed, and for each clang a stewardess appeared to be making a mark on a clipboard.

A steward appeared at Clara's side and invited her to board. The doors were held open for her as she emerged into the evening warmth and onto the waiting bus. The clanging sound was louder now, but soon the double doors hissed to a close and she was on her way across the tarmac towards the Boeing which stood shimmering in the day's residual heat.

She took her seat in the almost empty business class cabin where a steward immediately offered her the choice of iced champagne or freshly squeezed orange. She chose the juice and reached up to direct the overhead air nozzle onto her face, gratefully accepting a hot towel from the silver tongs. Pressing it to her face, and to the inside of each wrist, she looked forward to the uninterrupted hours. She had already decided that she would sleep for the ninety-minute hop to Bombay and then, on the long haul to London, she would focus her thoughts, coming to her decision before touching down in the early hours of the morning. In her mind she read again through her letter, wondering, as she would wonder for all the long hours ahead, whether she would put it into the out-tray on a Monday morning that seemed very far away. She caught the last faint smell of the warm, spicy air before the air conditioning overcame everything with its clean metallic cool. A few minutes later, the plane was banking steeply over the city.

She pressed her face to the window and traced the necklaces of lights on the main thoroughfares and the dimmer gleams of lesser roads criss-crossing the electrified quarters. Saw too the vast gaps of irregular darkness, and for the moment she had never felt more sure of what she must do, of the new heroism she must find, as she thought of Vijay somewhere in the jagged areas of the night below.

Later in the evening, lifting off from Santa Cruz airport, Bombay, she looked down on an infinitely vaster city than the one she had left. And as the plane fought its way up into the night, shuddering a little through the humid banks of air, she saw again the bright rivers of light fed by a million lesser tributaries. But once more her eyes were drawn to the irregular shapes where no lights burned, recognising the lands of darkness where a thousand times ten thousand Vijays lived beyond her knowing. The undercarriage locked reassuringly into place and the plane banked once more, replacing the city with the untroubled darkness as it headed out over the sea.

Author's Note

The hotel in which much of this story is set is similar in location and in some architectural details to the Galle Face Hotel in Colombo, Sri Lanka, as it was in the late 1980s. In all other respects, the hotel depicted here, its staff and services, are entirely imaginary. The hotel of the story is owned by an international conglomerate; the Galle Face Hotel was owned by the Sri Lankan businessman and philanthropist Cyril Gardiner until his death in 1996. Now under the Chairmanship of Sanjiva Gardiner, the Galle Face Hotel has been recently re-furbished, though it remains one of 'the last great unspoilt hotels of the east'. The author would like to acknowledge the help of the late Cyril Gardiner in researching some parts of this book.

Thanks are also due to Stephen Perera and Mohammed Jiffry for their kindness and help in the slums and shanties of Colombo, and to Leo Fonseca and Bertrand Mendis for reviewing the descriptions of Colombo life.